D0058333

Four Verse Plays

Maxwell Anderson was born in Atlantic, Pennsylvania, in 1888. He was graduated from the University of North Dakota in 1911 and received his M.A. from Stanford University in 1914. He taught briefly, then turned to newspaper work, being associated with the *Grand Forks* (North Dakota) *Herald, San Francisco Chronicle*, and *San Francisco Bulletin*. Later, he was an editorial writer for the *New Republic*, the *New York Globe*, and the *New York World*. His career as a playwright began in 1923; among his plays are *What Price Glory?* (with Laurence Stallings, 1924), *Saturday's Children* (1927), *Elizabeth the Queen* (1930), *Mary of Scotland* (1933), *Knickerbocker Holiday* (1938), *Key Largo* (1939), *Eve of St. Mark* (1942), *Joan of Lorraine* (1946), *Lost in the Stars* (1949), and *Bad Seed* (1954). He was awarded the Pulitzer Prize for *Both Your Houses* (1933) and the New York Drama Critics' Circle Award for *Winterset* (1935) and for *High Tor* (1936).

Four Verse Plays

by Maxwell Anderson

A Harvest ook

Harcourt, Brace & World, Inc.   New York

BY ARRANGEMENT WITH ANDERSON HOUSE

Preface

It has always been my conviction that the less a man says about his own work the better for him and the better for the work. Almost anybody is a fairer critic of a play than the playwright. Almost anybody comes to a play with fewer prejudices, for or against, than the writer of it. Even theater critics are more likely to know the worth of my plays than I am.

But some of the facts about them and how they came to be written I may remember better than anyone else. For example, my first produced play was in verse. (I had written one earlier, in prose, and discarded it because its story didn't hold together, but some of the dialogue was good enough to convince me that I should try again.) I didn't print *White Desert* because it was rather shapeless and came to nothing either in meaning or as drama.

After this first production (in verse), I tried a number of collaborations in prose, and a few prose plays of my own, some of them sufficiently successful to set me going as a playwright, though still not too happy with the theater I was a part of. In the nineteen twenties Broadway produced mainly realistic or melodramatic plays built to amuse or shock the dizzy and dazzled inhabitants of New York in the rather intoxicated decade after the First World War. For the first time in its history, the United States was a world power, and it was rapidly on its way to becoming the most potent of world powers. Our situation went to our heads. We felt a national elation that poured itself into our theater. We produced a great many vigorous plays, fast-talking and brilliant, colorful plays that filled a record number of theaters and trained a record crop of actors and writers that rode the economic boom right up to the crash.

The crash of '29 and '30 seemed to mark a transition. The elation of our times cooled into the apprehension of second thought.

It may have been quite by chance that my second play in verse, *Elisabeth the Queen*, was produced in 1930. It may have been that the shock of the depression made me feel that Broadway was ready to take an interest in more serious, or less razzle-dazzle, themes. Or it may be that I was trying to get back to the writing of verse simply because I enjoyed it and was at home in English literature and history.

As a child I had read my fill of the English novelists available to me, and as a high-school student I sought out and read with delight the English poets that could be found in libraries or on drugstore shelves in the Middle West. (I came across my first Shelley in a drugstore in New Hampton, Iowa, a reprint of Mary Shelley's edition, twenty-five cents. The Shakespeare, in the same drugstore, the Globe edition, fine print and hard on the eyes, was fifteen cents. I found a poem by Keats in an anthology and sent fifteen cents for the paper-bound copy of his work in the Riverside Literature Series. I still have the Shelley.) A new and magical world opened to me. The narratives of Dumas and Dickens began to seem childish things. I read poetry for the sheer pleasure of it, feeling as I read the way a porpoise must feel as he turns through the giant happiness of sea water. Then I tried writing it, and dis-

covered that the imagining, the word-finding, and the setting down of a poem were more intense delights than the
reading of even the greatest poems by other men. It wasn't
often that the impulse came over me, but when it did, and
a poem resulted, I had a taste of what, for lack of a better
figure, men call "heaven."

This was a quite private and personal thing. In the
Middle West poetry was not encouraged, nor in demand.
It was committed to paper in secret, like a crime, as Sidney
Howard used to say a play should be written. But I finished high school, by chance, in Jamestown, North Dakota, and a classmate, Garth Howland, persuaded me that
I should go on to the university. The university he planned
to attend was the University of North Dakota, and—
knowing nothing about universities, hardly aware that
they differed from each other—I set off, along with Howland, for Grand Forks, and managed to work my way
through the university in three years. In the University
of North Dakota I discovered, for the first time, that a
love of poetry and a desire to write it were honorable
predilections.

During those three college years, and during the teaching and journalism that followed, I continued to derive
my fun and to set my course by the few poems I managed
to write in occasional spare time. Whether they were good
or bad or mediocre, I wasn't sure, because none of them
got into a national magazine until after I'd spent two years
teaching high-school classes. After that the sale of poems
became fairly frequent, and gave a smack of literary excitement to a life otherwise devoted to the experiments in
living which we all make in marrying, having children,
and adjusting to the world. When, in the course of time,

my writing for the newspapers turned into writing for the stage, and I suddenly found myself a successful playwright, the temptation to try plays in verse grew inexcusably strong. Without doing much theorizing about it, I began to write plays in verse, and, since I was canny enough to choose subjects either far away and long ago or with romantic and colorful backgrounds, they were sometimes successful.

Some of them are in this volume. How good they are, how good the verse is, I can't tell. I suspect I wrote them in verse because I enjoyed writing verse—though I have found better reasons for the verse form, and once published an essay in defense of poetic plays. Actually, plays in verse are a rarity in our theater, and perhaps that's as it should be. Let the readers and the audiences decide.

MAXWELL ANDERSON

Contents

Elizabeth the Queen

CHARACTERS

(In the order of appearance)

SIR WALTER RALEIGH
PENELOPE GRAY
A CAPTAIN
SIR ROBERT CECIL
LORD ESSEX
FRANCIS BACON
QUEEN ELIZABETH
LORD BURGHLEY
LORD HOWARD
THE FOOL
CAPTAIN ARMIN
MARY
ELLEN
TRESSA
MARVEL
A COURIER
A HERALD
BURBAGE
HEMMINGS
FALSTAFF
PRINCE HENRY *Players in the*
GADSHILL *scene from*
PETO *Henry IV*
POINS

Also GUARDS, MEN-AT-ARMS, MAIDS-IN-WAITING,
and others

ACT ONE

Scene I

SCENE: *An entrance hall before a council chamber in the palace at Whitehall. The entrance to the council room is closed and four* GUARDS *with halberds stand at either side. A small door at the left of the entrance is also shut. It is early morning. The guards stand immobile.*

First Guard. The sun's out again, and it's guineas to pounds the earl comes back this morning.

Second Guard. I'll be glad of it, for one. You get nothing but black looks about the court when he's away.

First Guard. You'll get little else now he's back, my bully. They quarrelled too far for mending, this time.

Third Guard. Tut! They quarrel no more than the cock with the hen. The earl's been sick.

First Guard. Sick of the queen's displeasure. It's a disease a favorite can die of, and many have.

Fourth Guard. He's no sicker of her displeasure than she of his, if a man may judge. Once the earl's gone there's no dancing, no plays, no feasting . . . nothing to do nights but sleep. The very scullery-maids grow cold, and go to bed alone; like the queen.

First Guard. There are some even a scullery-maid would seldom kiss, save in moments of great excitement. Poor Wat looks forward to feast nights.

Fourth Guard. I've had my luck.

3

First Guard. You've had what was coming to you. Mucklemouth Jean, of the back kitchen.

Fourth Guard. You'd have been glad of her yourself if you could have had her.

First Guard. Consider, man. She may not have been true. When she wouldn't play with you, mayhap she was playing with somebody else. And if the queen could live without her Earl of Essex, it may have been because Sir Walter had a new suit of silver armor.

Third Guard. And there's a handsome man.

Fourth Guard. God defend me from speaking lightly of the queen!

First Guard. Eh? God defend you? Let no man accuse me of speaking lightly of the queen, nor of any other woman . . . unless she be a light woman, in which case, God defend me, I will speak lightly of her if I choose.

Third Guard. What say you of the queen?

First Guard. Of the queen? I say she is well-known to be the virgin queen, I say no more.

Second Guard. But do you think she is a virgin?

First Guard. She has doubtless been a virgin, bully, for all women have been virgins, but the question is: First, when . . . and, second, where?

Second Guard. Where?

First Guard. Where, bully, where?

Third Guard. Would you not say, in the proper place?

First Guard. No. I would not say in the proper place. Because it is hard to say if there is a proper place wherein to be a virgin . . . unless it be in church, and, God defend me, I do not go to church.

Second Guard. You do not go to church?

First Guard. No, for my sins, I do not go to church . . . or, if you like, I do not go to church for my sins.

Second Guard. Does it follow that the church is a proper place for virgins?

First Guard. It does. Did I not tell you I do not go there for my sins?

Fourth Guard. They say the queen's getting to be an old woman but I swear she looks younger than my wife, whom I married a young thing, six years come Easter.

Third Guard. It would age a girl fast, just the look of you.

First Guard. As for the queen, powder and paint accounts for some of it. To say nothing of the earl. A young lover will do much for a lady's face.

Fourth Guard. Now God defend me. . . .

First Guard. Aye, aye . . . God defend poor Wat.

    [*A* Nobleman *enters in silver armor. It is* Sir Walter Raleigh, *no other*]

Raleigh. Has the queen come forth yet?

First Guard. No, Sir Walter.

Raleigh. The Earl of Essex . . . is he here?

First Guard. No, my lord.

Raleigh. When he comes send me word. I shall be in the north corridor.

[*He turns*]

First Guard. Good, my lord.

[PENELOPE GRAY *comes in from the right, passing through*]

Raleigh.

[*Meeting her*]

Greetings, lady, from my heart.

Penelope. Good-morrow, lord, from my soul.

Raleigh. I take my oath in your face that you are rushing to the window to witness the arrival of my lord of Essex.

Penelope. And in your teeth I swear I am on no such errand . . . but only to see the sun-rise.

Raleigh. The sun has been up this hour, my dear.

Penelope. The more reason to hurry, gracious knight.

Raleigh. Do you think to pull the bag over my head so easily, Penelope? On a day when the earl returns every petticoat in the palace is hung with an eye to pleasing him. Yours not the least.

Penelope. I deny him thrice.

Raleigh. I relinquish you, lady. Run, run to the window! He will be here and you will miss him!

Penelope. Is there a lady would run from Sir Walter in his silver suiting? Since the sun is up . . . I have no errand.

Raleigh. Is there no limit to a woman's deception, wench? Would you go so far as to appear pleased if I kissed you?

Penelope. And no deception.

[*He kisses her*]

I call the Gods to witness . . . did I not blush prettily?

Raleigh. And meant it not at all. Tell me, did the queen send you to look out the casement for news of her Essex, or did you come at the prompting of your heart?

Penelope. Shall I tell you the truth?

Raleigh. Verily.

Penelope. The truth is I cannot answer.

Raleigh. Both, then?

Penelope. Both or one or neither.

Raleigh. Fie on the baggage.

Penelope. Is it not a virtue to be close-mouthed in the queen's service?

Raleigh. If you kept the rest of your person as close as your mouth what a paragon of virtue you would be!

Penelope. Indeed, my lord, I am.

Raleigh. Indeed, my lady? Have there not been certain deeds on dark nights?

Penelope. Sh! Under the rose.

Raleigh. Meaning under covers . . .

Penelope. Fie on my lord, to make me out a strumpet!

Raleigh. It is my manner of wooing, fair maid! I woo by suggestion of images . . .

Penelope. Like small boys on the closet wall . . .

Raleigh. Like a soldier . . .

Penelope. Aye, a veteran . . . of encounters . . .

Raleigh. I will have you yet, my love; I will take lessons from this earl . . .

Penelope. Take this lesson from me, my lord: You must learn to desire what you would have. Much wanting makes many a maid a wanton. You want me not . . . nor I you. You wear your silver for a queen.

[*A* CAPTAIN *enters from the left*]

Captain. Good-morrow, Sir Walter. Is the queen still under canopy?

Raleigh. I know not.

Captain. The earl is here and would see her.

Raleigh. Bid him hurry if he wishes to find her abed as usual.

Penelope. She is dressed and stirring, captain, and awaits my lord.

Raleigh. And many another fair maid awaits him likewise, captain. Take him that message from me. Run, girl, run. Tell the queen.

[*The* CAPTAIN *goes out left*]

Penelope.

[*Going*]

You make yourself so easily disliked.

[*She goes right.* CECIL *enters, passing her*]

Cecil. He is here?

Raleigh. So. The heavenly boy, clad in the regalia of the sun, even now extracts his gallant foot from his golden stirrup and makes shift to descend from his heaving charger. Acclamation lifts in every voice, tears well to every eye . . . with the exception of mine, perhaps, and yours, I hope. . . .

Cecil. I am at a pass to welcome him, myself. This Elizabeth of ours can be difficult on her good days . . . and there have been no good ones lately.

[*Two* MEN-AT-ARMS *enter with silver armor in their arms*]

Raleigh. And what is all this, sirrah?

First Man. Armor, my lord.

Raleigh. For whom?

First Man. We know not.

Raleigh. Now by the ten thousand holy names! Am I mistaken, Robert, or is this armor much like my own?

Cecil. Very like, I should say. Is it sterling?

Raleigh. And the self-same pattern. Has the earl gone lunatic?

Cecil. He means to outshine you, perhaps.

Raleigh. Has it come to this? Do I set the style for Essex? That would be a mad trick, to dress himself like me!

[BACON *appears in the doorway at right*]

What do you know of this, Sir Francis?

Bacon. Greeks, my lord, bearing gifts.

Raleigh. To hell with your Greeks! The devil damn him!
This is some blackguardry!

[*Two more* MEN-AT-ARMS *enter, carrying armor*]

There's more of it! Good God, it comes in bales!
I say, who's to wear this, sirrah? Who is it for?

[ESSEX *enters from corridor between the two files of soldiers,
    pushing them aside as he does so, and crosses to right of*
    RALEIGH, *speaking as he enters*]

Essex. Their name is legion, Sir Walter. Happily met!
Felicitations on your effulgence, sir!
You're more splendid than I had imagined! News came
    of your silver
Even in my retreat! I was ill, and I swear it cured me!
You should have heard the compliments I've heard
Passed on you! Sir Walter's in silver! The World's out-
    done
They said—the moon out-mooned. He gleams down
    every corridor
And every head's turned after him. The queen
Herself has admired it—the design—the workmanship!
There's nothing like it this side of Heaven's streets.
And I said to myself—the great man—this is what we
    have needed—
More silver everywhere—oceans of silver!
Sir Walter has set the style, the world will follow.
So I sent for the silver-smiths, and by their sweat
Here's for you, lads, tailored to every man's measure—
Shall Raleigh wear silver alone? Why, no,
The whole court shall go argent!

Raleigh. Take care, my lord.
   I bear insults badly.

Essex. And where are you insulted?
   For the queen's service you buy you a silver armor.
   In the queen's service I buy you a dozen more.
   A gift, my friends, each man to own his own,
   As you own yours. What insult?

Raleigh. Have your laugh,
   Let the queen and court laugh with you! Since you are
      envious
   You may have my suit. I had not thought even Essex
   Bore so petty a mind.

Essex. I misunderstood you
   Perhaps, Sir Walter. I had supposed you donned
   Silver for our queen, but I was mistaken . . .
   Keep these all for yourself. The men shall have other . . .
   Some duller color.

Raleigh. I have borne much from you
   Out of regard for the queen, my lord of Essex.

Essex. And I from you.
   By God . . .

Cecil. You have forgotten, Sir Walter,
   A certain appointment . . .

Raleigh. And you will bear more, by Heaven! . . .

Cecil. He is going to the queen,
   Remember. And we have an errand.

Essex. You presume to protect me,
   Master Secretary?

Cecil. I protect you both, and our mistress.
   There can be no quarrelling here.

Raleigh. That's very true. Let us go.
      [CECIL *and* RALEIGH *go out right*]

Bacon. And this armor? What becomes of it?

Essex. I have given it.
   Would you have me take it back?

Bacon. There has seldom been
   A man so little wise, so headstrong, but he
   Could sometimes see how necessary it is
   To keep friends and not make enemies at court.
   But you . . . God knows.

Essex. Let him make friends with me.
   He may need friends himself.
      [*To the* GUARDS]

   These are your armors.
   Keep them, wear them, sell them, whatever you like . . .
   Or your captain directs you.

First Guard. We thank you.
      [*They retire to examine the armor*]

Bacon. You are going to the queen?

Essex. Yes. God help us both!

Bacon. Then hear me a moment . . .

Essex. Speak, schoolmaster,
   I knew it was coming. You've been quiet too long.

Bacon. Listen to me this once, and listen this once
To purpose, my lord, or it may hardly be worth
My while ever to give you advice again
Or for you to take it. You have enough on your hands
Without quarrelling with Raleigh. You have quarrelled
   with the queen
Against my judgment ...

Essex. God and the devil! Can a man
Quarrel on order or avoid a quarrel at will?

Bacon. Why certainly, if he knows his way.

Essex. Not I.

Bacon. You quarrelled with her, because she wished to keep
   peace
And you wanted war ...

Essex. We are at war with Spain!
But such a silly, frightened, womanish war
As only a woman would fight ...

Bacon. She is a woman and fights a womanish war;
But ask yourself one question and answer it
Honestly, dear Essex, and perhaps you will see then
Why I speak sharply. You are my friend and patron.
Where you gain I gain ... where you lose I lose ...
And I see you riding straight to a fall today ...
And I'd rather your neck weren't broken.

Essex. Ask myself
What question?

Bacon. Ask yourself what you want:
To retain the favor of the queen, remain

Her favorite, keep all that goes with this,
Or set yourself against her and trust your fortune
To popular favor?

Essex. I'll not answer that.

Bacon. Then . . . I have done.

Essex. Forgive me, dear friend, forgive me.
I have been ill, and this silly jackanapes
Of a Raleigh angers me with his silver mountings
Till I forget who's my friend. You know my answer
In regard to the queen. I must keep her favor.
Only it makes me mad to see all this . . .
This utter mismanagement, when a man's hand and
   brain
Are needed and cannot be used.

Bacon. Let me answer for you;
You are not forthright with yourself. The queen
Fights wars with tergiversation and ambiguities . . .
You wish to complete your record as general,
Crush Spain, subdue Ireland, make a name like Cæsar's
Climb to the pinnacle of fame. Take care.
You are too popular already. You have
Won at Cadiz, caught the people's hearts,
Caught their voices till the streets ring your name
Whenever you pass. You are loved better than
The queen. That is your danger. She will not suffer
A subject to eclipse her; she cannot suffer it.
Make no mistake. She will not.

Essex. And I must wait,
Bite my nails in a corner, let her lose to Spain,
Keep myself back for policy?

Bacon. Even so.

Essex. I come of better blood than Elizabeth.
My name was among the earls around King John
Under the oak. What the nobles have taught a king
A noble may teach a queen.

Bacon. You talk treason and death.
The old order is dead, and you and your house will die
With it if you cannot learn.

Essex. So said King John
Under the oak, or wherever he was standing,
And little he got by it, as you may recall.
What the devil's a king but a man, or a queen but a
woman?

Bacon. King John is dead; this is Elizabeth,
Queen in her own right, daughter of a haughty line
There is one man in all her kingdom she fears
And that man's yourself, and she has good reason to fear
you.
You're a man not easily governed, a natural rebel,
Moreover, a general, popular and acclaimed,
And last, she loves you, which makes you the more to be
feared,
Whether you love her or not.

Essex. I do love her! I do!

Bacon. My lord, a man as young as you—

Essex. If she were my mother's kitchen hag,
Toothless and wooden-legged, she'd make all others
Colorless.

Bacon. You play dangerously there, my lord.

Essex. I've never yet loved or hated
    For policy nor a purpose. I tell you she's a witch—
    And has a witch's brain. I love her, I fear her,
    I hate her, I adore her—

Bacon. That side of it you must know
    For yourself.

Essex. I will walk softly—here is my hand.
    Distress myself no more—I can carry myself.

Bacon. Only count not too much on the loves of queens.

Essex. I'll remember.

    [CECIL *and* RALEIGH *reappear in the doorway at the right.*
    RALEIGH *is wearing ordinary armor and carries his silver suit.*
    ESSEX *looks at him, biting his lip*]

Sir Walter, take care of your health!

Raleigh. My health, sir?

Essex.

    [*Going out*]

Wearing no silver, in this chilly weather.

Raleigh.

    [*Tossing his silver armor into the pile*]

Put that with the others.

First Guard. Are we to wear them, sir?

Raleigh. No. Melt them down and sell the silver. And thus
see for yourself how soon a fool is parted from his
money. Take station in the outer hall and carry this
trash with you.

First Guard. Yes, sir.

[*The guards go out right*]

Raleigh.

[*To* BACON]

And you, sir, you are his friend . . .

Bacon. And yours, Sir Walter . . .

Raleigh. It's the first I've heard of it, but if you're mine too, so much the better. Carry this news to him: his suits go to the melting-pot.

Bacon. Willingly, my lord, if I see him. You have done quite properly.

Raleigh. I do not ask your commendation!

Bacon. No, but you have it.

[*He bows low and goes out to left*]

Raleigh. There's the viper under our flower, this Francis. He should be on the winning side.

Cecil. He will be yet . . .
Like all wise men. For myself, I no longer
Stomach Lord Essex. Every word he speaks
Makes me feel queasy.

Raleigh. Then why put up with him?

Cecil. The queen, my friend, the queen. What she wants she will have,
And she must have her earl.

Raleigh. Which does she love more,
Her earl or her kingdom?

Cecil. Yes, which? I have wondered.

Raleigh. Then you're less sapient
  Than I've always thought you, Cecil. She loves her kingdom
  More than all men, and always will. If he could
  Be made to look like a rebel, which he's close to being . . .,
  And she could be made to believe it, which is harder,
  You'd be first man in the council.

Cecil. And you would be? . . .

Raleigh. Wherever I turn he's stood
  Square in my way! My life long here at court
  He's snatched honor and favor from before my eyes . . .
  Till his voice and walk and aspect make me writhe . . .
  There's a fatality in it!

Cecil. If he could be sent from England . . . we might have a chance
  To come between them.

Raleigh. Would she let him go?

Cecil. No . . . but if he could be teased
  And stung about his generalship till he was
  Too angry to reflect . . . Suppose you were proposed
  As general for the next Spanish raid?

Raleigh. He would see it,
  And so would she.

Cecil. Then if you were named
  For the expedition to Ireland?

Raleigh. No, I thank you.
  He'd let me go, and I'd be sunk in a bog

This next three hundred years. I've seen enough
Good men try to conquer Ireland.

Cecil. Then how would this be?
We name three men for Ireland of his own supporters;
He will oppose them, not wishing his party weakened
At the court. Then we ask what he suggests
And hint at his name for leader . . .

Raleigh. Good so far.

Cecil. He will be angry and hint at your name; you will offer
To go if he will.

Raleigh. No. Not to Ireland.

Cecil. Yes!
Do you think he'd let you go with him and share
The military glory? It will go hard,
Having once brought up his name, if we do not manage
To ship him alone to Dublin.

Raleigh. We can try it, then,
Always remembering that no matter what
Is said . . . no matter what I say or you . . .
I do not go. You must get me out of that,
By Christ, for I know Ireland.

Cecil. I will. Be easy.

Raleigh. When is the council?

Cecil. At nine.

Raleigh. You'll make these suggestions?

Cecil. If you'll play up to them.

Raleigh. Count on me. I must look after
    These silver soldiers.

Cecil. At nine then.

Raleigh. Count on me.
    [*They go out in opposite directions*]

CURTAIN

ACT ONE

Scene II

Scene: *The queen's study, which adjoins her bed-chambers and the council hall. It is a severe little room, with chairs, a desk and a few books, huge and leather-bound.* Penelope *comes in from the bed-chamber and looks out through a curtain opposite. She returns to the chamber, then re-enters to wait.* Essex *enters.*

Penelope.
[*Rising*]
Good-morrow, my lord.

Essex. Good-morrow, Penelope. Have I kept the queen?

Penelope. If so, would I acknowledge it?

Essex. I commend me to your discretion.

Penelope. Only to my discretion?

Essex. Take her what message you will . . . only let it be that I am here.

Penelope. May I have one moment, my lord? She is not quite ready.

Essex. As many as you like. What is it, my dear?

Penelope. Do you love the queen?

Essex. Is that a fair question, as between maid and man?

Penelope. An honest question.

Essex. Then I will answer honestly. Yes, my dear.

Penelope. Dearly?

21

Essex. Yes.

Penelope. I would you loved someone who loved you better.

Essex. Meaning . . . whom?

Penelope. Meaning . . . no-one. Myself, perhaps. That's no-one. Or . . . anyone who loved you better.

Essex. Does she not love me, sweet?

Penelope. She loves you, loves you not, loves you, loves you not . . .

Essex. And why do you tell me this?

Penelope. Because I am afraid.

Essex. For me?

Penelope. I have heard her when she thought she was alone, walk up and down her room soundlessly, night long, cursing you . . . cursing you because she must love you and could not help herself . . . swearing to be even with you for this love she scorns to bear you. My lord, you anger her too much.

Essex. But is this not common to lovers?

Penelope. No. I have never cursed you. And I have good cause.

Essex. But if I were your lover, you would, sweet. So thank God I am not.

Penelope. I must go and tell her you are here.
    [*She lifts her face to be kissed*]
Goodbye.

Essex. Goodbye, my dear.
  [*He kisses her*]
  And thank you.

Penelope. Will you beware of her?

Essex. Lover, beware your lover, might well be an old
  maxim.
  I will beware.

Penelope. For I am afraid.
  [*A* MAID-IN-WAITING *appears in the doorway*]

Maid. Her Majesty is ready.

Penelope. I will tell her my lord is here.
      [*She runs out hastily.* ELIZABETH *enters, signing imperiously
      to the maid, who disappears. There is a moment's
      silence*]

Elizabeth. When we met last it was, as I remember,
  Ill-met by moonlight, sir.

Essex. Well-met by day,
  My queen.

Elizabeth. I had hardly hoped to see you again,
  My lord of Essex, after what was vowed
  Forever when you left.

Essex. You are unkind.
  To remind me.

Elizabeth. I think I also used
  The word forever, and meant it as much, at least . . .
  Therefore, no apology. Only my Penelope
  Passed me just now in the door with eyes and lips

That looked the softer for kissing. I'm not sure
But I'm inopportune.

Essex. She's a crazy child.

Elizabeth. A child! That's for me, too, no doubt! These children
Have their little ways with each other!

Essex. Must we begin
With charges and counter-charges, when you know . . .

Elizabeth. Do I indeed? . . .
You have been gone a week, at this Wanstock of
yours . . .
And a week's a long time at court. You forget that I
Must live and draw breath whether I see you or not . . .
And there are other men and women, oh yes, all fully
Equipped for loving and being loved! Penelope . . .
You find Penelope charming. And as for me
There's always Mountjoy . . . or Sir Walter . . . the
handsome,
Sir Walter, the silver-plated . . .

Essex. He'll wear no more
Silver at your door.

Elizabeth. What have you done . . . come, tell me.
I knew this silver would draw fire. What happened?

Essex. Nothing . . . but the fashion's gone out.

Elizabeth. No, but tell me!

Essex. He happened to be in the way
When the upstairs pot was emptied.
He's gone to change his clothes.

Elizabeth. You shall not be allowed
   To do this to him. . . .

Essex.

   [*Moving toward her*]

   You shall not be allowed
   To mock me, my queen.

   [*He kisses her*]

Elizabeth. Isn't it strange how one man's kiss can grow
   To be like any other's . . . or a woman's
   To be like any woman's?

Essex. Not yours for me,
   No, and not mine for you, you lying villain,
   You villain and queen, you double-tongued seductress,
   You bitch of brass!

Elizabeth. Silver, my dear. Let me be
   A bitch of silver. It reminds me of Raleigh.

Essex. Damn you!

Elizabeth. Damn you and double-damn you for a damner!
   Come some day when I'm in the mood. What day's
      this? . . .
   Thursday? Try next Wednesday . . . or any Wednesday
   Later on in the summer . . . Any summer
   Will do. Why are you still here?

Essex. Oh, God, if I could but walk out that door
   And stay away!

Elizabeth. It's not locked.

Essex. But I'd come back!
   Where do you think I've been this last week? Trying,
   Trying not to be here! But you see, I am here.

Elizabeth. Yes, I see.

Essex. Why did you plague me without a word?

Elizabeth. Why did you not come?

Essex. You are a queen, my queen. You have proscribed
   me,
   Sent formal word I'd not be admitted if I came.

Elizabeth. I may have meant it at the time.

Essex. I think I have a demon, and you are it!

Elizabeth. If ever a mocking devil tortured a woman
   You're my devil and torture me! Let us part and
     quickly,
   Or there'll be worse to come. Go.

Essex. I tell you I will not.

Elizabeth. Come to me, my Essex. Let us be kind
   For a moment. I will be kind. You need not be.
   You are young and strangely winning and strangely
     sweet.
   My heart goes out to you wherever you are.
   And something in me has drawn you. But this same
     thing
   That draws us together hurts and blinds us until
   We strike at one another. This has gone on
   A long while. It grows worse with the years. It will end
     badly.

Go, my dear, and do not see me again.

Essex. All this
Is what I said when last I went away.
Yet here I am.

Elizabeth. Love someone else, my dear.
I will forgive you.

Essex. You mean you would try to forgive me.

Elizabeth. Aye, but I would.

Essex. What would you have to forgive?
I have tried to love others. It's empty as ashes.

Elizabeth. What others?

Essex. No one.

Elizabeth. What others?

Essex. Everyone.

Elizabeth. Everyone?

Essex. That too has been your triumph! What is a cry
Of love in the night, when I am sick and angry
And care not? I would rather hear your mocking
laughter—
Your laughter—mocking at me—defying me
Ever to be happy—with another.

Elizabeth. You have done this to me?

Essex. You have done this to me! You've made it all
empty
Away from you! And with you too!

Elizabeth. And me—what of me while you were gone?

Essex. If we
Must quarrel when we meet, why then, for God's sake,
Let us quarrel. At least we can quarrel together.

Elizabeth. I think if we are to love we must love and be
silent—
For when we speak—

Essex. I'll be silent then.
And you shall speak—

Elizabeth.
[*Her finger to her lips*]
Hush!

Essex. If you would sometimes heed me—

Elizabeth. Hush!

Essex. Only sometimes—only when I'm right. If you would
Say to yourself that even your lover might be
Right sometimes, instead of flying instantly
Into opposition as soon as I propose
A shift in policy!

Elizabeth. But you were wrong! You were wrong!
A campaign into Spain's pure madness, and to strike at
Flanders
At the same moment . . . think of the drain in men
And the drain on the treasury, and the risks we'd run
Of being unable to follow success or failure
For lack of troops and money . . . !

Essex.
[*Letting his arms fall*]
But why lack money . . .

And why lack men? There's no richer country in Europe
In men or money than England! It's this same ancient
Unprofitable niggardliness that pinches pennies
And wastes a world of treasure! You could have all
      Spain,
And Spain's dominions in the new world, an empire
Of untold wealth . . . and you forgo them because
You fear to lay new taxes!

Elizabeth. I have tried that . . .
      And never yet has a warlike expedition
      Brought me back what it cost!

Essex. You've tried half-measures . . .
      Raids on the Spanish coast, a few horsemen sent
      Into Flanders and out again, always defeating
      Yourself by trying too little! What I plead for
      Is to be bold once, just once, give the gods a chance
      To be kind to us . . . walk through this cobweb Philip
      And take his lazy cities with a storm
      Of troops and ships!
      If we are to trifle we might better sit
      At home forever, and rot!

Elizabeth. Here we sit then,
      And rot, as you put it.

Essex. I'm sorry . . .

Elizabeth. It seems to me
      We rot to some purpose here. I have kept the peace
      And kept my people happy and prosperous.

Essex. And at what a price . . .
      What a cowardly price!

Elizabeth. I am no coward either.
It requires more courage not to fight than to fight
When one is surrounded by hasty hot-heads, urging
Campaigns in all directions.

Essex. Think of the name
You will leave . . . They will set you down in histories
As the weasel queen who fought and ran away,
Who struck one stroke, preferably in the back,
And then turned and ran . . .

Elizabeth. Is it my fame you think of,
Or your own, my lord? Have you not built your name
High enough? I gave you your chance at Cadiz,
And you took it, and now there's no name in all England
Like yours to the common people. When we ride in
 the streets
Together, it's Essex they cheer and not their queen.
What more would you have?

Essex. Is it for fear of me
And this hollow cheering you hold me back from Spain?

Elizabeth. It's because I believe in peace, and have no faith
In wars or what wars win.

Essex. You do not fear me?

Elizabeth. Yes, and I fear you, too! You believe yourself
Fitter to be king than I to be queen! You are flattered
By this crying of your name by fools! You trust me no
 more
Than you'd trust . . . Penelope . . . or any other woman
To be in power! You believe you'd rule England better
Because you're a man!

Essex. That last is true. I would.
And that doesn't mean I don't love you . . . remember
that.
I love you, my queen, madly, beyond all measure,
But that's not to say I cannot see where you fail
As sovereign here, and see that why you fail
When you do is merely because a woman cannot
Act and think like a man.

Elizabeth. Act and think like a man . . . !
Why should I
Think like a man when a woman's thinking's wiser?
What do you plan? To depose me, take over the king-
dom?

Essex.
[*Smiling*]
You are a touchy queen.

Elizabeth. I had bad bringing up.
I was never sure who my mother was going to be
Next day, and it shook my nerves.

Essex. You're your father's daughter,
I'll swear to that. I can tell by your inconstancy.

Elizabeth. I wish you had need
To fear for me . . . or at any rate that I'd never
Let you see how much I'm yours.

Essex. But why?

Elizabeth. Tell me, my dear,
Do you tire of me . . . do I wear upon you a little?

Essex. Never.

Elizabeth. But you'd have to say that, you can see . . .
   You'd have to say it, because you wouldn't hurt me,
   And because I'm your queen. And so I'll never know
   Until everyone else has known and is laughing at me,
   When I've lost you. Wait, let me say this, please . . .
      When the time
   Does come and I seem old to you, and you love
   Someone else, tell me, tell me the first . . .

Essex. You are not old! I will not have you old!

Elizabeth. Will you do that, in all kindness, in memory
   Of great love past? No. You could not, could not.
   It's not in a man to be kind that way, nor in
   A woman to take it kindly. I think I'd kill you,
   In a first blind rage.

Essex. Kill me when I can say it.

Elizabeth. Love, will you let me
   Say one more thing that will hurt you?

Essex. Anything.

Elizabeth. Your blood's on fire to lead a new command
   Now that you've won so handsomely in Spain,
   And when I need a general anywhere
   You'll ask to go. Don't ask it . . . and don't go.
   You're better here in London.

Essex. Was this all you wanted?

   [*Stepping back*]

   To make me promise this?

Elizabeth.
  [*Softly*]
  Not for myself,
  I swear it, not because I think you reckless
  With men and money, though I do think that,
  Not because you might return in too much triumph
  And take my kindgom from me, which I can imagine,
  And not because I want to keep you here
  And hate to risk you, though that's also true . . .
  But rather . . . and for this you must forgive me . . .
  Because you're more a poet than general . . .
  And I fear you might fail, and lose what you have gained
  If you went again.

Essex. God's death! Whom would you send?

Elizabeth. I asked you not to be angry.

Essex. Not to be angry!
  How do you judge a leader except by whether
  He wins or loses? Was it by chance, do you think,
  That I took Cadiz?

Elizabeth. Very well. You shall go.
  Go if you will. Only I love you and I say
  What would be wiser.

Essex. You choose the one thing I must have
  And ask me not to ask it! No. Forgive me.

Elizabeth. I'll not say it again.

Essex. But if I'm more poet than
  General, why poets make better generals
  Than generals do, on occasion.

Elizabeth. You've proved it so
  One more than one occasion.
    [*A clock strikes. She rises*]
  There's the chime.
  The council's waiting, and we shall hear about Ireland,
  If Cecil has his way. One thing remember,
  You must not go to Ireland.

Essex. No. That's a war
  I'm content to miss.

Elizabeth. Thank God for that much then. I've been afraid
  Ireland might tempt you. And one more thing remember . . .
  I'll have to oppose you in the council on
  The Spanish hostages . . . You'll have your way . . .
  But I'll have to oppose you, lest they think it's your
    kingdom . . .
  Will you understand . . . ?

Essex. I'll play my part perfectly.
    [*He kisses her hand, then her lips*]

Elizabeth. Now what can come between us, out of heaven
  or hell,
  Or Spain or England?

Essex. Nothing . . . never again.

CURTAIN

ACT ONE

Scene III

Scene: *The same as Scene I, save that the doors to the council room have been thrown back, revealing a chair of state for the queen, and beneath it a table at which her councillors sit. The* Guards *are placed at left and right. The* Queen *sits in her chair.* Raleigh, Cecil, Essex, Burghley, Howard, *and one or two others are at the table. The queen's* Jester *sits cross-legged on at mat.* Burghley *is speaking.*

Burghley. It is quite true we shall have an enemy
In Spain while Philip lives and his state has power
To wage war on us, but there is little he can do
Against an island as well walled as ours.
He has tried his best, and failed. My lord of Essex
Says it costs more to fight Spain every year
In this chronic fashion than it would to throw
A challenge down, raid the Escurial
And sack the empire. With this the weight of the council
Disagrees, and we may hold it settled
That our tactics continue defensive till the queen
Rule otherwise.

Elizabeth. You'll wait some time for that.

Burghley. But in the matter
Of the Spanish ransoms it appears to me
Lord Essex has right on his side. The English soldiers
Who brought their prisoners home from the last raid
Deserve their prize money. By immemorial custom
The ransom belongs to the taker of the prisoner
And not to the state.

Elizabeth. That I intend to change,
  That same immemorial custom. I thought you had been
  Informed, Lord Burghley, that it was my will
  That the Spanish ransoms be paid to the treasury.

Burghley. But my lord of Essex . . .

Elizabeth. My lord of Essex does not speak for me.
  I was told this expedition into Spain
  Would be paid for in booty. The cost, so far,
  Has not been made up; and since there are Spanish
    nobles
  To be ransomed, I think they should pay it.

Essex. Your Majesty,
  I do not speak for myself . . . I took no prizes . . .
  But only to redeem my word. I assured
  My followers that they would have for their own
  Whatever ransoms they earned.

Elizabeth. And by what right
  Did you make this promise?

Essex. By this same ancient custom
  Of which Lord Burghley speaks. A custom so well
  Established there's not a soldier anywhere
  But takes it for granted.

Elizabeth. Your word is pledged?

Essex. It is.

Elizabeth.
    [*Smiling*]
  And if the state should confiscate these ransoms
  You would make them good to the captors?

Essex. No. To speak frankly . . .

   [*He smiles*]

   No.

Elizabeth. Then the issue lies between the queen
   And her soldiers . . . and your lordship need feel no
   Concern in the matter.

Essex. When I made these promises
   I spoke for Your Majesty . . . or believed I did.

Elizabeth. Master Cecil, advise us; am I as queen
   Bound by Lord Essex' promise?

Cecil. No, my liege;
   It is well-known a regent may repudiate
   Treaty or word of a subject officer.
   The throne is not bound.

Essex. If it comes to repudiation,
   The throne can, of course, repudiate what it likes.
   But not without breaking faith.

Elizabeth. I fear we are wrong, Sir Robert;
   And what has been promised for me and in my name
   By my own officer, my delegate in the field,
   I must perform. The men may have their ransoms.
   The state will take its loss; for this one time
   Only, and this the last. In the future a prisoner
   Is held in the name of the state, and whatever price
   Is on his head belongs to the crown. Our action
   Here is made no precedent. What further
   Business is there before us?

Cecil. There is one perpetual
　　Subject, Your Majesty, which we take up
　　Time after time, and always leave unsettled,
　　But which has come to a place where we must act
　　One way or another. Tyrone's rebellion in Ulster
　　Is no longer a smouldering coal, but a running fire
　　Spreading north to south. We must conquer Ireland
　　Finally now, or give over what we have won.
　　Ireland's not Spain.

Elizabeth. I grant you.

The Fool. I also grant you.

Elizabeth. Be quiet, fool.

The Fool. Be quiet, fool.
　　[*He slaps his own mouth*]

Elizabeth. Lord Burghley,
　　You shall speak first. What's to be done in Ireland?

Burghley. If my son is right, and I believe him to be,
　　We can bide our time no longer there. They have
　　Some help from Spain, and will have more, no doubt,
　　And the central provinces are rising. We must
　　Stamp out this fire or lose the island.

Elizabeth. This means
　　Men, money, ships?

Burghley. Yes, madam.

Cecil. And more than that . . .
　　A leader.

Elizabeth. What leader?

Cecil. A Lord Protector
Of Ireland who can carry sword and fire
From one end of the bogs to the other, and have English
 law
On Irish rebels till there are no rebels.
We've governed Ireland with our left hand, so far,
And our hold is slipping. The man who goes there now
Must be one fitted to master any field . . .
The best we have.

Elizabeth. What man? Name one.

Cecil. We should send,
Unless I am wrong, a proved and able general,
Of no less rank, say, than Lord Howard here,
Lord Essex, Sir Walter Raleigh, Knollys, or Mount-
 joy . . .
This is no slight matter, to keep or lose the island.

Elizabeth. I grant you that also.

The Fool. I also grant you. Be quiet,
Fool!
 [*He slaps his mouth*]

Elizabeth. I ask you for one and you name a dozen,
Sir Robert.

Raleigh. Why should one go alone, if it comes
To that? Why not two expeditions, one
To Dublin, one into Ulster, meeting half-way?

Elizabeth. Are there two who could work together?

Cecil. Knollys and Mountjoy.
They are friends and of one house.

Essex. Yes, of my house.

Elizabeth. Essex, whom would you name?

Essex. Why, since Lord Cecil
Feels free to name my followers, I shall feel free
To name one or two of his . . .

Elizabeth. In other words,
You would rather Knollys and Mountjoy did not go?

Essex. I would rather they stayed in England, as Sir
Robert knows.
I have need of them here. But I will spare one of them
If Lord Cecil will let Sir Francis Vere go with him.

Elizabeth. Let Vere and Knollys go.

Cecil. Lord Essex names
Sir Francis Vere because he knows full well
I cannot spare him, my liege.

Elizabeth. Is this appointment
To wait for all our private bickerings?
Can we send no man of worth to Ireland, merely
Because to do so would weaken some house or party
Here at court?

The Fool. Your Majesty has said . . .

Elizabeth. Be quiet . . .

The Fool. Fool!

Elizabeth. Be quiet!

The Fool. Fool!

Elizabeth. Be quiet!

[*The* FOOL *forms the word "fool" with his lips, but makes no sound*]

Cecil.

[*Rising*]

I hope I betray no secret, Sir Walter,
If I tell the council that I spoke with you
Before the session, and asked you if you would go
Into Ireland if the queen requested it . . . and that you
    said
Yes, should the queen desire it.

Burghley. That would answer.

Cecil. But I believe, and Sir Walter believes, there should
    be
More than one hand in this . . . that if he goes
Lord Essex should go with him.

Elizabeth. With him?

Essex. In what
    Capacity?

Cecil. Leading an equal command. Two generals
    Of coeval power, landing north and south
    And meeting to crush Tyrone.

Essex. Would you set up
    Two Lord Protectors?

Cecil. It was my thought that we name
    Raleigh as Lord Protector.

Essex. And I under him?

Cecil. Since the Azores adventure
  Which my Lord Essex led, and which came off
  A little lamer than could be wished, but in which
  Sir Walter showed to very great advantage,
  It has seemed to me that Raleigh should receive
  First place if he served in this.

Essex.
  [*Rising*]
  This is deliberate,
  An insult planned!

Cecil. It is no insult, my lord,
  But plain truth. I speak for the good of the state.

Essex. You lie! You have never spoken here or elsewhere
  For any cause but your own!

Elizabeth. No more of this!

Essex. The good of the state! Good God!
  Am I to swallow this from a clerk, a pen-pusher . . .
  To be told I may have second place, for the good of the
    state?

Cecil. Were you not wrong at the Azores?

Essex. No, by God!
  And you know it!

Elizabeth. Whoever makes you angry has won
  Already, Essex!

Essex. They have planned this!

Cecil. I say no more.
  Raleigh will go to Ireland as Lord Protector

And go alone, if the queen asks it of him,
And since you will not go.

Essex. I have not said
I would not go. But if I were to go I would go
Alone, as Lord Protector!

Elizabeth. That you will not.
I have some word in this.

Essex. If this pet rat
Lord Cecil wishes to know my mind about him,
And it seems he does, he shall have it! How he first crept
Into favor here I know not, but the palace is riddled
With his spying and burrowing and crawling under-
      ground!
He has filled the court with his rat friends, very gentle,
White, squeaking, courteous folk, who show their teeth
Only when cornered; who smile at you, speak you fair
And spend their nights gnawing the floors and chairs
Out from under us all!

Elizabeth. My lord!

Essex. I am
Not the gnawing kind, nor will I speak fair
To those who don't mean me well . . . no, nor to those
To whom I mean no good! I say frankly here,
Yes, to their faces, that Cecil and Walter Raleigh
Have made themselves my enemies because
They cannot brook greatness or power in any but
Themselves! And I say this to them . . . and to the
      world . . .
I, too, have been ambitious, as all men are

Who bear a noble mind, but if I rise
It will be by my own effort, and not by dragging
Better men down through intrigue! I admit
Sir Walter Raleigh's skill as a general
And Cecil's statecraft! I could work with them freely
And cheerfully, but every time I turn
My back they draw their knives! When Cecil left Eng-
    land
I guarded his interests as I would my own
Because he asked me to . . . but when I left,
And left my affairs in his hands . . . on my return
I found my plans and my friends out in the rain
Along with the London beggars!

Cecil. I did my best . . .

Essex. Aye . . . the best for yourself! For the good of the
    state!

Raleigh. If Lord Essex wishes
    To say he is my enemy, very well . . .
    He is my enemy.

Essex. But you were mine first . . .
    And I call the gods to witness you would be my friend
    Still, if I'd had my way! I take it hard
    That here, in the queen's council, where there should be
    Magnanimous minds if anywhere, there is still
    No trust or friendship!

Elizabeth. I take it hard that you
    Should quarrel before me.

Essex. Would you have us quarrel

Behind your back? It suits them all too well
To quarrel in secret and knife men down in the dark!

Burghley. This is fantastic, my lord. There has been no
  knifing.
  Let us come to a decision. We were discussing
  The Irish protectorate.

Cecil. And as for Ireland,
  I am willing to leave that in Lord Essex' hands
  To do as he decides.

Essex. Send your Sir Walter
  To Ireland as Protector! And be damned to it!

Cecil. As the queen wishes.
  It is a task both difficult and dangerous.
  I cannot blame Lord Essex for refusing
  To risk his fame there.

Essex. There speaks the white rat again!
  Yet even a rat should know I have never refused
  A task out of fear! I said I would not go
  As second in command!

Cecil. Then would you go
  As Lord Protector?

Elizabeth. You have named your man . . .
  Sir Walter Raleigh.

Raleigh. I'll go if Essex goes.

Essex. What! Is our Raleigh
  Afraid to go alone?

Raleigh. I don't care for it . . .
  And neither does our Essex!

Essex. Why, what is this
   That hangs over Ireland? Is it haunted, this Ireland?
   Is it a kind of hell where men are damned
   If they set foot on it? I've never seen the place,
   But if it's a country like other countries, with people
   Like other people in it, it's nothing to be
   Afraid of, more than France or Wales or Flanders
   Or anywhere else!

Cecil. We hear you say so.

Essex. If I
   Am challenged to go to Ireland, then, Christ, I'll go!
   Give me what men and horse I need, and put me
   In absolute charge, and if I fail to bring
   This Tyrone's head back with me, and put the rebellion
   To sleep forever, take my sword from me
   And break it . . . I'll never use it again!

Elizabeth. Will you listen . . . ?

Essex. They've challenged me!

Elizabeth. If you volunteer
   To go to Ireland there is none to stop you.
   You are first soldier here, first in acclaim
   And in achievement, but since the decision lies
   With yourself alone, reflect a little.

Essex. My queen,
   I can see that Raleigh and Cecil have set themselves
   To bait me into Ireland! They know and I know
   That Ireland has been deadly to any captain
   Who risked his fortunes there; moreover, once

I'm gone they think to strip me here at home
Ruin me both ways! And I say to them "Try it!"
There are men who are greater than Ireland or their
  chicane . . .
Since this is a challenge I go, and go alone,
And return victorious, and, by God, more of a problem
To Cecils and Raleighs than when I went!

[*The* Fool *rises and approaches* Essex *from behind*]

Burghley. If Essex
Will go, it solves our problem, Your Majesty.
We could hardly refuse that offer.

Elizabeth. No.

Essex. I will go,
And I will return! Mark me!

The Fool.
    [*Touching* Essex]
My lord! My lord!

Essex.
    [*Turning suddenly with an instinctive motion that sweeps the*
        Fool *to the floor*]
Take your hands off me! You touch me for a fool?
    [*He helps the* Fool *up*]
Get up!

The Fool. Do not go to Ireland!

Essex.
    [*Impatiently*]
You too?

The Fool. Because, my lord, I come from Ireland.
  All the best fools come from Ireland, but only
  A very great fool will go there.

Essex. Faugh!

The Fool. It's not too late yet!

Elizabeth. Break up the council, my lords.
  We meet tomorrow.

Burghley. And this is decided?

Essex. Yes!

Elizabeth. Yes, if you wish it. Go now.
      [*The council rises when the queen does and files out silently,*
            leaving ESSEX *and* ELIZABETH]
  You should have had
  The fool's brain and he yours! You would have bettered
  By the exchange.

Essex. I thank you kindly, lady.

Elizabeth. What malicious star
  Danced in my sky when you were born, I wonder?

Essex. What malicious star danced in the sky
  Of Ireland, you should ask.

Elizabeth. Oh, my dear,
  You are a child in council. I saw them start
  To draw you into this, and tried to warn you . . .
  But it was no use.

Essex. They drew me into nothing.
  I saw their purpose and topped it with my own.
  Let them believe they've sunk me.

Elizabeth. You will withdraw.
  I'll countermand this.

Essex. And give them the laugh on me?
  I'll have the laugh on them yet.

Elizabeth. Better they should laugh
  A little now than laugh at you forever.

Essex. And why not win in Ireland?

Elizabeth. No man wins there.
  You're so dazzled
  With the chance to lead an army you'd follow the devil
  In an assault on heaven.

Essex. No, but I'd lead him.
  Heaven is always taken by storm. That's one thing
  The devil doesn't know. Ireland is only
  A country, and this is superstition.

Elizabeth. I know.
  You were quite right. I thought so as you said it.
  Only somehow here in my breast something con-
    stricts . . .
  Is it the heart grows heavy? I must let you go . . .
  And I'll never see you again.

Essex. Mistrust all these
  Forebodings. When they prove correct we remember
    them,
  But when they're wrong we forget them. They mean
    nothing.
  Remember this when I'm back and all turns out well . . .
  That you felt all would turn out badly.

Elizabeth. Oh, my love,
Come touch me, tell me all will happen well.

Essex. And so it will.

Elizabeth. Do you want to go?

Essex. Why yes . . .
And no. I've said I would and I will.

Elizabeth. It's not yet
Too late. There are no announcements made, no orders
Given. If you win, that will divide us . . .
And if you lose, that will divide us too.

Essex. I'll win, and it will not divide us. Is it so hard
To believe in me?

Elizabeth. No . . . I'll believe in you . . .
And even forgive you if you need it. Here.
My father gave me this ring . . . and told me if ever
He lost his temper with me, to bring it to him
And he'd forgive me. And so it saved my life . . .
Long after, when he'd forgotten, long after, when
One time he was angry.

Essex. Darling, if ever
You're angry rings won't help.

Elizabeth. Yes, but it would.
I'd think of you as you are now, and it would.
Take it.

Essex. I have no pledge from you. I'll take it
To remember you in absence.

Elizabeth. Take it for a better reason. Take it because

The years are long, and full of sharp, wearing days
That wear out what we are and what we have been
And change us into people we do not know,
Living among strangers. Lest you and I who love
Should wake some morning strangers and enemies
In an alien world, far off; take my ring, my lover.

Essex. You fear
    You will not always love me?

Elizabeth. No, that you
    Will not love me, and will not let me love you.
        [*She puts the ring on his finger*]

CURTAIN

ELIZABETH THE QUEEN
ACT TWO

ACT TWO

Scene I

Scene: *The queen's study.* Penelope *is sitting reading. The* Fool *enters. She does not see him.*

The Fool. Sh! Make no noise.

Penelope. What do you mean?

The Fool. Silence! Quiet!

Penelope. I am silent, fool.

The Fool. You silent? And even as you say it you are talking!

Penelope. You began it.

The Fool. Began what?

Penelope. Talking.

The Fool. Oh, no. Talking began long before my time. It was a woman began it.

Penelope. Her name?

The Fool. Penelope, I should judge.

Penelope. Fool.

The Fool.

[*Looking away*]

No, for with this same Penelope began also beauty and courage and tenderness and faith . . . all that a man could desire or a woman offer . . . and all that this early Penelope began has a later Penelope completed.

55

Penelope.
   [*Rising*]
   It lacked only this . . . that the court fool should make
   love to me.

The Fool. I am sorry to have been laggard. But truly I
   have never found you alone before.

Penelope. How lucky I've been!

The Fool. Are you angered?

Penelope. At what?

The Fool. At my loving you.

Penelope. I've learned to bear nearly everything.

The Fool. A lover's absence?

Penelope. Among other things.

The Fool. The presence of suitors undesired?

Penelope. That, too.

The Fool. I am not a suitor, my lady. I ask nothing. I know
   where your heart lies. It is with my lord Essex in Ireland.
   I do not love you.

Penelope. Good.

The Fool. I lied to you. I do love you.

Penelope. I am sorry.

The Fool. You will not laugh at me?

Penelope. No.

The Fool. Then there is yet some divinity in the world . . .

while a woman can still be sorry for one who loves her without return.

Penelope. A woman is sadly aware that when a man loves her it makes a fool of him.

The Fool. And if a fool should love a woman . . . would it not make a man of him?

Penelope. No, but doubly a fool, I fear.

The Fool. And the women . . . how of the women?

Penelope. They have been fools, too.

The Fool. The more fool I, I tried to save Lord Essex from Ireland . . . but he needs must go . . . the more fool he.

Penelope. Let us not talk of that.

The Fool. May I kiss you?

Penelope. No.

The Fool. Your hand?

Penelope. Yes.

    [*He kisses her hand*]

The Fool. I thank you.

    [*She touches his fool's cap gently with her hand*]

Penelope. The more fool you, poor boy.

    [Robert Cecil *enters from the left*]

Cecil. This is hardly a seemly pastime, Mistress Gray.

Penelope. And are you now the judge of what is seemly, Sir Robert?

Cecil.
[*To the* FOOL]
Be off with you!
[*To* PENELOPE]
The queen is expecting Master Bacon here?
[*The* FOOL *goes*]

Penelope. I am set to wait for him.

Cecil. You will not be needed.

Penelope. Excellent.
[*She goes out right, passing* RALEIGH, *who enters*]

Cecil. This Bacon keeps himself close. I have been unable
to speak with him. She has this news?

Raleigh. Yes.

Cecil. She believes it?

Raleigh. Burghley himself believes it.

Cecil. Then she does.

Raleigh. Beyond question.
[*The curtains part at the left and* BACON *enters*]

Cecil. Good-morrow, Master Bacon.

Bacon. And to you, my lords.

Cecil. I have sent everywhere for you, sir, this three hours
. . . and perhaps it was not altogether by accident that
I could not find you.

Bacon. I was not at home. You must forgive me.

Cecil. You are here to see the queen?

Bacon.

    [*Bowing*]

The queen has also been good enough to send for me.

Cecil. It was my wish to speak with you first . . . and it is my opinion that it will be the better for all of us, if I do so now . . . late as it is.

Bacon. I am but barely on time, gentlemen.

Cecil. You need answer one question only. You have been in correspondence with Lord Essex in Ireland?

Bacon. Perhaps.

Cecil. The queen has this morning received news warning her that Lord Essex is allied with the Irish rebels and is even now leading his army back to England to usurp her throne. Had you heard this?

Bacon. No.

Cecil. Do you credit it?

Bacon. It is your own scheme, I believe.

Cecil. That Essex should rebel against the queen?

Bacon. Even so.

Raleigh. You accuse us of treason?

Bacon. If the queen were aware of certain matters she would herself accuse you of treason.

Cecil. What matters?

Bacon. I prefer that the queen should question me.

Cecil. Look to yourself, Master Bacon. If you intend to

accuse any man of the suppression of letters written by Essex to the queen, or of the suppression of letters sent by the queen to Essex, you will be unable to prove these assertions and you will argue yourself very neatly into the Tower.

Bacon. My lord . . . I had no such business in mind.

Raleigh. Then what? . . .

Bacon. I hope I can keep my own counsel. The truth is, my lords, you are desperate men. You have overreached yourselves, and if wind of it gets to the royal ears you are done.

Raleigh. We shall drag a few down with us if we are done, though, and you the first.

Cecil. You have but a poor estimate of me, Master Bacon. If you go in to the queen and reveal to her that her letters to Essex have not reached him . . . as you mean to do . . . the queen will then send for me, and I will send for Lord Essex' last letter to you, containing a plan for the capture of the city of London. It will interest you to know that I have read that letter and you are learned enough in the law to realize in what light you will stand as a witness should the queen see it.

Bacon. I think it is true, though, that if I go down I shall also drag a few with me, including those here present.

Cecil. I am not so sure of that, either. I am not unready for that contingency. But to be frank with you, it would be easier for both you and us if you were on our side.

Bacon. You must expect a man to side with his friends.

Cecil. And a man's friends . . . who are they? Those who can help him to what he wants.

Bacon. Not always.

Cecil. When he is wise. You have served Lord Essex well and I believe he has made you promises. But the moment Essex enters England in rebellion, he is doomed, and his friends with him.

Bacon. One word from the queen to him . . . one word from him to the queen . . . one word from me, revealing that their letters have been intercepted, and there can be no talk of rebellion. There has been some underhand traffic with the couriers between here and Ireland. Their letters have been lost, you have induced the queen to promulgate arbitrary orders . . . and since they are both proud, you have bred distrust in her and defiance in him. Your machinations have been so direct, so childish, so simple . . . and so simply exposed . . . that I wonder at you!

Cecil. My friend, a child could trip him. Not so simple as your own. I have news this morning that Lord Essex has already landed in England and set up his standard here. He is a rebel, and when a man is once a rebel, do you think there will be any careful inquiry into how he happened to become one?

Bacon. Essex in England!

Cecil. In England.

Raleigh. And has neglected to disband his army.

Cecil. You speak of explanations between the queen and

Essex. Unless you betray us there will be no explanations. They are at war and will never meet again.

Bacon. That is, if your plan succeed.

Cecil.

[Standing aside]

Very well, then. Go in. You have chosen your master.
I have done with you.

Bacon.

[Not moving]

And if I say nothing?

Cecil. Then . . . whatever you have been promised, whatever you have desired, that you shall have. There is no
place in the courts you could not fill. You shall have your
choice. If you need excuse, no-one should know better
than you that this Essex is a danger to the state, a danger to the queen, a danger to liberty.

Bacon. If I need excuse I shall find one for myself.

[There is a pause. Then the curtain parts to the right and
PENELOPE enters. She holds the curtain back]

Penelope. Yes, Your Majesty; he is here.

Elizabeth. Why was I not told?

[She enters]

Is this an ante-chamber, Sir Robert? Am I never to look
out of my room without seeing you?

Cecil. Your pardon, Your Majesty. I was just going.

Elizabeth. Then go. You need not pause to explain why
you came. I am weary of your face!

Cecil. Yes, Your Majesty.

[CECIL *and* RALEIGH *bow and depart*]

Elizabeth. I have heard that you are a shrewd man, Master
Bacon.

Bacon. Flattery, Majesty, flattery.

Elizabeth. I have heard it,
And in a sort I believe it. Tell me one thing . . .
Are you Cecil's friend?

Bacon. I have never been.

Elizabeth. He is a shrewd man; he's
A man to make a friend of if you'd stand well
In the court, sir.

Bacon. It may be so.

Elizabeth. Why are you not
His friend then?

Bacon. We are not on the same side.

Elizabeth. You follow Lord Essex?

Bacon. Since I have known him.

Elizabeth. There's
A dangerous man to follow.

Bacon. Lord Essex?

Elizabeth. Lord Essex.

Bacon. I am sorry, madam,
If I have displeased you.

Elizabeth. You have displeased me.

Bacon. I repeat then . . .
I am sorry.

Elizabeth. You will change, then? You will forget
This Essex of yours?

Bacon. If you ask it . . . if there is reason . . .

Elizabeth. Well, there is reason! He has taken up arms
Against me in Ireland.

Bacon. You are sure of this?

Elizabeth. I have reports. Is it so hard to believe?

Bacon. Without proofs, it is.

Elizabeth. I have proof.

Bacon. May I ask of what sort?

Elizabeth. Proof good enough. You know the punishment
For treason? From what I have heard
Of late both you and Essex should remember
That punishment.

Bacon. Madam, for myself I have
No need to fear, and if Lord Essex has
I am more than mistaken in him.

Elizabeth. I am very sorry
That I must do this . . . but all friends of Essex
Go straightway to the Tower. I have sent for you
To give you a last chance to change your mind
Before this blow falls. Are you still his friend?

Bacon. Yes, Majesty.

Elizabeth. I am sorry for it.

Bacon. That is all?

Elizabeth. Why, no. You do not believe me?

Bacon. I do not.

Elizabeth. And why?

Bacon. I neither believe our Essex a rebel
Nor that you believe so. If you intended to place me
In the Tower . . . I would be in the Tower . . . and no
talk about it.

Elizabeth. You are shrewd indeed.

Bacon. I am Essex' friend.

Elizabeth. If that
Were true . . . if I could speak to you . . . if there were
only
The sound of one honest voice!
. . . I must rule England,
And they say he is rebel to me . . . and day and night,
Waking, sleeping, in council, there is still always
One thing crying out in me over and again . . .
Waking and sleeping I hear it crying: He cannot,
Cannot fail me! But I have written him my love
And he has not answered. What you know of this
Answer me truly, truly . . . bitter or not,
And you shall not lose!

Bacon. He has not answered?

Elizabeth. No.

Bacon. If I
Knew why I would know much. Have you angered
him . . .
Sent arbitrary orders?

Elizabeth. I have ordered him to disband
His forces and return. I have cut off
Revenue and supplies.

Bacon. But this was rash . . .
To send a popular leader out with an army
And then check him suddenly, heap disgrace upon
   him . . .
He has great pride.

Elizabeth.
   [*Getting up*]
He has rebelled then?
I wrote him lovingly.

Bacon. And he answered? . . .

Elizabeth. Nothing.

Bacon. That could not be excused.

Elizabeth. And it cannot be. It's true. It will not be!

Bacon. Dear queen, I fear
I have turned you against him!

Elizabeth. No, no! I needed that!

Bacon. And if there were something wrong . . .
Some misunderstanding? . . .

Elizabeth. No, no . . . don't try comfort now . . .
He had my letters. That could not go wrong.
Did he not have my letters?

Bacon. Could it be otherwise?

Elizabeth. You would know that. You would know if he
   had not.
You've had word from him?

Bacon. Yes.

Elizabeth. He has written you,
  But not me! Or are you traitor to him also? . . .
  I think you are! I think you lie to me! I am
  Encompassed by lies! I think you, too, betray him . . .
  But subtly, with infinite craft, making me believe
  First that you would not wrong him! No, no . . . I'm
    gone mad
  Pacing my room, pacing the room of my mind.
  They say a woman's mind is an airless room,
  Sunless and airless, where she must walk alone
  Saying he loves me, loves me, loves me not,
  And has never loved me. The world goes by, all shadows,
  And there are voices, all echoes till he speaks . . .
  And there's no light till his presence makes a light
  There in that room. But I am a queen. Where I walk
  Is a hall of torture, where the curious gods bring all
  Their racks and gyves, and stretch me there to writhe
  Till I cry out. They watch me with eyes of iron
  Waiting to hear what I cry! I am crying now . . .
  Listen, you gods of iron! He never loved me . . .
  He wanted my kingdom only . . .
  Loose me and let me go! I am yet a queen . . .
  That I have! That he will not take from me.
  I shall be queen, and walk his room no more.
  He thought to break me down by not answering . . .
  Break me until I'd say, I'm all yours . . . what I am
  And have, all yours! That I will never, never,
  Never say. I'm not broken yet.

Bacon. Nor will be, majesty.

Elizabeth. We must not follow him.
We must forget him, break him as he would break us,
Bow that bright head . . . I shall be as I was.
See him no more, my friend,
He walks on quicksand. Avoid him.

Bacon. Yes, my queen.

Elizabeth. Go, my friend.
You have done well. I trust you.

Bacon. I thank Your Majesty.

> [*He goes out.* ELIZABETH *claps her hands twice. After a moment* CAPTAIN ARMIN *enters*]

Elizabeth. Captain Armin, keep a watch on Master Bacon,
On his house and on his correspondence.
I wish to know all he knows.

Armin. Yes, Your Majesty.

Elizabeth. Wait. I have found you true of word,
And sure of hand. Moreover, you can keep counsel—

> [ARMIN *bows. She beckons him to come to her. He does so*]

What we say now is forever secret between us—
Between us two—not one other.

Armin. I'll hold it so.

Elizabeth. It is reported there is an army risen
Against me—

Armin. God forbid!

Elizabeth. It is so reported. The rebellion I speak of's the force
Lord Essex has brought back with him from Ireland.

I wish to make this preparation for it: Whatever orders
You receive from your superiors, whatever broils
Occur, he is to have free access to my presence.

Armin. There would be danger to your person, madame.

Elizabeth. I will risk that.

Armin. You would be hostage if he were in command.

Elizabeth. Be ready for danger—and if need be, death.

Armin. Yes, Majesty.

> [*He goes out.* ELIZABETH *stands motionless for a moment.
> There is a sudden burst of girls' laughter in an adjoining
> room, and the* FOOL *runs in with a garment in his hand.
> Three* GIRLS *run after him, the foremost tripping him
> so that he falls in a corner and is instantly pounced
> upon by all three*]

Mary.
> [*Entering*]

Thief! Thief! Stop thief!

Ellen. Kill the slobber thief! Fall on him!

Tressa. Can a maid not keep a silk smock?

The Fool. Help! Salvage! Men-at-arms to the rescue! I am
boarded by pirates!
> [*They tickle him*]

Ellen. Tear it from him! He will exhibit it!

Tressa. No, no! Don't tear it!

The Fool. If you sit on me in that fashion, darling, you will
regret it. There will be issue!

Ellen. What issue?

The Fool. Twins! Seven or eight!
> [ELLEN *slaps him*]

Mary. Rise! Rise quickly! The queen is here. Rise!
> [*They all get up in confusion*]

Tressa. We are sorry, Your Majesty.
> ELIZABETH *looks at them without seeing them and goes out to her bedroom*]

Ellen. What is it? She seemed not to see.

Mary. It's not like her not to strike us.

Tressa. We'll be whipped.

The Fool. No, no. She strikes instantly or not at all.

Tressa. Give me that.
> [*She snatches her smock from the* FOOL]

Mary. Come.
> [*They tiptoe out*]

CURTAIN

ACT TWO

Scene II

Scene: *The interior of Essex' tent on the coast of England.* Essex *sits in the light of a candle, reading dispatches. A* Guard *stands in the shadow.* Marvel, *an aide, enters.*

Marvel. There is a courier from the queen, my lord.

Essex. At last, then.

Marvel. You will see him at once?

Essex. Yes . . . Wait. Bring him in and stay here while I read the dispatches. If I give orders to torture or kill him, show no surprise. You understand?

Marvel. You will not torture him?

Essex. Am I not tortured? And you, too, sirrah. You will remember?

The Guard. Yes, my lord.

Essex. Good.

> [Marvel *goes out.* Essex *rises and stands out of the light, waiting.* Marvel *enters with the* Courier, *who falls on his knee before* Essex]

The Courier. My lord of Essex?

Essex. Yes.

Courier. Dispatches from the queen.

Essex. When did you leave London?

Courier. Four days ago, my lord. We were delayed.

Essex. What delayed you?

Courier. Robbers.

Essex. And they took what from you?

Courier. Our horses and money.

Essex. And the letters? . . .

Courier. Were returned to me untouched.

Essex. When did this happen?

Courier. This side of the ford. There were four armed men
against us two.

Essex. Give me the letters.
[*The* COURIER *does so.* ESSEX *reads briefly*]
This is all?

Courier. Yes, my lord.

Essex. You are sure you have lost nothing?

Courier. Indeed yes, my lord. There was but one missive
and the seal was returned unbroken. The cut-throats
told us they cared the less about our letters for they
could not read.

Essex. You are a clever liar, sirrah, and you are the third
liar who has come that same road to me from London.
You are the third liar to tell this same tale. You shall
pay for being the third.

Courier. My lord, I have not lied to you.

Essex. Take his weapons from him, lieutenant.
[MARVEL *obeys*]

Set him against the post there. Not so gently. He shall
lose his ears first and then his lying tongue.

Courier. Your lordship does not mean this?

Essex. And why not? We shall then cut him in pieces ...
But gradually, with infinite delicacy.
  [MARVEL *approaches the* COURIER *with a knife. The* GUARD
  holds him]

Courier. No, no, no, no! Oh, God! Oh, my lord! My lord!

Essex. What are you waiting for?

Marvel. We must tie him to the pole first, sir.

Essex. Then tie him!

Courier. No, no ... oh, God, no! What do you want of me?
I swear to you I haven't lied to you! I swear ... ugh!
  [*He is choked*]

Essex. Let him speak. What do you swear?

Courier. My lord, I have not lied ... I speak truth ...

Essex. Tie him up.

Courier. Let me speak ... I can ... ugh ...

Essex. Silence him. We know too well what you have done,
sirrah. We need no evidence of that. What we ask is that
you tell us who set you on ... and your accomplices.
Tell us this and I want no more of you. You shall have
your freedom ... and this ...
  [*He tosses a clinking bag at his feet*]
Speak.

Courier. My lord, if I knew ...

Essex. Bind him. Truss him up and cut him open. Dispense
with these niceties. Have you no knife?
  [*He is bound*]
We have heard enough! Take out his tongue!
  [*They approach him. He becomes calm*]

Courier. My lord, I am not a coward, though it may seem
    to you
  I am, for I have cried out . . . but I cried out
  Not so much for pain or fear of pain
  But to know this was Lord Essex, whom I have loved
  And who tortures innocent men.

Essex. Come, silence him!

Courier. Come then. I am innocent. If my lord Essex
  Is as I have believed him, he will not hurt me;
  If he will hurt me, then he is not as I
  And many thousands believe him, who have loved him,
  And I shall not mind much dying.
    [*A pause*]

Essex. Let him go.
  [*They unbind the* COURIER]
  I thought my letters had been tampered with.
  You'd tell me if it were so.

Courier. My honored lord,
  By all the faith I have, and most of it's yours,
  I'd rather serve you well and lose in doing it
  Than serve you badly and gain. If something I've done
  Has crossed you or worked you ill I'm enough punished
  Only knowing it.

Essex. This letter came
From the queen's hands?

Courier. It is as I received it
From the queen's hands.

Essex. There was no other?

Courier. No other.

Essex. Take this and go.
   [*He tosses the bag to the* COURIER]

Courier. I have brought misfortune ...

Essex. You bring good news. We break camp tomorrow for
London ... Go ... take that news with you. They'll
welcome you outside. Remain with my guard and return
with us.
   [*The* COURIER *goes out*]

Marvel. We march tomorrow?

Essex. Yes.

Marvel. Under orders?

Essex. No.
   [*He reads*]
"Lord Essex is required to disperse his men
And return to the capital straightway on his own
Recognizance, to give himself up."

Marvel. And nothing with this?

Essex. Give out the necessary orders, we shall
Move at daybreak.

Marvel. Yes, my lord.

Essex. And it is
As well it falls out this way! By right of name
And power and popular voice this is my kingdom . . .
This England under my feet, more mine than hers,
As she shall learn. It is quite as well.

Marvel. There is no man
But will think so. There is victory in your path,
My lord. The London citizens will rise
At the first breath of your name.

Essex. Yes . . . that I'm sure of.

Marvel. And with London in your hands . . . well . . . it's
your world then . . .
As far as you like.

Essex. And I am glad for England.
She has lain fallow in fear too long! Her hills
Shall have a spring of victory. Goodnight.

Marvel. Goodnight.

Essex. And for this order, I received it not.
[*He tears the paper*]

CURTAIN

ACT TWO

Scene III

SCENE: *The council hall of Act I is cleared here for a court assembly. Those who attended the council are present, save for* ESSEX, *also the* FOOL, ELLEN, MARY, TRESSA, PENELOPE. BACON *and other* LORDS-AND-LADIES-IN-WAITING. BURGHLEY *and* CECIL *are standing to one side in earnest talk. Across from them a group made up of* RALEIGH, BACON, *the* FOOL *and a number of others.*

Burghley. These players should be put down with an iron hand. They have neither conscience nor morals. They will make any display for money. In my young days they were allowed only interludes and instructive entertainment. The queen has been too lax . . .

Cecil. Have you seen this play of Richard II?

Burghley. I see no plays.

Cecil. It's high treason. Richard is deposed in it. High treason.

Bacon. Treason to depose a king? Not if you succeed.

Cecil. No, but treason to teach treason.

Bacon. What is treason?

Raleigh. Said jesting Pilate.

Cecil. Is it not treason to depose a king?

Raleigh. What if it makes a king of you?

The Fool. It would then be treason not to have done it.

77

Bacon. The Fool is a Jesuit.

The Fool. In truth, he was deposed. It is treason to all his successors to deny it.

Bacon. An excellent Jesuit.

The Fool. What? I a Jesuit? Jesu!

Penelope. And a wit.

Bacon. Bad.

Penelope. Very bad.

Raleigh. Unutterably bad. What? Jesu-wit! Poisonous! Shall we allow this?

Penelope. I am guilty. I surrender.

Raleigh. What did you do with the body?

Penelope. There was none. I did eat my words.

Raleigh. A cannibal, a monster, a word-swallower!

The Fool. A man-eater.

Penelope. Nay, nay!

Bacon. Do you eat your men with butter or salt?

Penelope. With salt if they are buttery and with butter if they are salty.

Raleigh. Ready then. Here comes a salty man to be buttered.

Penelope. A butter-in.

The Fool. A salt-butter.

Bacon. A cheese . . . a whole cheese.

Tressa. Full of holes, holey.

Ellen. Pitted.

Penelope. What? Am I pitted against a cheese?

Raleigh. Let but this cheese roll into your pit, lady . . .
and you are answered.

Penelope. No . . . you are answered. You are answered no.

Burghley.

> [*To* CECIL]

There can be no doubt the Essex faction sent money to
the actors to purchase a performance of Richard. It is
an old play; it would draw no public.

Cecil. The actors are then accessory.

Burghley. Think you so?

Cecil. They could hardly be unaware of the purposes of the
Essex party.

Bacon. Is it so certain that Essex has a purpose?

Cecil. He has led his army into London.

Bacon. The men live in London. Moreover the order to
disperse on landing may not have been received. Such
things have happened.

Cecil. Yes?

Bacon. Aye, indeed.

Cecil.

> [*To* BURGHLEY]
> You are to see these actors?

Burghley. They are sending spokesmen today.

The Fool. Let them put on the play for us.

Tressa. Yes . . . the deposition scene. It may convince us. We may all turn rebel.

Burghley. Tut!

The Fool. Tut? What does this mean . . . this tut?

Burghley. Will you learn manners, sirrah? In my young days there was no such loose speaking about the court.

The Fool. There was no tutting, neither.

Penelope. You are mistaken. There used to be tutting parties. They all brought their tutting.

The Fool. Fie on you! Also pooh on you!

Penelope. Yes . . . there were fieing and poohing parties also.

Raleigh. True, true. Well I remember the old days when all the young people would get together and try which could make the greatest pooh.

Tressa. There was such laughter and jesting!

Raleigh. Ah, yes, at the old Tut, Fie and Pooh Tavern! It's torn down now, but what a place it was!

The Fool. The game went out of fashion, alas, when it was discovered that a virgin could always pooh farther than anybody else.

Tressa. Tut!

Mary. Fie!

Ellen. Pooh!

The Fool. I beg pardon. I had forgotten there were virgins present.

Penelope. We are all virgins.

Raleigh. The proof then, quickly. Show me.

Penelope. It is nothing that can be seen, my lord.

Raleigh. They say seeing is believing.

Penelope. Virginity is rather a state of mind.

Ellen. Nay . . . a state of preservation.

The Fool. I have seen these preserved virgins.

Raleigh. You have seen them?

The Fool. Seen them? I've been bothered by them. The whole court used to be driven indoors by them regularly on our progress through Middlesex.

Raleigh. They are worse at night, I believe? Middlesex . . . Middlesex . . .

Penelope. Change the subject, gentles. This virginity begins to wear thin.

The Fool. It has worn clear through, and a great hole appears in the center.

Penelope. A hole in your wit.

Raleigh. His Jesuit.

Penelope. His half-wit.

[*A* HERALD *enters and speaks to* CECIL]

The Herald. My lord, there are two fellows here who ask for audience with the queen.

Cecil. Who are they?

Herald. Players, my lord.

Cecil. Tell them to wait. The queen will see them presently.
[*The* HERALD *goes out*]

Burghley. To my mind it was one of these same players writ the ballad that was posted up at St. Paul's.

Cecil. No, no . . . the man has been discovered . . . and will have his ears cropped for it.

Burghley. But he could not have written it . . . he was but an instrument. The actors are too devilish ingenious at writing ballads. I cannot put it out of my mind they are all treasonous scoundrels.

Raleigh. Is this the ballad on the Earl's return?

Cecil. Aye . . .
"When England needeth victories
She calleth Essex on . . ."
And more to the same purpose. What I cannot understand is that the queen should take no steps to put the city in a posture of defense. Essex draws near with his army . . . and we swing the gates as usual.

Bacon. Is that a symptom of danger . . . that an English general should return with his army to the English capital?

Cecil. Are you not aware that Essex' house in the Strand

is a camp brimming full of armed nobles going and coming?

The Fool. It is much more likely to be brimming with
drunken nobles going and coming brim full.

Cecil. Be quiet!

The Fool. Fool.

[CECIL *lays a hand on his sword angrily. The* FOOL *points to
his own breast and repeats:*]

Fool.

[CECIL *turns away. There is a rustling among those present.
Several rise. At the rear the* QUEEN *appears silently,
two* LADIES *following her. She comes forward without
speaking, her eyes seeking for someone. She fixes on*
LORD BURGHLEY]

Elizabeth. Is it true, then, my dear Burghley, that you
have taken to attending the Theatre?

Burghley. No, madam.

Elizabeth. It was not you, then, who forbade the per-
formances of Richard II without asking my advice?

Burghley. It was, madam.

Elizabeth. On what ground?

Burghley. Your Majesty, the play is treasonous. It shows
the deposition of a king, and its performance was pro-
cured by rebels.

Elizabeth. Rebels? What rebels?

Burghley. I know not, madam. I have sent for the players
to discover that.

Elizabeth. You have sent for them?

Burghley. Aye, madam . . . and they are here.

Elizabeth. They will laugh at you, dear Burghley.

Burghley. Others have laughed at me, Majesty.

Elizabeth. They will laugh at you, sir, and you will deserve it. Is my kingdom so shaky that we dare not listen to a true history? Are my people so easily led that the sight of a king deposed in play will send them running thither to pull the queen out of her chair? Have we not passion plays in every little town showing the murder of our Lord? You are nervous, Lord Burghley. Let these children play their plays.

Cecil. Your Majesty, I very much fear they are not all children, and that they mean to do harm.

Elizabeth. Then let them. Let them do all the harm they can. Are we too stupid to see that to prohibit a rebellious play is to proclaim our fear of rebellion? Who is there here who fears a rebellion against me? I do not.

Cecil. It is dangerous to let these mutterings grow, dear queen.

Elizabeth. It is dangerous to touch them. Let them mutter, if they will. Let them cry out . . . let them run the streets, these children! When they have worn themselves weary running and crying "Up with Essex!" "Down with Elizabeth!" and got themselves drunk on mutual pledges, they will go to bed and sleep soundly and wake up wiser. Let me speak to these players. Bring them to me.

Burghley. Here, madam?

Elizabeth. Here.

Cecil. Majestas, adsunt legati de curia Galliæ. Placetne eos recipere antequam . . .

Elizabeth. Cras illos recipiam.

Cecil. Sed maxime præstat . . .

Elizabeth. Si bene mihi videbitur, cras redituros recipiam! Nay, I can bang you in Latin too!

> [CECIL *goes out.* ELIZABETH *sits and turns to the* FOOL]
> You, sirrah . . . I hear that you have fallen in love.
> Do you wish to be whipped?

The Fool. I would rather have been whipped, madam; much rather.

Elizabeth. Why?

The Fool. It would hurt less.

Elizabeth. Good. You shall be whipped.

The Fool. Madam, if you can whip it out of me I will give you my lucky shilling.

Elizabeth. You shall be whipped and keep your shilling.

The Fool. You would better take it, madam queen.

Elizabeth. Your shilling?

The Fool. Yes, madam queen, to buy another whip with for yourself. Nay, you had perhaps better buy several. But in truth, dear queen, I have not fallen in love, only a pretty little strumpet has fallen in love with me and I beg leave that we be allowed to marry.

Elizabeth. Is she of the court?

The Fool. Yes, madam.

Elizabeth. What, are there strumpets at court?

The Fool. Oh, they are all strumpets here at court. Some are here because they are strumpets and some are strumpets because they are here, but strumpets they all are.

Elizabeth. Which is it you wish to marry?

The Fool. It is not that I wish to marry her, madam, but she wishes to marry me.
   [*Walking about to choose finally pointing to* TRESSA]
This one, Majesty.

Tressa.
   [*Leaping at him*]
Scoundrel! . . .

The Fool.
   [*Pointing to* ELLEN]
No, no . . . I mean this one.

Ellen. You dog! You . . .
   [*The* FOOL *passes* PENELOPE *by*]

The Fool.
   [*Pointing to Mary*]
Or that one . . .

Mary. What!

The Fool. I feel sure it was one of them, Majesty . . . but it was dark at the time . . . and in truth I gave her my word of honor in the dark that I would make an honest woman of her by daylight. It is thus that most marriages are made.

Elizabeth. How, fool?

The Fool. In the dark, my lady. Quite in the dark.

Elizabeth.

[*To a soldier*]

Take this fool, captain, and put him in the dark for three days with but little bread and water. I have a distaste for this fooling.

The Fool. No, no, madam.

Elizabeth. I am tired of your strumpets! And let him not see his lady Penelope meanwhile. You will be sure of that, mistress?

Penelope. I have no desire to see him.

Elizabeth. Whom do you desire to see?

Penelope. No-one, your Majesty.

Elizabeth. You lie! This Mistress Gray, take her too! Let her have bread and water!

[*She looks at* PENELOPE *with hatred*]

Penelope. Your Majesty . . . what is this?

Elizabeth. I am weary to death of you! I am weary of all men and women, but more of you than any! You have written. You have had letters! I say, take her out of my sight!

[*The soldiers start to take out* PENELOPE *and the* FOOL]

Whip them first, whip them both!

[*The two are taken to the door*]

Nay, leave them here, leave them, knaves ... leave
them! Damn you, do you hear me! You are too quick
to obey orders! You like this whipping too well, sirrah!
You have an itch for laying on! You beef-witted bas-
tards! And now let us have entertainment, gentle lords!
Let us be merry! The players are here! Let us have a
play!

[*A* HERALD *runs in to the queen without ceremony, calling out
as he comes*]

The Herald. Your Majesty, Your Majesty! Lord Scroop
sends me from the city to tell you there is a rising in
London! There is a mob rising in the city!

Elizabeth. What ... is this one of the players? Are you
playing Richard II for us?

The Herald. No, no, Your Majesty! A great number of
people came through Fleet Street ... and they have
sacked a grocer's and broken into a wine-merchant's
cellar! It is said they will break into Fleet Prison and
set all free ...

Elizabeth. Not they. If they've broken into a wine-cellar
they'll get no farther. We're a marvellous people, we
English, but we cannot hold liquor. Now if they were
Scotch one might worry. What are they saying, these
wine drinkers?

The Herald. I cannot tell you that, Your Majesty.

Elizabeth. Are they not crying "Up with Essex!" "Down
with Elizabeth!"?

The Herald. Yes, madam!

Elizabeth. Why surely. What else would they be crying? "Up with Essex!" Viva! "Down with Elizabeth!" À bas! The queen is dead, long live the king! If I were there I would cry it myself! It has a marvellous ring! "Up with Essex!" "Down with Elizabeth!"

Burghley. What are we to do, madam?

Elizabeth.

[*To the* HERALD]

What is the Lord Mayor doing about this?

Herald. Nothing, madam.

Elizabeth. How like a Lord Mayor and how sensible. That's the first principle of government. Never do anything. Let the others make all the mistakes.

Cecil. But madam . . . there are five hundred of the royal guard at the Tower . . .

Elizabeth. Let the mayor of London look out for his people. If he allows them to run up and down breaking into wine-cellars, it's his own affair.

Burghley. But if it spreads to the palace, Majesty?

Elizabeth. Why yes . . . let them bring their revolution here to me. I should be amused to see it. They are children, Burghley, drunken children. Would you fire on children?

Burghley. Then let me go into London, madam . . .

Elizabeth. And call out the guard and put down these traitors with powder and ball? No! They are to be allowed to get quite drunk and then go to sleep. Where are these players?

[CECIL *enters with* BURBAGE *and* HEMMINGS]

Cecil. Here, madam.

Elizabeth. Ah, yes, bold Burbage and handsome Hemmings. Well, my masters, I understand that you have come to me to have your noses slit and your thumbs branded? Is it so?

Burbage. Only if unavoidable, Your Majesty.

Elizabeth. You have put on a play, I believe?

Burbage. Many, Your Majesty.

Elizabeth. You have revived the old play of Richard II, including in it the deposition scene which was censored on its first presentation, and you have done this to foster treasonous projects.

Burbage. No, Your Majesty, I swear it.

Elizabeth. You have not played this play?

Burbage. But not to foster treason, that I swear.

Elizabeth. If you played Richard with that pot-belly it was treason indeed. Then for what purpose?

Burbage. To make money.

Elizabeth. On an old play?

Burbage. We were paid in advance . . .

Elizabeth. By whom?

Burbage. By Lord Southampton.

Burghley. You see? A friend of Essex.

Elizabeth. You have much too handsome a nose for slitting, Master Hemmings, yet you say nothing.

Hemmings. There is only this to say, Your Majesty . . . that we knew nothing of any traitorous intent in the matter . . . and that, had we known of such intent, we would not have given the performance.

Elizabeth. I think you are all traitorous knaves and rascals, as a matter of fact, in league with Essex and Southampton and the smoothest liars in Christendom. Is there something in this?

Hemmings. No, madam.

Elizabeth. You know Essex and Southampton?

Hemmings. We know Lord Southampton.

Elizabeth. How much were you paid for the revival of Richard?

Hemmings. Three pounds, Your Majesty.

Elizabeth. No more?

Hemmings. No more.

Elizabeth. Play it again this afternoon, masters, play it at my request this afternoon, and you shall have ten pounds for it. Lord Cecil, pay Master Burbage ten pounds from the royal exchequer for one performance of Richard. And let it stand in the record.

Cecil. Yes, madam.

Elizabeth.

[*To* HEMMINGS]

And tell Lord Southampton when you see him that I paid ten to his three. Will you tell him?

Hemmings. Yes, Your Majesty.

Elizabeth. And when you have all this treason out of your systems be ready to play Sir John Falstaff for me at the end of the week. I should like to see your Falstaff again, sir.

Burbage. Yes, Your Majesty.

Elizabeth. You may go.

[BURBAGE *and* HEMMINGS *go out*]

Cecil.

[*Waiting till they are gone*]

You are mad, Your Majesty! This is a rebellion, and you play into their hands. The outer court is thronging with messengers from the city! Half the town is in uprising!

Elizabeth. I know.

Cecil. Madam . . .

Elizabeth. Little man, little man, let me alone.

Cecil. This much I must tell you. Lord Essex has been seen with an armed force in the city.

Elizabeth. Lord Essex?

Cecil. With an army. Where he is now no-one can say.

Elizabeth. And if one were to guess?

Cecil. He is on his way hither.

Elizabeth. So I think. I shall be glad to see him. Let him bring his revolution here. How long think you it will last after I have looked on it?

Burghley. Madam, the palace is unprotected from the waterside. The guard must be drawn up.

Elizabeth. With your permission, my lord, I would rather not.

Cecil. I took the liberty of ordering a guard posted along the river.

> [*A door is opened without and a sudden snarl of angry voices breaks in on the conference*]

The Voices. "Who has given these orders?"
"Back there . . . back!"
"Not the queen, by God!"
"The queen . . . the queen! Defend the queen!"
"An Essex!"
"Hold your mouth!"
"Stand back, fellow!"

Essex.

> [*Outside*]

I say the queen will see me! Stand back!

> [*There is a clank of armor in the hallway and* ESSEX *appears in the doorway, soldiers following him*]

Elizabeth. You come with a file of soldiers at your back, my lord of Essex.

Essex. Do I need them, Your Majesty?

Elizabeth. No.

Essex. Then be off with you. Follow my orders . . . They
told me you would not see me.

Elizabeth. They were wrong. I will see you. It seems you are
  in rebellion,
My good lord. Enter and state your grievance,
If you have grievance. For myself, I have
A great affection for rebels, being one myself
Much of the time.

Essex. I am no rebel, Your Majesty . . .
But, newly arrived from Ireland, and bearing news
Of your subjects there, I venture to come to see you,
No more.

Elizabeth. And your army? . . . You have an army with
  you?

Essex. I have brought my men home to London.

Elizabeth. You received
My orders, no doubt, directing you to disband?

Essex. I believed them to be mistaken. To disband on the
  coast
And leave my expedition there, seemed strange,
And dangerous to the country. An army turned loose
Becomes a mob.

Elizabeth. And you tell me this! You are informed in these
  matters
But I am not!

Essex. Indeed, that is quite true . . .
I do know about armies . . . and you do not.

Elizabeth. Oh, yes . . .
   Oh, indeed. And who paid them then? I believe
   Your supplies were cut off?

Essex. I have paid them.

Elizabeth. They are then
   In your service?

Essex. In my service and therefore
   Devoted yours.

Elizabeth. And Ireland? How of Ireland?

Essex. I could have conquered Ireland had you given me
      time.
   I left it worse than I found it.

Elizabeth. An honest answer,
   At any rate.

Essex. Why should I lie? The fault,
   If any, was yours. To conquer Ireland requires
   More than the months you gave me. Years, perhaps.

Elizabeth. You were engaged in subduing the rebels, then,
   When I summoned you home?

Essex. Just so.

Elizabeth. You were not, by chance,
   Joined with the rebels?

Essex. Never.

Elizabeth. You held no parleys
   With our friend Tyrone?

Essex. I did. They were part of my plan.

Elizabeth. Your plans! Your plans! Why did you write me
    nothing
Of these your plans? Am I a witch to find out
What happens on the far side of the Irish Sea
Without being told?

Essex. I wrote you . . .

Elizabeth. Masterly letters,
    Brief, to the point, wasting no words, in short,
Nothing.

Essex. I know not what Your Majesty means
    By that. I wrote you fully, and in answer
Received no reply.

Elizabeth. You wrote me?

Essex. Many times.

Elizabeth. And had no letters from me?

Essex. None.

Elizabeth. Before God,
    If the couriers were tampered with there shall be
Some necks stretched here! My lords, I wish to speak
With Lord Essex here alone! Leave us.

Cecil. Dear queen,
    Do you think it safe . .

Elizabeth. Leave us!

    [BURGHLEY *makes a sign and the stage is silently emptied*
        save for the QUEEN *and* ESSEX. *A pause*]

What did you write me?

Essex. I wrote you my love—for I thought you loved me
  then—
And then I pled with you not to bring me home
In the midst of my mission—and then at last angrily—
For I had not heard—but always to say I loved you—
Always.

Elizabeth. But is this true?

Essex. Would I lie?

Elizabeth. Some one
Has lied and will pay with his life if this is true!—
Before God and hell—Some one will pay for this.

Essex. What did you write me?

Elizabeth. I wrote—my love—
God keep you safe—I know not—and then, not hearing
I wrote God knows what madness—as to a rebel—
Thinking you no longer mine—faithless!
Thinking—

Essex. I would I had known—I was in torment—
I—forgive me—

Elizabeth. You should never have gone away.
God, how I've hated you!—

Essex. No!

Elizabeth. Planned to put you to torture!

Essex. I have been in torture!
  [*He steps toward her*]

Elizabeth. Not yet—I can't breathe yet—I can't breathe—
Or think or believe—

Essex. Nor I.

Elizabeth. Can we ever—
   Believe again? Can it be as it used to be?

Essex. We can make it so.

Elizabeth. Come, kill me if you will. Put your arms round
   me—
   If you love me. Do you still love me?

Essex. Yes.

Elizabeth. Yes, yes—
   If this were false, then, then truly—then I should die.
   I thought because I was older—you see—some one
   else—

Essex. No one—never a breath—

Elizabeth. Is it all, all as before?

Essex. We have not changed.

Elizabeth. No. Yes, a little, perhaps.
   They have changed us a little.

Essex. Not I. I have not changed.

Elizabeth. Can I trust you now?

Essex. Sweet, think back, all those months,
   All those hideous months! No word, no love.
   And when word did come, it was to make me prisoner!
   Christ, I have pride!
   And though I came here in defiance, I came truly to
   find you
   Who have been lost from me.

Elizabeth. Do you ask forgiveness?
It is all forgiven.

Essex. Then, why then, hell's vanished—
And here's heaven risen out of it, a heaven of years
In the midst of desolate centuries.

Elizabeth. We have so few years.
Let us make them doubly sweet, these years we have,
Be gracious with each other, sway a little
To left or right if we must to stay together—
Never distrust each other—nay, distrust
All others, when they whisper. Let us make this our pact
Now, for the fates are desperate to part us
And the very gods envy this happiness
We pluck out of loss and death.

Essex. If two stand shoulder to shoulder against the gods,
Happy together, the gods themselves are helpless
Against them, while they stand so.

Elizabeth. Love, I will be
Your servant. Command me. What would you have?

Essex. Why nothing—

Elizabeth. Take this my world, my present in your hands!
You shall stand back of my chair and together we
Shall build an England to make the old world wonder
And the new world worship!—What is this doubt in
your brow?

Essex. I am troubled to be dishonest. I have brought my
army

Here to the palace—and though it's all true what we've
    said—
No letters—utter agony over long months—
It is something in myself that has made me do this,
Not Cecil—nor anyone. No one but myself.
The rest is all excuse.

Elizabeth. Speak what you will.

Essex. If you had but shown anger I could have spoken
Easily. It's not easy now, but speak I must!
Oh, I've thought much about this
On lonely marches and in distant tents,
Thinking of you and me. I say this now
Without rancor—in all friendliness and love—
The throne is yours by right of descent and by
Possession—but if this were a freer time,
And there were election, I should carry the country be-
    fore me,
And this being true, and we being equal in love,
Should we not be equal in power as well?

Elizabeth. We are equal.
I have made you so.

Essex. Yes, but still it's all yours—
Yours to grant me now or take away.

Elizabeth. How could this well be otherwise?

Essex. Am I not—and I say this too in all love—
As worthy to be king as you to be queen?
Must you be sovereign alone?

Elizabeth. You are young in policy,

My Essex, if you do not see that if I
Should grant high place to you now it would show ill to
   the kingdom—
It would be believed that you had forced this on me,
Would be called a revolution. It would undermine
All confidence. What is built up for years
In people's minds blows away like thistledown
When such things get abroad.

Essex. But is this your reason
   Or have you another? Would you trust me as king?

Elizabeth. No.

Essex. And are you still reluctant to give up
   Your prerogatives?

Elizabeth. Yes.

Essex. Then now, when the country is mine, the court in
   my hands,
   You my prisoner, I must send my men away,
   Disband my army, give back your kingdom to you,
   And know I have been king for a moment only
   And never will be again?

Elizabeth. I am your prisoner?

Essex. The palace and the city are in my hands.
   This England is mine now for the taking—

Elizabeth. This is your friendship! This is your love!

Essex. As water finds its level, so power goes
   To him who can use it, and soon or late the name
   Of king follows where power is.

Elizabeth. Oh, my Essex,
　You are a child in war as you are in council.
　Why all this talk of power? No army opposed you
　When your troops came the road from Ireland. No guard
　　was set
　To stop your entrance with your thousand halberds.
　Shall I tell you why? Because I wished to keep
　A semblance of peace between us. And for that,
　I am your prisoner!

Essex. Yes. My dear prisoner.

Elizabeth. Now I do know at least
　What it was you wanted. You wanted my kingdom. You
　　have it.
　Make the best of it. And so shall I.
　What are your plans?

Essex. I have none.

Elizabeth. The Tower, the block—
　You could hardly take a queen prisoner and have no
　　thought
　Of her destiny. I am my mother's daughter,
　I too can walk the path my mother walked.

Essex. These are heroics. You know you are free as air.

Elizabeth. If I do as you ask.

Essex. Is it so hard to share your power with your love?
　I could have all—and I offer to share with you.

Elizabeth. Let's have no more pretending.
　I'd have given all—but you came with an army, de-
　　manding—

In short, you don't love—nor trust me—no—nor want
me—

Essex. God knows I have wanted you. I have wanted
power—
Believed myself fitted to hold it—but not without you.

Elizabeth. If you had wanted me would you rise and strike
At me with an army? Never, never! You'd have come
To me quietly, and we'd have talked of it together
As lovers should—and we'd both have our way—
And no one the wiser. But now, to take the palace,
Hold me prisoner—no—what you wanted you've
taken—
And that is all you shall have. This is your kingdom—
But I—I am not yours.

Essex. But I am yours
And have been.

Elizabeth. Who will believe that? Not the world,
No, and not I. I'd rather go to the Tower
Than share my place on terms like these. Put me where I
Will do least harm.

Essex. I cannot, could not, will not.

Elizabeth. If I could have given freely—
But not now. Not surrendering. Not to a victor,

Essex. I am no victor if I lose you. The only gift
That I could take from you, is that we are equals.

Elizabeth. Yes, but not now.

Essex. I ask one word from you.
Give me this word—this one word—and these soldiers
Shall leave, and you shall be free.

Elizabeth. I'll believe that
When it happens.

Essex. I'll believe you when you promise.

Elizabeth. Then you have my promise.
You shall share the realm with me. As I am queen,
I promise it.

Essex. Then this is my answer.
[*He kisses her, then calls*]
Marvel!—Marvel!
[MARVEL *enters*]
Carry out the order of release. Dismiss my guard—
Return the palace into the queen's hands.
Retire with all our forces to the Strand.
Release all prisoners. Release the queen's guard
And send them to their stations.
[MARVEL *goes out*]
The palace will be
Returned as quickly as taken. This is our last quarrel.

Elizabeth. Yes—our last.

Marvel's Voice.
[*Offstage*]
Form for retire!

Another Voice. Form for retire!

A More Distant Voice. Form for retire!

A Voice.
    [*In the distance*]
  Ready to march!

Another Voice. Ready to march!

Another. All ready!

Another. Ready, captain!
    [MARVEL *enters*]

Marvel. The order is obeyed, my lord.

Essex. Follow your men.

Marvel. Yes, my lord.
    [*He goes out*]

Essex. It is as I planned. They are leaving the palace.
  Now let us talk no more of this tonight—
  Let us forget this matter of thrones and kingdoms
  And be but you and me for a while.

Elizabeth.
    [*Immobile*]
  Yes—yes—
  Let us forget. Have you kept your word indeed?

Essex. I have kept my word.

Elizabeth. If I clapped my hands
  Would my guard come now—or yours?

Essex. Yours only. Shall I call them?

Elizabeth. No—I'll call them.
    [*She claps her hands four times.* CAPTAIN ARMIN *appears in
    the entrance followed by four* BEEF-EATERS *with hal-
    berds. They stand at attention in the entrance*]

To be sure I have a guard
Once more.
The palace has been returned? It is in
Our hands?

Captain. Yes, Majesty.

Elizabeth. I have ruled England a long time, my Essex,
And I have found that he who would rule must be
Quite friendless, without mercy, without love.
Arrest Lord Essex!
Arrest Lord Essex! Take him to the Tower
And keep him safe.

Essex. Is this a jest?

Elizabeth. I never
Jest when I play for kingdoms, my lord of Essex.

Essex. I trusted you.

Elizabeth. I trusted you,
And learned from you that no one can be trusted.
I will remember that.

Essex. Lest that should be all
You ever have to remember, Your Majesty,
Take care what you do.

Elizabeth. I shall take care.

[ESSEX *unsheathes his sword, breaks it across his knee, flings
it at the foot of the throne, turns and walks out between
the two files of guards*]

CURTAIN

ELIZABETH THE QUEEN
ACT THREE

ACT THREE

SCENE: *The queen's apartments in the Tower, a square and heavy room, long and with a raised stone platform at one end of which stands a regal chair. It is dawn, the light filtering in coldly. ELLEN stands in the doorway at the left, weeping, with one arm before her face. THE FOOL, who has been sleeping wrapped in the draperies of the queen's chair, uncoils himself from among them and rolls over to rub his eyes. TRESSA hurries in.*

Tressa. Come back quickly, dear, quickly! She's sorry she hurt you. She'll have no one else read to her.

Ellen.

[*Weeping*]

I can't read now. I'm—I don't mind if she strikes me—only—it wasn't my fault—We're all so weary.

Tressa. She's sorry—

The Fool.

[*Waking*]

One, two—there should be three.

[MARY *comes to the door*

Mary.

[*Very low*]

Ellen—

The Fool. Three.

Mary. Ellen! She wants you at once.

[ELLEN *runs out*]

The Fool. Where am I?

Mary. Yes—and what are you doing there?

The Fool. Trying to sleep.

Mary. Sleep? In the Tower?

The Fool. Come and help me. I have heard that you are perfect at lying down.

> [MARY *and* TRESSA *go out.* THE FOOL *looks about him sleepily, then remembers something and hunts for it under a chair. When he extracts it it proves to be a roasted bird on a wooden platter, covered with leaves. He examines it, then replaces a large leaf over it.* PENELOPE, *fully dressed, comes in from the rear*]

Penelope?

Penelope. Yes?

The Fool. Have you slept?

Penelope. No.

The Fool. Then you should break your fast. You are hungry?

Penelope. No. I can't eat.

The Fool.

> [*Showing his capon*]

Look.

Penelope. What's that?

The Fool. Breakfast. I brought it from Whitehall.

Penelope. Eat it then.

> [*She sits on a step disconsolately*]

The Fool. You won't have any?

Penelope. No.

The Fool.
> [*Pushing the food away*]
> I'm not hungry either.

Penelope. Eat it, poor fool.

The Fool. I don't want it. I brought it for you.

Penelope. I know. But eat it.
> [*She wipes her eyes*]

The Fool. Why should you weep?

Penelope. God knows. He never wept for me.

The Fool. The earl's not dead yet, remember.

Penelope. No.

The Fool. And she'll never let it happen.

Penelope. The clock's struck five. He's to die at six.

The Fool. Why has she not sent to him?

Penelope. She has. We were awake all night. She has sent messages but he's not answered. She's been waiting for word from him. But he's as silent as if he wanted to die.

The Fool. Will she let them kill him if he says nothing?

Penelope. She's a strange woman. She wants him to beg her pardon . . . or something like that.

The Fool. Would you beg her pardon if you were he?

Penelope. No.

The Fool. Then he won't. For I think he's as proud as you.

Penelope. He has not said a word or sent a message since his arrest.

The Fool. And the queen has not slept?

Penelope. No.

The Fool. Nor you?

Penelope. No.

The Fool. God help these women.

Penelope. She says she gave him a ring once. If he ever wanted forgiveness he was to send the ring. And he sits there stubbornly with the ring on his finger. Oh, God, will nothing happen?

> [*The* FOOL *has absent-mindedly pulled the capon toward him again, and begins to eat.* ELIZABETH *emerges from the rear*]

Elizabeth. Penelope?

Penelope. Yes.

Elizabeth. Have the players come?

Penelope. Not yet.

> [*The* FOOL *has pushed the food guiltily behind him*]

Elizabeth. These cheating grooms! I'll have them carbonadoed for this dallying! I shall go mad here! Bring me the little book of prayers . . . from the window-sill. No . . . leave it. The gods of men are sillier than their kings and queens . . . and emptier and more powerless. There is no god but death, no god but death!

> [*She sees the food the* FOOL *has been hiding*]

Gnaw your bones somewhere else!

> [*The* FOOL *goes out left*]

Come here, my dear. I heard the clock strike five.

Penelope. Yes. I heard it.
[*They sit together on the steps, and* PENELOPE *puts her arm round* ELIZABETH]

Elizabeth. Do you love him well, my dear?

Penelope. Yes, Your Majesty.
[ELIZABETH *bows her head wearily on* PENELOPE]

Elizabeth. I love him. He has never loved me.

Penelope. Yes, yes. He does love you. I've been madly jealous of you.

Elizabeth. Of me? Poor child.

Penelope. But he loved you . . . and never me at all.

Elizabeth. How do you know?

Penelope. He told me.

Elizabeth. What did he say?

Penelope. He said, "I love her dearly." I wanted him for myself, and I warned him against you. He laughed at me. He said, "I love her very dearly."

Elizabeth. You tell me this because you want to save him.

Penelope. No, dear queen. It's true.

Elizabeth. This is the end of me, dear. This is the end.
It comes late. I've been a long while learning,
But I've learned it now. Life is bitter. Nobody
Dies happy, queen or no. Will he speak, think you?
Will he send to me?

Penelope. No. Not now.

Elizabeth. You see,
This is the end of me. Oh, I shall live,
I shall walk about and give orders . . . a horrible
while . . .
A horrible old hag.

Penelope. You must send for him.
He's proud as you are, and you have the upper hand.
He'll say nothing. You must send for him, bring him
here.
[*The chimes ring the quarter hour*]

Elizabeth. Not yet. Not yet.
[*She rises*]
Where are the players? I sent
For the players hours ago! They shall pay for this,
The insolent servants! Mary . . . Tressa, God's head!
I'm bestially served! Ellen!
[ELLEN *looks in, partly dressed*]
Find out if the players
Are here? And be quick.

Ellen. Yes, madam.
[*She disappears*]

Elizabeth. Where's my fool?

The Fool.
[*Looking in with a bone in his hand*]
Here, madam.

Elizabeth. Where are you when I need you?
Look at the oaf! Say nothing! You're funny enough

The way you are with your capon in your mouth!
Eat! Eat! Let me see you!

The Fool. I don't seem to be hungry!

Elizabeth. Eat, I say!

The Fool. Yes, madam.
  [*He tries to eat*[

Elizabeth. Now wipe your fingers.
  Here, take my napkin, child. Come here! You're dis-
  gusting!
  [*She gives him a kerchief*]
  Can you not clean your face?

The Fool. With this?

Elizabeth. Aye, with that.
  [*She takes his bone and throws it*]
  Why do you make mouths at it? It's clean.

The Fool. Yes, madam!
  [*He begins to wipe his mouth, then starts to cry, and sitting
      down on the step, sobs heavily, his head in his hands*]

Elizabeth. What is it now? What good's a fool that cries
  When you need comfort? What's the matter?

The Fool. Please,
  I don't know. You aren't like the queen.

Elizabeth. I am
  The queen, though.

Tressa.
  [*Looking in*]
  The players, madam.

Elizabeth. Bring them here.

Penelope. The time's grown short. Will you send for him?

Elizabeth. Wait . . . he may come.

Penelope. No, no. He won't. You'll let it go too long
Watching the players.

Elizabeth. Let them come in.
   [TRESSA *is seen at the doorway with the actors*]

Penelope. You should eat
A little something first.

Elizabeth. No, no. Bring them in.
   [*The* ACTORS *enter*]
Come in, my masters, let us have a play . . .
Let us have revels and amusements quickly . . .
If ever you played play now. This is my bad
Quarter of an hour.

Penelope. Please, please . . .

Elizabeth. Quick! Quick . . .
You are late, sirs . . . never mind . . . some scene from
   Falstaff . . .
The one where he lies to the prince about running away
And the prince catches him . . .

Hemmings. Where, Majesty?

Elizabeth. There, anywhere. Come, sit down. Sit down.
   [*The girls and the* FOOL *group about her*]
Begin, Falstaff! "I call thee coward! I'll see thee
Damned ere I call thee coward!"

Falstaff. I call thee coward! I'll see thee damned ere I call thee coward: but I would give a thousand pound I could run as fast as thou canst.

Prince Henry. What's the matter?

Falstaff. What's the matter! there be four of us here have ta'en a thousand pound this day morning.

Prince Henry. Where is it, Jack? where is it?

Falstaff. Where is it! taken from us it is: a hundred upon poor four of us.

Prince Henry. What, fought ye with them all?

Falstaff. All! I know not what ye call all; but if I fought not with fifty of them, I am a bunch of radish: if there were not two or three and fifty upon poor old Jack, then am I no two-legged creature.

Elizabeth. Come, come . . . this is not to the purpose . . . I had thought this witty . . .

[*The Players pause*]

Play! Play!

Prince Henry. Pray God, you have not murdered some of them.

Falstaff. Nay, that's past praying for: I have peppered two of them; two I am sure I have paid, . . . two rogues in buckram suits. I tell thee what, Hal, . . . if I tell thee a lie, spit in my face, call me horse. Thou knowest my old ward . . . here I lay, and thus I bore my point. Four rogues in buckram let drive at me . . .

Prince Henry. What, four? thou saidst but two even now.

Falstaff. Four, Hal; I told thee four.

Poins. Ay, ay, he said four.

Falstaff. These four came all a-front, and mainly thrust at me. I made me no more ado but took all their seven points in my target, thus.

[*The* QUEEN *walks from place to place, restlessly*]

Prince Henry. Seven? why, there were but four even now in buckram.

Poins. Ay, four in buckram suits.

Falstaff. Seven, by these hilts, or I am a villain else.

Prince Henry. Pr'ythee, let him alone; we shall have more anon.

Falstaff. Dost thou hear me, Hal?

Prince Henry. Ay, and mark thee too, Jack.

Elizabeth. Aye, aye . . . we are listening . . . Play!

Falstaff. Do so, for it is worth the listening to. These nine in buckram that I told thee of . . .

Prince Henry. So, two more already.

Falstaff. Began to give me ground: but I followed me close, came in foot and hand; and with a thought seven of the eleven I paid.

Prince Henry. O monstrous! eleven buckram men grown out of two!

Falstaff. But, as the devil would have it, three misbegotten knaves in Kendal green came at my back and let drive at me . . . for it was so dark, Hal, that thou couldst not see thy hand.

Prince Henry. These lies are like the father that begets them . . . gross as a mountain, open, palpable. Why, thou clay-brained guts, thou nott-pated fool, thou whoreson, obscene, greasy tallow-ketch . . .

Falstaff. What, art thou mad? art thou mad? is not the truth the truth?

Prince Henry. Why, how couldst thou know these men in Kendal green, when it was so dark thou couldst not see thy hand? come, tell us your reason: what sayest thou to this?

Poins. Come, your reason, Jack . . . your reason.

Falstaff. What, upon compulsion? Give a reason on compulsion! if reasons were as plenty as blackberries I would give no man a reason on compulsion, I.

Prince Henry. I'll be no longer guilty of this sin; this sanguine coward, this bed-presser, this horse back-breaker, this huge hill of flesh . . .

Falstaff. Away, you starveling, you elf-skin, you dried neat's tongue . . . O for breath to utter what is like thee! . . . you tailor's yard, you sheath, you bow-case, you vile standing-tuck . . .

Prince Henry. Well, breathe awhile, and then to it again: and when thou hast tired thyself in base comparisons, hear me speak but this.

Poins. Mark, Jack.

Prince Henry. We two saw you four set on four; you bound
them, and were masters of their wealth . . . Mark now,
how a plain tale shall put you down . . . Then did we
two set on you four; and, with a word, out-faced you
from your prize, and have it: yes, and can show it you
here in the house: . . . and, Falstaff, you carried your
guts away as nimbly, with as quick dexterity, and roared
for mercy, and still ran and roared, as ever I heard bull-
calf. What a slave art thou, to hack thy sword as thou
hast done, and then say it was in fight! What trick, what
device, what starting-hole, canst thou now find out to
hide thee from this open and apparent shame?

Poins. Come, let's hear, Jack; what trick hast thou now?

Falstaff. By the Lord, I knew ye as well as He that made
ye. Why, hear ye, my masters: was it for me to kill the
heir-apparent? Should I turn upon the true prince?
Why, thou knowest I am as valiant as Hercules: but beware instinct; the lion will not touch the true prince.
Instinct is a great matter; I was a coward on instinct. I
shall think the better of myself and thee during my life;
I for a valiant lion, and thou for a true prince. But, by
the Lord, lads, I am glad you have the money. What,
shall we be merry? Shall we have a play extempore?

Elizabeth. My God, my God . . . can one not forget for a
moment?
Who are these strangers? What is this interlude?
Go! Go! It's a vile play and you play it vilely!
Go! By my God, will no-one deliver me from this tor-
ment?
    [*The players start out*]

Take your trappings and go!
[*They leave. The chimes strike*]
Again ... the half-hour ...
[CECIL *enters*]
Yes?
[*To* PENELOPE]
Was I not wise to wait? He has spoken first! Yes?

Cecil. Your Majesty, a citizen rabble has gathered
To protest the execution of Essex. The captain
Begs permission to use your guard. There's no other
Force at hand to disperse them.

Elizabeth. It's your day, Cecil
I daresay you know that. The snake-in-the-grass
Endures, and those who are noble, free of soul,
Valiant and admirable ... they go down in the
    prime,
Always they go down ...

Cecil. Madam, the guard
Is needed at once ...

Elizabeth. Aye ... the snake-mind is best ...
One by one you out-last them. To the end
Of time it will be so ... the rats inherit the earth.
Take my guard. Take it. I thought you brought word
    from ...
Go, call Lord Essex for me
From his cell ... and bring him thither! I'll wait no
    longer!

Cecil. Lord Essex is prepared for execution.
The priest has been sent to him.

Elizabeth. Bring him here, I say,
   And now . . . at once!

    [CECIL *bows and goes out*]

   Go out from me, all of you,
   All save Penelope. Go quickly, quickly . . .
   All . . .

    [*They leave*]

   Penelope, bring my robe, the one
   Laid out . . .

    [PENELOPE *goes.* ELIZABETH *seats herself in the royal chair.*
      PENELOPE *returns with the robe*]

   Look here in my face, Penelope. He's so young,
   And I'm old, girl, I'm old. It shows in my eyes.
   Dear, you're so young. Do not be here when he
    comes . . .
   Do you mind? You'll look so young.

Penelope. Yes, madam . . . but you . . .
   You're beautiful.

Elizabeth. Beautiful still? But I was once . . . I was . . .
   You'd not believe it now.

Penelope. Oh, yes . . .
   You're always beautiful. You've always been.

Elizabeth. Thank you,
   My dear. Go now. He'll come.

Penelope. Yes.

    [*She goes out to the rear. After a moment* ESSEX *enters from
    the left with a Guard. The Guard leaves him and steps
    out.* ESSEX *is dressed in black and is very pale*]

Essex. You sent for me?
  Or so they said.

Elizabeth. Yes.

Essex. It would have been kinder
  To leave me with my thoughts till the axe came down
  And ended them. You spoil me for death.

Elizabeth. Are you
  So set on dying?

Essex. I can't say I care for it.
  This blood that beats in us has a way of wanting
  To keep right on. But if one is to die
  It's well to go straight toward it.

Elizabeth. You must have known
  I never meant you to die.

Essex. I am under sentence
  From Your Majesty's courts. There's no appeal that
    I know of.
  I am found guilty of treason on good evidence,
  And cannot deny it. This treason, I believe,
  Is punishable with death.

Elizabeth. God knows I am proud . . .
  And bitter, too . . . bitter at you with much cause,
  But I have sent for you. I've taken the first step
  That way. Do not make me take the next!

Essex. The next is to the scaffold. It's only a step
  Now, and I've made ready.

Elizabeth. Aye, you are bitter,
  Too; we have let it go late; we've both

Waited for the other. But it was I who spoke
First . . . Will you make me tell you first how much
I've longed for you? It's hard for me.

Essex. My dear,
You can tell me so gracefully, for you
Have nothing to gain or lose by me . . . but I
Have life and love to gain, and I find it less
Than fitting to speak like a lover, lest you suppose
I do it to save my head.

Elizabeth. It's true that you never
Loved me, isn't it? You were ambitious, and I
Loved you, and it was the nearest way to power,
And you took the nearest way? No, no . . . one moment . . .
This is an hour for truth, if there's ever truth . . .
I'm older than you . . . but a queen; it was natural
You'd flatter me, speak me fair, and I believed you.
I'm sorry I believed you. Sorry for you
More than for me.

Essex. Why, yes . . . that's true enough.
Now may I go? This dying sticks in my mind,
And makes me poor company, I fear.

Elizabeth. It was true.
It was true then?

Essex. If you wish to make me tell you
What you well know, how much I used to love you,
How much I have longed for you, very well, I will
say it.

That's a small victory to win over me now,
But take it with the rest.

Elizabeth. You did love me?

Essex. Yes.

Elizabeth. And love me still?

Essex. Yes. You should know that, I think.

Elizabeth. You kept my ring. You never sent my ring.
I've been waiting for it.

Essex. You may have it back
If you have use for it . . . I had thought to wear it
As far as my grave, but, take it.

Elizabeth. I'd have forgiven
All that had passed, at any hour, day or night,
Since I last saw you. I have waited late at night
Thinking, tonight the ring will come, he will never
Hold out against me so long, but the nights went by
Somehow, like the days, and it never came,
Till the last day came, and here it is the last morning
And the chimes beating out the hours.

Essex. Dear, if I'd known . . .
But I could not have sent it.

Elizabeth. Why?

Essex. If I'd tried
To hold you to a promise you could not keep
And you had refused me, I should have died much more
Unhappy than I am now.

Elizabeth. I'd have kept my promise.
I'd keep it now.

Essex. If I offered you this ring?

Elizabeth. Yes . . . even now.

Essex. You would pardon me, set me free,
Cede back my estates to me, love me as before,
Give me my place in the state?

Elizabeth. All as it was.

Essex. And what would happen to your throne?

Elizabeth. My throne?
Nothing.

Essex. Yes, for I'd take it from you.

Elizabeth. Again?
You'd play that game again?

Essex. The games one plays
Are not the games one chooses always. I
Am still a popular idol of a sort.
There are mutterings over my imprisonment,
Even as it is . . . and if you should set me free
And confess your weakness by overlooking treason
And setting me up in power once more, the storm
That broke last time would be nothing to the storm
That would break over you then. As for myself,
I played for power and lost, but if I had
Another chance I think I'd play and win.

Elizabeth. Why do you say this?

Essex. I say it because it's true.
I have loved you, love you now, but I know myself.
If I were to win you over and take my place
As it used to be, it would gall me. I have a weakness
For being first wherever I am. I refuse
To take pardon from you without warning you
Of this. And when you know it, pardon becomes
Impossible.

Elizabeth. You do this for me?

Essex. Why, yes,
But not altogether. Partly for England, too.
I've lost conceit of myself a little. A life
In prison's very quiet. It leads to thinking.
You govern England better than I should.
I'd lead her into wars, make a great name,
Perhaps, like Henry Fifth and leave a legacy
Of debts and bloodshed after me. You will leave
Peace, happiness, something secure. A woman governs
Better than a man, being a natural coward.
A coward rules best.

Elizabeth. Still bitter.

Essex. Perhaps a little.
It's a bitter belief to swallow, but I believe it.
You were right all the time.
    [*The chimes ring three-quarters*]
And now, if you'll pardon me,
I have an appointment near-by with a headsman.
He comes sharp on the hour.

Elizabeth. You have an hour yet.
It's but struck five.

Essex. It struck five some time since.

Elizabeth. It cannot go this way!

Essex. Aye, but it has.
It has and will. There's no way out. I've thought of it
Every way. Speak frankly. Could you forgive me
And keep your throne?

Elizabeth. No.

Essex. Are you ready to give
Your crown up to me?

Elizabeth. No. It's all I have.
[*She rises*]
Why, who am I
To stand here paltering with a rebel noble!
I am Elizabeth, daughter of a king,
The queen of England, and you are my subject!
What does this mean, you standing here eye to eye
With me, your liege? You whom I made, and gave
All that you have, you, an upstart, defying
Me to grant pardon, lest you should sweep me from
power
And take my place from me? I tell you if Christ his
blood
Ran streaming from the heavens for a sign
That I should hold my hand you'd die for this,
You pretender to a throne upon which you have

No claim, you pretender to a heart, who have been
Hollow and heartless and faithless to the end!

Essex. If we'd met some other how we might have been
  happy . . .
  But there's been an empire between us! I am to die . . .
  Let us say that . . . let us begin with that . . .
  For then I can tell you that if there'd been no empire
  We could have been great lovers. If even now
  You were not queen and I were not pretender,
  That god who searches heaven and earth and hell
  For two who are perfect lovers, could end his search
  With you and me. Remember . . . I am to die . . .
  And so I can tell you truly, out of all the earth
  That I'm to leave, there's nothing I'm very loath
  To leave save you. Yet if I live I'll be
  Your death or you'll be mine.

Elizabeth. Give me the ring.

Essex. No.

Elizabeth. Give me the ring. I'd rather you killed me
  Than I killed you.

Essex. It's better for me as it is
  Than that I should live and batten my fame and fortune
  On the woman I love. I've thought of it all. It's better
  To die young and unblemished than to live long and
    rule,
  And rule not well.

Elizabeth. Aye, I should know that.

Essex. Is it not?

Elizabeth. Yes.

Essex. Goodbye, then.

Elizabeth. Oh, then I'm old, I'm old!
  I could be young with you, but now I'm old.
  I know now how it will be without you. The sun
  Will be empty and circle round an empty earth . . .
  And I will be queen of emptiness and death . . .
  Why could you not have loved me enough to give me
  Your love and let me keep as I was?

Essex. I know not.
  I only know I could not. I must go.

Elizabeth.
  [*Frozen*]
  Yes.
  [*He goes to the door*]
  Lord Essex!
  [*He turns*]
  Take my kingdom. It is yours!
  [Essex, *as if not hearing, bows and goes on.* Penelope *runs
    in, meeting him*]

Penelope. My lord! She has forgiven you?

Essex. Goodbye, my dear.
  [*He kisses her*]

Penelope. No, no! She loves you! Go to her.
  [Essex *goes out*]
  Run to her! She waits you still! See, if you turn

She waits you still! Dear queen, would you let him
    go?
He goes to his death! Send, send after him!

[*The* QUEEN *lifts her head and shows a face so stricken that*
    PENELOPE, *who has gone to her, says no more. The clock*
    strikes six. ELIZABETH *bows her head on* PENELOPE'S
    knees, her hands over her ears]

CURTAIN

Mary of Scotland

CHARACTERS

(In the order of their appearance)

First Guard, JAMIE
Second Guard
Third Guard
JOHN KNOX
JAMES HEPBURN, Earl of Bothwell
CHATELARD
MARY STUART
DUC DE CHATELHERAULT
MARY BEATON
MARY SETON
MARY LIVINGSTONE
MARY FLEMING
ELIZABETH TUDOR
LORD BURGHLEY
HENRY, LORD DARNLEY
LORD GORDON
DAVID RIZZIO
JAMES STUART, Earl of Moray
MAITLAND of Lethington
LORD HUNTLEY
LORD MORTON
LORD ERSKINE
LORD THROGMORTON
A Porter
LORD RUTHVEN
LORD DOUGLAS
Young RUTHVEN
First Sentinel
Second Sentinel
A Sergeant
A Warden
Soldiers and others

ACT ONE

Scene I

Scene: *A half-sheltered corner of the pier at Leith. It is a sleety, windy night, and the tall piles of the background and the planks underfoot shine black and icy with their coating of freezing rain. Long cables stretch away into the dark. The only light comes from the lantern of two iron-capped* Guards *who are playing cards morosely on the head of a fish-tub in the lee of a great coil of rope.*

First Guard. Na, na, put them away. I'm fair clabbered with cold.

Second Guard. Aye, you'd say that, wi' ma siller-piece laced in your brogues!

First Guard. Gie me the hand, then. But man, it's an unco bitter nicht for indoor pleasures.

Second Guard.
　[*Throwing out cards*]
It's a blastit wonner—

First Guard. Put out, put out!

Second Guard.
　[*Laying down a coin*]
Aye.

First Guard. And we'll just stop now, forbye to go on 'ud strain your two-year credit.
　[*He shows his hand*]

3

Second Guard. Dod, mon, ye hae luck wi' the titties. Ye'll no refuse me ma revenge, Jamie?

[*A tall bearded* FIGURE, *muffled in a cloak, has come in from the left*]

First Guard. When ye can afford it. No earlier.

Second Guard. Ye see yoursel', Jamie. I'm gouged out clean—

First Guard. And is that a reason I should risk my gains—?

The Old Man. Aye, dicing, gaming, cards, drinking, dancing, whoring, and all the papistical uses of the flesh— they run before her like a foul air—

Second Guard. It's the Master—wheest—put them awa'.

First Guard. An' what of it? I'm na member of his congregation.

[*A third* GUARD *runs in from the right*]

Third Guard. I was right, Jamie! 'Tis the Queen's ship!

First Guard. The Queen's ship, you goik! How could it be the Queen's ship? She's to come in a galley, and she's none due this month yet.

Third Guard. My word on it, Tod, I rid out wi' the fishermen, and she's a galley wi' oars, and by God she carries the oriflamme!

Second Guard. Would the queen's ship dock without notice to the lords, and no retinue at the pier?

Third Guard. There it lies—yon wi' the lights!

First Guard. She's lights aplenty, afore God. Aweel, we've no orders aboot it.

Third Guard. But we can do no less than give her what escort we can—

First Guard. We're set to guard the pier, and for nowt else. —And why are you so hot for a Romish sovereign to set foot on Scottish soil, do you mind if I ask?—For myself, I'm no member of the congregation, I'm a sojer doing what I'm set to, but it runs in my head we've had enough of the Guises and their Holy Father. Let them stick to their warm climates where they're welcome—and may they come to a hotter place before they set up another standard here!

The Ola Man. Ye may be na member of the congregation, friend, but you will be if you keep in that opinion. For her or against her it's to be in this land, and no half-way to stand on. The kirk of Christ or the hussy of Rome, drowned in wine, bestial with fornication, corrupt with all diseases of mind and blood—

Second Guard. Is it the queen's galley, Master?

The Old Man. Aye, is it.

Second Guard. For there's been no herald of it, nor anyone told—

The Old Man. I have my ways of knowing. And, hearing of it, I came myself to see this white face they speak of, and these taking graces, and to tell her to that white face of hers and despite her enchantments that we want and will have none of her here. For whatever beauty she may possess, or whatever winning airs, they are given her of the devil to cozen us, they are born solely of the concupiscence of hell and set upon her like a sign. They say when she speaks she drips honey and she smells sweet with boughten perfumes, but I say the man who tastes of her or the people who trust in her will chew on dry ashes in the last day and find no remedy for that thirst! I say she comes with a milk-white body and a tongue of music, but beware her, for she will be to you a walking curse and a walking death!

Third Guard. You will say this to the queen?

The Old Man. I will say this to her whey face!
   [BOTHWELL *enters from the right*]

Bothwell. Leg it over to the inn, one of you lads, and fetch a chair—

First Guard. We're on guard here, my lord.

Bothwell. Damn your guard duty! The queen of Scotland's stepping out of a boat 'n velvet shoes—

Third Guard. I doubt there's a chair nearer than Edinburgh town—

Bothwell. There's one at the Leith inn, as ye well know—

First Guard. We'd need the silver for that, in any case—

Bothwell. My mannie, if I was to lay a fist to the side of that iron pot of yours I doubt the dinge would come out in a hurry—. What the devil do ye mean bauchling over a dirty chair? Seize it, seize it in the queen's name!

Third Guard. I'll fetch it, sir.
   [*He starts out*]

Bothwell. And do you go with him. I suspect ye of being a psalm-singer with that face.

[*The first* GUARD *goes with the third*]

A verra braw evening to you, Master Knox.

The Old Man. And to you, my lord.

Bothwell. It seems some here heard of her coming, though not perhaps those she'd have chosen. You're not here, by chance, to greet the daughter of Mary of Guise?

The Old Man. If I have aught to say to her, it will be for her own ears.

Bothwell. No doubt, no doubt. And I have a little observe to make to you about that, too, sir. Whatever it is you have to say to her you won't say it.

The Old Man. And why not? Are the Papists muzzling the ministers of God?

Bothwell. I'm no Papist, as ye're aware, Master Knox, and if I were I'm no such fool as to try to muzzle a minister, nevertheless, whatever it was you were going to say, you won't say it, that's my observe to you—

Knox. I shall say what I have come to say.

[BOTHWELL *follows the Soldiers. A man's voice, speaking French in a light tenor comes in from the right*]

Chatelard.

[*Outside*]

It is a badge of honor, I assure Your Majesty.

Mary.

[*Outside*]

Still, when next you toss your cloak in the mud, take note whether there are any watching to report it—

Chatelard.

[*Outside*]

But if my queen and lady note it—ah, what other advertisement would a man desire?

[MARY *the Queen enters with* CHATELARD, CHATELHERAULT, *and the* FOUR MARYS-IN-WAITING]

Mary. Tut, if it were not known, or suspected, that I was queen, I should have stepped in bog like a drover's daughter—

Chatelard. Madame, that you are queen would be known if the world were stripped of subjects. The very trees and frozen mountains would bow down to you!

Mary.

[*Laughing*]

I can well imagine.

Body o' me, I could wish the clouds would stoop less to their queen in my native land.

Chatelherault. One forgets how damn dismal this Scotland can be.

Mary. Dismal? Traitor, have you never plucked a gowan in spring—a fairy fresh gowan—?

Chatelherault. Late—it comes late here—

Mary. Or gorged with bright thorn-apples in mid-August?

Chatelherault. Is there an August in this heathenish climate? God, I can't remember it!

Mary. They are sweeter here than in France, as I recall, and all fruits are sweeter here, of those that grow—and the summer's sweeter—

Chatelherault. They're short enough, God knows.

The Old Man. And when they come they will bring excellent devices of masks and ornament to deceive the eye, and soft words and stenches to cumber the senses of mankind. Adulterers, jig-masters and the like will come in authority, and their counsel will be whoring and carousing, the flowers and fruits of evil, of that great sin, that sin that eats at the heart of the world, the church of abominations, the church of Rome.

[*He pauses.* MARY *stops to look back at him*]

Mary. Chatelherault, I have been long away, and the speech of Scotland falls strangely on my ears, but is this talk usual among my people?

The Old Man. Yet is there a place reserved for them, where the fire is unending and abates not, even as their desires abate not, where their tender flesh shall be torn from them with white-hot pincers, nor shall rank or station avail them, whether they be queens or kings or the lemans of queens and kings—!

Mary.

[*Tremulous*]

Surely this is some jest, sir. Surely this is not said in welcome to me.

The Old Man. And what other welcome shall we give the

whore of Babylon—the leprous and cankerous evangel of the Beast!

[BOTHWELL *returns from the right*]

Bothwell. Your Majesty, they are preparing a room at the inn, and the chair will be here at once. If you would deign to take my cloak for your shoulders—

    [*He lays his cloak around her*]

Mary. Thank you. I wish to speak to this gentleman—

Bothwell. This is Master John Knox, of whom your Grace may have heard.

Mary. Nay, then I have heard of him, and I wish to speak to him. Master Knox, it is true that I am Mary Stuart, and your queen, and I have come back from France after many years away, to take up my rule in this country. It is true, too, that I am sad to leave the south and the sun, and I come here knowing that I shall meet with difficulties that would daunt many older and wiser than I am—for I am young and inexperienced and perhaps none too adept in statecraft. Yet this is my native place, Master Knox, and I loved it as a child and still love it—and whatever I may lack in experience, whatever I may have too much of youth, I shall try to make up for, if my people will help me, in tolerance and mercy, and a quick eye for wrongs and a quick hand to right them—

The Old Man. Aye, they told me you spoke honey—

Mary. And cannot you also—you and your people and those you know—cannot you too be tolerant toward me a little space while I find my way? For it will be hard enough at the friendliest.

The Old Man. Woman, I remember whose daughter and whose voice you are—

Mary. If I were your daughter, Master Knox, and this task before me, would you think it fitting to lay such hard terms on me, beast and whore and I know not what? For I am not a whore, I can say truly, but the daughter of a prince, softly nurtured and loving honor and truth. Neither is my body corrupt, nor my mind Nay, I am near to tears that you should think so, and I was not far from tears before, finding myself unexpected on this coast, and no preparation to receive me. What you have said comes as very cold comfort now when I need greeting and reassurance.

Bothwell. Your Majesty, if the old goat has said anything that needs retracting—

Mary. He shall retract nothing in fear! I would have all men my friends in Scotland!

Bothwell. I'm afraid that's past praying for.

Mary. Look on me, sir—and judge my face and my words. In all fairness, am I the evangel of the Beast? Can we not be friends?

The Old Man. I fear not, madam.

Mary. I strongly desire it. I have no wish for any enemy of mine except that he become my friend. You most of all, for I have met you first, and it is an augury.

The Old Man. Your Majesty, I have said what I came to say.

Mary. But you no longer mean it! See—I give you my hand, Master Knox—it is a queen's hand, and fair—and I look at you out of honest eyes—and I mean well and fairly—you cannot refuse me! Do you still hesitate? It is clean.

[*She smiles. He bows stiffly over her hand*]

And will you come to see me at Holyroodhouse, and give me counsel? For God knows I shall need counsel —and I shall listen, that I promise.

The Old Man. Your Majesty, I should be untrue to myself and my calling if I refused counsel where it is asked.

Mary. You will come?

The Old Man. I will come.

Mary. I will send for you, and soon.

[*Her words are a kindly dismissal*]

The Old Man. Good night, Your Majesty—

Mary. Goodnight, Master Knox.

[Knox *goes to the left*]

Now I wonder, will he hate me more or less?

Bothwell. More, probably. However, it's just as well to have him where you can watch him.

Mary. You're an outspoken man yourself, Captain.

Bothwell. I am.

Mary. You will forgive, me, but so far I have not heard your name.

Chatelherault. The Captain is James Hepburn, madame—the Earl of Bothwell.

Mary. Ah—you fought ably for my mother.

Bothwell. I have been of some slight service here and there.

Mary. You have indeed! Tell me, my lord of Bothwell, have I done well so far? Shall I not make this Scotland mine?

Bothwell. Madame, it is a cold, dour, sour, bastardly villainous country, and the folk on it are a cold, dour, sour, bastardly lot of close-shaving psalm-retching villains, and I can only hope no harm will come here to that bonny face of yours, and no misery to the spirit you bring.

Mary. Now here's a new kind of courtesy!

Bothwell. You'll hear far and wide I'm no courtier, madame—but I have eyes, and I can see that the new sovereign is a sonsie lass and a keen one, and I was for her from the first I saw her face—but from my heart I could wish her a better country to rule over—

Mary. Now, will no one speak well of this poor Scotland of mine—?

Bothwell. Your Majesty, shall I praise it for you—as high as it deserves—?

Mary. Say whatever good you can!

Bothwell. Then this is Scotland, my lady: To the north a few beggarly thousands of Highland Catholics who have not yet learned the trick of wearing britches, and to the south a few beggarly thousands of Lowland Protestants whose britches have no pockets to them—Their pleasures are drinking and fighting, both of which they do badly, and what they fight about is that half of them are willing to sell their souls for a florin, whereas the other half has no expectation of getting so much. What business they have is buying cheap and selling dear, but since none of them will sell cheap, and none will pay dear, the upshot is there's no business done—

Mary. Enough, enough!—solemnly and truly, sir—it may be they are not a happy race, but they have beliefs—and what they believe they believe from the heart! Even this Master Knox—

Bothwell. He? He believes whatever's to his own advantage, and prophesies whatever will line his nest if it comes to pass. He makes his living yelling nonsense into the lugs of these poor, benighted, superstitious savages—he's split the country wide open over your coming and leads the pack against you, brawling from his dung-hill! We'll have bloodshed over it yet—

Mary. Blood-shed?

Bothwell. And plenty.

Mary. No. If I thought that I should turn now and bid the mariners hoist sail and put back for France. I shall win, but I shall win in a woman's way, not by the sword.

Bothwell. Let us hope so.

Mary. Hope so! But I shall!

Bothwell. I am no courtier, madame. I say, let us hope so.

Mary Beaton. The chair has come, madame.

Mary. Yes, and in time. We're chilled to the heart here.
Come.

> [*She goes out with* Bothwell, *the others following. The first
> and third* Guards *return*]

First Guard. Did the old man spit his venom?

Second Guard. You'll not believe it. He kissed her hand.

Third Guard. She's a witch, then.

Second Guard. Aye, is she. The kind a man wouldna mind
being bewitched by.

Third Guard. No.

Second Guard. I tell you she fair wenched him. The old
man doddert a bit and then bent over like a popinjay.

First Guard. She's tha' kind then?

Second Guard. She's tha' kind.

CURTAIN

ACT ONE
Scene II

Scene: *A corner of Queen Elizabeth's study at Whitehall. It is morning, but the sun has not yet risen. She is up early to go over plans with* Lord Burghley, *who sits opposite her at a small table on which an hour-glass stands like a paper-weight on their notes. She is a young woman, still beautiful, with a crafty face. Tall candles burn behind them in a sconce. Outside the circle of light the scene is indefinite.*

Burghley. It still lacks something of dawn, Your Majesty.

Elizabeth. We have one more hour before the palace will be stirring. You said, I believe, that you have made memoranda in regard to Mary Stuart?

Burghley. I have set down the facts as we must face them, and alternative policies.

Elizabeth. Read them, if you will. And turn the glass. It's run out.

Burghley.

[*Turning the glass and taking up a paper*]

They are not in order, but the main points are covered. First, Mary Stuart has crossed from France to Scotland against your advice and without your safe-conduct. This is in itself a slight to Your Majesty, and almost a challenge, though not one of which you can take public cognizance.

Elizabeth. Yes.

Burghley. Second, she has been crowned queen of Scotland, this also against your wish and in defiance of your

16

policy. This may be construed as an open breach of friendship, or may be overlooked, as Your Majesty may desire—and as it may seem best.

Elizabeth. Yes.

Burghley. Third, she is a Catholic and related by blood to the most powerful Catholic house in France, which constitutes her a public danger to Protestant England. Fourth, she is next heir after Your Majesty to the throne of England, and is held by Catholic Europe to be the rightful queen of England at the present time, Your Majesty being regarded by all Catholics as a pretender, unjustly seated on your throne.

Elizabeth. True. Proceed. You have more on that point. They believe me a bastard and say so. Very well, let us face that, too.

Burghley. Fifth, then—you are held by the Catholic Europe to be the illegitimate daughter of Henry the Eighth, the divorce of Henry from Catherine of Aragon being unrecognized by the Church of Rome and his marriage to your mother, Anne Boleyn, deemed invalid. Sixth, these things being true, Your Majesty must not allow Marie Stuart to succeed as Queen of Scotland. For in so far as she is secure in Scotland you are insecure in England. Your Majesty will forgive my bad habit of setting down in writing what is so obvious, but it is only by looking hard at these premises that I am able to discover what must be done.

Elizabeth. Out with it then. What must be done?

Burghley. She must be defeated.

Elizabeth. How?

Burghley. Is there more than one way? We must pick our quarrel and send an army into Scotland.

Elizabeth. Declare war?

Burghley. Perhaps not openly—but we have excuse for it.

Elizabeth. And reason?

Burghley. She must be defeated.

Elizabeth. Truly, but not so quick, not so quick with wars and troops and expenses. Have you no better counsel?

Burghley. In all my reading I have found no case of a sovereign deposed without violence.

Elizabeth. And in all those voluminous notes of yours you have set down no other method save warfare? The last resort, the most difficult, costly and hazardous of all?

Burghley. It is the only sure method, and you cannot afford to fail.

Elizabeth. My dear Burghley, in any project which affects England and our own person so nearly we have no intention of failing. But you have overlooked in your summary two considerations which simplify the problem. One is the internal dissension in Scotland, half Protestant, half Catholic, and divided in a mortal enmity—

Burghley. Overlooked it! Madame, it is the main argument for an immediate declaration of war—Edinburgh would rally to your arms overnight! This is our opportunity to unite England and Scotland!

Elizabeth. A war would unite Scotland against us—unite Scotland under Mary. No—it is necessary first to undermine her with her own subjects.

Burghley. And how would that be accomplished?

Elizabeth. This brings me to the second consideration which you overlook—the conduct and reputation of Mary herself.

Burghley. Would that affect our policy?

Elizabeth. It will make it. Merely to remind us, will you read over again the report of Mary's character in Randolph's latest budget of news?

Burghley. This? "As for the person of Marie, our new Queen, I must say in truth that she is of high carriage, beautiful in a grave way—"?

Elizabeth. So—go on.

Burghley. "Beautiful, in a grave way, somewhat gamesome and given to lightness of manner among her lords as well as with other company, very quick-witted to answer back, and addicted to mirth and dancing, wherewith she hath made many converts to her cause among those most disaffected, though there be also those found to say her manners might more beseem the stews or places of low resort than so ancient a palace and line—"

Elizabeth. You see, she is a Stuart.

Burghley. "Moreover, she hath allowed herself to be seen much in the company of certain men, among them the

Earl of Bothwell, and hath borne herself among these men, they being known of somewhat loose report, in such fashion as to give scandal to the stricter sort here, she not scanting to lend her eyes or hands or tongue to a kind of nimble and facile exchange of smiles and greetings which might better become the hostess of an alehouse, seeking to win custom. Natheless she is liked, and greatly liked by those on whom she hath smiled closely, they being won not as a wise sovereign wins subjects, but as a woman wins men."

Elizabeth. Yes, a Stuart.

Burghley. "Yet to be true again I must say also that she is of noble mind, greatly religious in her way, and the whispers against her name not justified by what she is in herself, but only by her manners, which she hath brought from France."

Elizabeth. She has won our Randolph among others. He shall go north no more.

Burghley. "And in addition she hath borne her power thus far with so discreet and tolerant a justness, impartial to north and south, to Catholic and Protestant alike, that if she persevere in this fashion she is like to reconcile the factions and establish herself firmly on the throne of Scotland. For vast numbers who thought to curse her now remain her fast friends."

Elizabeth. Have you yet seen what we must do?

Burghley. I find in this only a graver and more malicious danger.

Elizabeth. And you would still make war?

Burghley. Your Majesty, it will be war whether we like it or not—and there is imminent danger, danger to your throne and life. The more suddenly you act the less effort will be needed—

Elizabeth. My lord, my lord, it is hard to thrust a queen from her throne, but suppose a queen were led to destroy herself, led carefully from one step to another in a long descent until at last she stood condemned among her own subjects, barren of royalty, stripped of force, and the people of Scotland were to deal with her for us?

Burghley. She would crush a rebellion.

Elizabeth. She would now, but wait. She is a Catholic, and for that half her people distrust her. She has a name for coquetry and easy smiling, and we shall build that up into a name for wantonness and loose behaviour. She is seen to have French manners; we shall make it appear that these manners indicate a false heart and hollow faith.

Burghley. Can this be done?

Elizabeth. She is a woman, remember, and open to attack as a woman. We shall set tongues wagging about her. And since it may be true that she is of a keen and noble mind, let us take care of that too. Let us marry her to a weakling and a fool. A woman's mind and spirit are no better than those of the man she lies under in the night.

Burghley. She will hardly marry to our convenience, madame.

Elizabeth. Not if she were aware of it. But she is next heir to my throne; she will hope for children to sit on it, and she will therefore wish to marry a man acceptable as the father of kings. We can make use of that.

Burghley. Only perhaps.

Elizabeth. No, certainly. She is a woman and already jealous for the children she may bear. To my mind the man she marries must be of good appearance, in order that she may want him, but a fool, in order that he may ruin her, and a Catholic, in order to set half her people against her.

Burghley. We know that she is seen much with Bothwell.

Elizabeth. And he is a Protestant.

Burghley. He is a Protestant. Now suddenly it occurs to me. If she were to marry a Protestant and turn Protestant herself, would she not make an acceptable ally?—

Elizabeth.

[*Rising*]

I do not wish her for an ally! Have you not yet understood? I wish her a Catholic and an enemy, that I may see her blood run at my feet! Since Bothwell is a Protestant, the more reason for dangling some handsome youngster instantly in the north, as if by accident, nay, as if against my will, some youngster with courtly manners, lacking in brain, a Catholic, and of a blood-strain that would strengthen pretensions to the throne of England.

Burghley. You have thought of someone?

Elizabeth. I have thought of several. I shall even let it be rumored that I oppose such a marriage. I shall let it go abroad that I favor someone else.

Burghley. Who is the man?

Elizabeth. I have thought of Darnley.

Burghley. But after herself Darnley is in fact heir to the English throne. An alliance with him would actually strengthen her claim to succeed to your place.

Elizabeth. The better, the better. He is handsome, and of good bearing?

Burghley. Yes.

Elizabeth. And a fool?

Burghley. A boasting, drunken boy.

Elizabeth. And a Catholic.

Burghley. As you know.

Elizabeth. If I give out that I am determined against it, she will marry him, and he will drag her down, awaken her senses to become his slave, turn her people against her, make her a fool in council, curb this pretty strumpetry that gains her friends, haul her by the hair for jealousy, get her big with child, too, and spoil her beauty. I tell you a queen who marries is no queen, a woman who marries is a puppet—and she will marry—she must marry to staunch that Stuart blood.

Burghley. This will take time.

Elizabeth. It may take many years. I can wait.

Burghley. And we shall need many devices.

Elizabeth. You shall not find me lacking in devices, in the word to drop here, the rumor started there. We must have constant knowledge of her, and agents about her continually, so that her acts and sayings may be misconstrued and a net of half-lies woven about her, yes, till her people believe her a voluptuary, a scavenger of dirty loves, a bedder with grooms. Aye, till she herself think ill of herself and question her loves, lying awake in torment in the dark.—There is a man called Knox who can be used in this.

Burghley. But that—to accomplish that—

Elizabeth. We live in a world of shadows, my lord; we are not what we are, but what is said of us and what we read in others' eyes. More especially is this true of queens and kings. It will grow up about her in whispers that she is tainted in blood, given over to lechery and infamous pleasures. She will be known as double-tongued, a demon with an angel's face, insatiable in desire, an emissary of Rome, a prophetess of evil addicted to lascivious rites and poisonous revenges. And before all this her own mind will pause in doubt and terror of what she may be that these things should be said of her—she will lie awake in torment in the dark—and she will lie broken, nerveless there in the dark. Her own people will rise and take her sceptre from her.

Burghley.
   [*Rising*]
   But Your Majesty—you—

Elizabeth. However, I am not to appear in this. Always, and above all, I am to seem her friend.—You would say that I am in myself more nearly what will be said of her.

Burghley. No, no—

Elizabeth. Why, perhaps. But that is not what is said of me. Whatever I may be, it shall be said only that I am the queen of England, and that I rule well.

CURTAIN

ACT ONE

Scene III

Scene: *A great hall in Mary Stuart's apartments at Holyroodhouse. The room is rectangular with wide fireplaces glowing to the left and right. An entrance door opens to the right, and two doors at the left lead, one to Mary's study, and the other to her bedroom. The stone of the walls is largely covered with stamped leather hangings. A chair, slightly elevated, stands in the middle of the rear wall, the royal arms of Scotland draped above it. The floor is stone with a few Eastern rugs. There are two high, heavily draped windows at the rear, on either side of the queen's chair.*

Mary Beaton, Mary Seton, *and* Mary Livingstone *are concerning themselves with the hanging of the ensign behind the chair, and* Livingstone *has stepped upon a stool to reach a fold of it.* Lord Darnley *and* Lord Gordon *are warming themselves at one of the fires, having just come in.*

Beaton.

[*To the men*]

It's to hang there because she wants it there. Isn't that enough?

Gordon. I've heard my father say the kings of Scotland were always plain folk, but queens are a fancy breed, and their ways are fancy.

Darnley. A thought higher with that fold, my dear—just a thought higher.

Livingstone.

[*Turning*]

And why?

26

Darnley. Dod, lady, it's a neat turn of ankle you show when you reach up. Reach a bit higher.

Livingstone.

[*Back to her work*]

Look your eyes full if it does you any good, my Lord Darnley.

Darnley. Man, man, but that's a pretty foot!

Gordon. Aye.

Darnley. Ye have heard it said, no doubt, what they say about a woman's foot?

Gordon. Aye.

Seton. What do they say?

Darnley. About a woman's foot? Only that it's, in a sort, a measure of her capacities.

Beaton. Oh, is it, indeed? I've heard the same in respect to a man's nose, and I can only say if it's true your nose is no great advertisement for you.

Darnley. The nose is a fallible signal, my lady, as I'll prove to you—you naming your own place and time.

Beaton. I to name the place?

Darnley. It is your privilege.

Beaton. Your own bed-chamber, then.

Livingstone. Beaton!

Darnley. Accepted! Accepted! My own bed-chamber! And the time?

Beaton. The night of your wedding, by God!

Darnley. My dear lady—

Gordon. She has you there, Darnley.

Beaton. Moreover, if there is one kind of a man a woman dislikes more than another it's one so little experienced that he goes peeping at ankles for lack of better satisfaction.

Darnley. Stop there! I will furnish you with data—

Beaton. Unless indeed it be the kind of man whose experiences with women have been like nothing so much as those of a dog with lamp-posts—

Livingstone. Beaton!

    [MARY FLEMING *enters from the queen's study*]

Beaton.

    [*Clapping a hand to her mouth in mock chagrin*]

Oh, what have I said, what have I said?

Seton. A great plenty!

Darnley. Mistress Fleming, is it true our sovereign is inaccessible this day?

Fleming. Quite true, I fear.

Darnley. God help the man who tries to woo a queen.

Fleming. And so he might if your Lordship prayed to him with any serious intent.

Darnley. Perhaps. And yet I doubt it might do more good if a man were to have studied in France.

Fleming. Studied?

Darnley. The arts. The arts of Ovid. The arts of pleasing a maid.

Beaton. They are the same in France as elsewhere, no doubt.

Darnley. No doubt, says she, and a very pretty innocence.

Gordon. Aye, as though she'd never been there.

Fleming. We're not denying that we've been in France.

Darnley. Then don't tell us that the art of Love is the same there as in England and Scotland, for the report runs different.

Gordon. It's a kennt thing that French love is none the same.

Livingstone. Will you tell us how?

Gordon. Eh, we're to tell you who've lived among them?

Fleming. Aside from better manners the people of France are like the people of Scotland, both in love and war.

Darnley. It's not an easy matter to go into with my lady's bevy of beauty, nevertheless they say there are no virgins there above four years old.

Livingstone. Then they lie who say it, and you're fools to believe it.

Darnley. Nay, it may be a bit exaggerated, but I'd lay no more than a groat on any piece of French virginity. They have summat to tell in confession; they have had their three of a night; they have had their what-for, and come up all the fresher and more lisping for it.

Beaton. I must say I've never met nastier minds than here-
about, and that's something for John Knox to ponder
on, too.

Gordon. Will ye come, man? Ye'll have no sight of the
queen today, and these trollops have no time for plain
Scotchmen.

Darnley. Aye.

Fleming. Lord Darnley is to remain within call. It is her
Majesty's pleasure.

Darnley. Ah, well that's something.

Gordon. It's dangling, to give it a plain name.
    [BOTHWELL *enters from the right*]

Livingstone. Oh, my lord Bothwell.

Bothwell. By God, my name's remembered, and that's a
    triumph,
Tell the sweet queen Lord Bothwell would see her
    alone.

Livingstone. Sir, she is closeted with her secretary—
We are not free to speak with her.

Bothwell. Closeted? So?
I like not that word closeted. Who is there here
Who can speak with her and tell her?

Fleming. My Lord, she has spaced
This day off into hours, so many to each,
And I fear your name is not scheduled.

Bothwell. Distrust your schedule,
Then, my prim, for I'll see her.

Fleming. The ambassador
From England arrives today, for his audience,
And before that Her Majesty plans to hold
A conclave with the lords.

Darnley. We've been sloughed off
Much the same way, my lord

Bothwell. Run along then, and practise
Wearing that tin sword you've got hung on you,
Before it trips you.

Darnley. Trips me?

Bothwell. Aye, run and play!
This one's been used. The nicks along the edge
Were made on tougher than you. Tell my lady queen
I wish to see her now.

Fleming. I cannot myself.
I might speak to Master Rizzio.

Bothwell. Then do that. Is Scotland grown so formal
That a man's received like a money-lender?
   [FLEMING *goes out*]

Livingstone. No,
But these matters must be arranged.

Bothwell.
   [*To* DARNLEY]
Are you still here?

Darnley. Still here.

Bothwell. I knew a pimp in Paris had much your look,
But the women he brought me were foul.

Darnley. But good enough,
  I daresay.

Bothwell. You might have thought so.

  [RIZZIO *enters,* FLEMING *following*]

Rizzio. Oh, my lord Bothwell,
  There's such great pressure on our time today—
  Matters that must be seen to; if you could come
  Tomorrow—

Bothwell. Well, I cannot come tomorrow.
  Tomorrow will not do. I am here today.
  And will not be here tomorrow. Is that understood?

  [RIZZIO *pauses*]

Darnley. Let him run his suit into the ground.

Gordon. Aye, and himself.

  [DARNLEY *and* GORDON *go out*]

Rizzio. My orders are strict, my lord. Her Majesty
  Has great problems of state—

Bothwell. And they concern me
  More than some others. Now, before Christ, I've
  argued
  Enough with women and women-faced men! A room's
  a room
  And a door's a door! Shall I enter without warning
  Or will you announce me to her? Great pressure on
  Our time! Our time, he says! My fine Italian—

  [MARY STUART *enters. There is sudden quiet*]

Mary. I will speak with my lord alone.

  [*One by one, and silently,* RIZZIO *and the girls go out*]

Do I find you angry?

Bothwell. At these pests and midges.

Mary. You saw me yesterday.

Bothwell. I have been standing since this early morning—
I and some hundred crows, out in the coppice
On the cliff's edge, waiting for the smoke to rise
From your breakfast chimney. And by the Lord these
  crows
Are a funny company. I've had four full hours
To study them.

Mary. You come to tell me this?

Bothwell. I come to tell you
I've never shown such patience for a woman,
Not in my life before.

Mary. Did you call it patience
On a time when I could not see you, to wreck an inn,
Leave mine host in the road with a broken head
And lie with his daughter?

Bothwell. That was not true. Or at least
I had her good will for it.

Mary. And another time
To besiege the governor's house with your border
  knaves
And rouse all Edinburgh? Are you a man
Or a storm at sea, not to be brought indoors?

Bothwell. When I would see my girl, why I must see her
Or I am a storm, and indoors, too.

Mary. Your girl? Give me leave,
Since I am a queen, with a kingdom to reign over,
To queen it once in a while.

Bothwell. I tell you truly
I've the manners of a rook, for we're all crows here,
And that's what's understood in this town, but I
could
Be tame and split my tongue with courtly speeches.
If I could be sure of you—if I could know from one
day
To another what to make of your ways. You shut
yourself up
With secretaries and ministers, harking for weeks
On end to their truffle—while I perch me on the rocks
And look my eyes out.

Mary. When I was but thirteen
A pretty lad fell in love with me; he'd come,
Oh, afternoons, late midnight, early dawn
Sopping with dew-fall; he'd stand there, waiting for a
glance—
I've never had such tribute.

Bothwell. This is no boy.
This is a man comes beating your door in now.
It may be you're too young to know the difference,
But it's time you learned.

Mary. You've had your way, my lord;
We've spoken together, though I had no time to give,
And now, with your pardon—

Bothwell. You'll go about the business

Of marrying someone else. That's what this mangy
Meeting of councillors means, and that's what por-
   tends
From Elizabeth's ambassador! I warn you,
Make no decisions without me!

Mary. I cannot marry you.
  I beg you, ask it not; speak not of it. Our day
  Has come between us. Let me go now.

Bothwell. My lady,
  I will speak softly. Have no fear of me
  Or what I intend. But there have been days I remember
  When you had less care what hostages you gave
  The world. I think you showed more royally then
  Than now, for you loved then and spoke your love,
    and I
  Moved more than mortal for that while. Oh, girl,
  If we would be as the high gods, we must live
  From within outward! Let the heavens rain fire
  Or the earth mud. This is a muddy race
  That breeds around us. Will you walk in fear of mud-
    slingers,
  Or walk proudly, and take my hand?

Mary. I am a queen.

Bothwell. They've made a slave of you,
  This bastard half-brother of yours, this fox of a Mait-
    land,
  This doddering Chatelherault! They frighten you
  With consequences. They're afraid of men's tongues
  And they've made you afraid. But what they truly fear

Is that you'll win the country, be queen here truly.
And they'll be out of it. What they'd like best of all
Is to wreck you, break you completely, rule the country
   themselves,
And why they fear me is because I'm your man alone,
And man enough to stop them.

Mary. Yes. You are man enough.
It's dangerous to be honest with you, my Bothwell
But honest I'll be. Since I've been woman grown
There's been no man save you but I could take
His hand steadily in mine, and look in his eyes
Steadily, too, and feel in myself more power
Then I felt in him. All but yourself. There is aching
Fire between us, fire that could take deep hold
And burn down all the marches of the west
And make us great or slay us. Yet it's not to be trusted
Our minds are not the same. If I gave my hand
To you, I should be pledged to rule by wrath
And violence, to take without denial,
And mount on others' ruin. That's your way
And it's not mine.

Bothwell. You'll find no better way.
There's no other way for this nation of churls and
   cravens.

Mary. I have been queen of France—a child-queen and
   foolish—
But one thing I did learn, that to rule gently
Is to rule wisely. The knives you turn on your people
You must sometime take in your breast.

Bothwell. You know not Scotland
  Here you strike first or die. Your brother Moray
  Seeks your death, Elizabeth of England
  Seeks your death, and they work together.

Mary. Nay—
  You mistrust too much—and even if this were true
  A sovereign lives always with death before and after,
  And many have tried to murder their way to safety—
  But there's no safety there. For each enemy
  You kill you make ten thousand, for each one
  You spare, you make one friend.

Bothwell. Friends? Friends? Oh, lass,
  Thou'lt nurse these adders and they'll fang thee—
    Thou'rt
  Too tender and too just. My heart cries for thee—
  Take my help, take my hands!

Mary. I would I could take both.
  God knows how I wish it. But as I am queen
  My heart shall not betray me, what I believe
  And my faith. This is my faith, dear my lord, that all
    men
  Love better good than evil, cling rather to truth
  Than falseness, answer fair dealing with fair return;
  And this too; those thrones will fall that are built on
    blood
  And craft, that as you'd rule long, you must rule well—
  This has been true, and is true.

Bothwell. God help thee, child.

Mary. Be staunch to me. You have been staunchest of all.

Let me not lose your arm. No, nor your love—
You know how much you have of mine. I'm here
Alone, made queen in a set, hard, bitter time.
Aid me, and not hinder.

Bothwell. So it shall be.

Mary. And give me the help I'd have.

Bothwell. That I can't promise.
I'll help thee and defend thee. Lady dear,
Do you use guile on me?

Mary. No, sweet, I love thee,
And I could love thee well.
  [*She goes to him. He kisses her hand and then her lips*]
Go now, and leave me.
We've been seen too much together.

Bothwell. You must lay this hand
In no one's else. It's mine.

Mary. I have but lease on it,
Myself. It's not my own. But it would be yours
If it were mine to give.
  [MARY LIVINGSTONE *comes to the right hand door*]

Livingstone. Your Majesty,
The Lords of the council are here.

Mary. Let them be admitted.
  [LIVINGSTONE *goes out*]

Bothwell. Has Your Majesty forgotten
That I am of the council, under your seal?

Mary. I could wish you were elsewhere. These are the men I least

Have wanted to find us alone. But stay, now you're here.

[*She goes pensively to her chair of state and seats herself.* LORD JAMES STUART, *Earl of Moray*, MAITLAND OF LETHINGTON, *the* DUC DE CHATELHERAULT, HUNTLEY, MORTON, *and* ERSKINE *are ushered in by* MARY LIVINGSTONE, *who withdraws. There is a brief silence*]

Maitland. We have not interrupted Your Majesty?

Mary. No. The Earl of Bothwell is of the council. I have asked him to take part.

Maitland. There was some agreement
That since the Earl's name might come up, it would be as well
If he were not here.

Bothwell. And then again, since my name
May be mentioned, and there's none so able as I
To defend it, it may be as well that I'm here.

Maitland. My lord,
There was small thought to attack you.

Bothwell. Less now, perhaps,

Mary. Lord Bothwell will remain.

Moray. Sister, it may be that Bothwell will be offended
By something said.

Mary. You are courtier enough
To couch it not to offend, my brother.

Maitland. Nay, then,
What we have come to say must be softly said,

But meant no less strictly. The question of our queen's
 marriage,
Of which everyone has spoken, let me add,
But which we have avoided here, must now come up
Whether or no we like it.

Mary. Be not so tender
With me, dear Maitland. I have been married. I am
A widow, and free to marry again.

Huntley. That's the lass!
They say widows are always ready.

Mary. Do they say that?
Do they not say ready but—wary?

Huntley. Aye, that too.

Mary. But the truth is I should prefer my own time for
 wedding.
I know of no prince or king whose hand is offered,
And whose hand I'd take.

Maitland. It's not to be treated lightly
I'm much afraid. The thrones of all the world
Are shaken with broils even as we stand here. The
 throne
On which you sit, our sovereign, is shaken, too,
Though Your Majesty has done more than I'd have
 dreamed
Could be done to still the factions. It's our belief
That a marriage, if the right one, would seat you more
 firmly,
Put an end to many questions.

Mary. There's more of this?

Maitland. That's all we wish—to see you safe on your throne
So that we may be safe in our houses. Until men know
What alliance we're to make, what hangs over us
In the way of foreign treaties, the clans will sleep
With dirks in their brogans, and a weather eye still open
For fire in the thatch. And yet to choose the man—
That's a point we can't agree on.

Mary. I'm with you there.
For you see, I'm hard to please.

Maitland. And more than that,
Of princes that offer, or have been suggested, each one
Commits us to some alliance of church or state
We'd find embarrassing. Philip of Spain, the Duke
Of Anjou—these are Catholic—

Bothwell. Has it crossed your mind
That there are lords in Scotland?

Maitland. And there, too—
If the choice were to fall on a Scottish earl, the houses
Passed over would take it ill—and it might well lead
To a breach in our peace—

Bothwell. Yes?

Maitland. Nay, even to civil war.

Mary. I cannot give myself out
As a virgin queen, yet our cousin Elizabeth's plan
Has virtues. Must I marry at all?

Morton. Your Majesty,
    We have not yet said what we came to say,
    And it needs saying bluntly. The people of Scotland
    Are given to morals almost as much as to drink.
    I'll not say they're moral themselves, but they'll insist
    On morals in high places. And they've got in their heads
    That you're a light woman.
      [MARY *rises*]
    I don't know how it got there,
    And I daresay it's not true—

Mary. Thank you. For your daresay.

Maitland. I could have wished to speak more delicately
    Of this, but it's before us, and can't be denied.
    Your Majesty, when you came to us from France
    And I saw you first, I said to myself in my heart,
    All will be well with Scotland. What I thought then
    I can say now, for you are wiser even
    Than I had supposed, and you have dealt more justly
    Than any could have hoped, yet still it's true
    Some spreading evil has gone out against you,
    A crawling fog of whispers.

Mary. Who believes them?

Maitland. I'll not say they're believed. I'm not sure they
    are.
    But there was the episode of the boy who was hidden
    In your bed-chamber

Erskine. Chatelard.

Maitland. Aye, he, and
    That may have begun it. I believed at first it stemmed

From John Knox's preaching, for he holds all Catholics
To be the devil's own, but there's more than that—
A much more seeded, intentional crop of lyings
Planted here, till I've wondered if Chatelard
May not have been an agent, or one of many.

Mary. Planted by whom?

Huntley. Why, by Elizabeth.
Who else?

Maitland. But that's not certain, either.
Chatelard came from France, and in all this scurril
I've traced no word to London.

Mary. It's what they say.
Not what they believe.

Huntley. You've lent them some color for it,
Your Majesty. You've been no statue.

Mary. No,
Nor wish to be. My lord of Lethington,
What you have said of me, how I was when you saw me,
How I seem to you now, I swear to you, you were not
    wrong.
I have not betrayed myself as woman or queen.

Maitland. I would swear that, too.

Mary. And since I know that is true,
I have thought very little of whispers. For there is
    judgment
Somehow in the air; what I am will be known, what's
    false

Will wash out in the rains.

[*She seats herself again*]

Maitland. My sovereign, you are yet young.
I once believed that. But I have lived long enough
To see error grow up and prosper, and send its roots
A century deep. There's force enough in these winds
Of malice to blow us all down—

Mary. I'll try to be serious,
For I see you are. It's your thought, then, that a marriage
Would end the rumors?

Maitland. Aye.

Mary. But as to whom I'll marry—
Happily, that's not decided for me yet.

Morton. By God.
If it was we'd see you to bed with him tonight.

Mary. Has the woman no voice in such matters?

Morton. Not in such cases.

Mary. And what is my case, may I ask?

Morton. Why, we've said nothing
About my Lord Bothwell. It's his name's coupled with yours;
His young Rizzio's.

Bothwell. I've thought often, Morton,
One of us would die before the other. Now
I'm sure of it. And soon.

Morton. I have you.

Mary. My lords,
   Will you quarrel in council over your queen's virtue?
   Let me defend my own honor, and let you
   Defend your own. Do I understand that I
   Am accused with Bothwell or Rizzio? Or both?

Maitland. You are accused of nothing.

Morton. You are not accused,
   Your Majesty. Moreover, you are queen
   Of Scotland, and therefore no man here would dare
   Accuse you—

Mary. Oh, speak out, man! Are you afraid?
   When have I punished plain dealing?

Morton. Why, then, you are queen,
   And may set your own customs, but if my wife were seen
   Abroad as you are, and half so free of contact
   With young and old as you are, I'd not answer
   For what was said about her!

Mary. I'm no man's wife.

Morton. No. And the sense of this council
   Is that it might be better if you were,
   Better for your good name and better for Scotland.

Mary. I will answer these things: as for Rizzio,
   He is my secretary; if I spend time
   In private with him, that is the reason. If I
   Had not liked him, he would not be my secretary.
   As for Lord Bothwell, he has put more strength
   Behind what I wished to do than any among you,
   And at times when I had despaired. He is my good
      friend.

We were here alone before this conference
And we differed in opinion. To wipe that out
I went to him of myself and kissed his lips.
We had kissed but once before, may not kiss again,
But that's at my option, not yours.

Huntley. Lassie, ye've been
Too honest for your own good.

Mary. Why, if so much weight
Is placed on a kiss in Scotland, come now, each one
And take your kiss—or if that's no recompense
Come to me then in private, and you shall have,
Each one, one kiss.

Morton. And after that, there are kisses
Elsewhere—and when you've finished, whether you'll
  marry
Or not may not be the question, but whether we can find
A prince who'll have you.

Mary.
  [*Rising and taking a step down*]
And having heard that word—
My lords, when you wish to talk with me again
As civilized men, and not barbarians,
You shall have audience. This Scottish kirk of yours
Has misled you as to the meaning of kisses. I am
Unsullied and young, and have my own faith to plight
And more to think of than these maunderings
Over pantry gossip. I shall not marry till
I find it wise, nor until I have made quite sure
What effect it will have on my inheritance

Of the throne of England. You come here in high con-
clave
And spend three-farthing's worth of wit to chaffer
Over a kiss in my audience-chamber! The question
Is not to save my name, I hope, nor my throne,
But how best to meet the destiny that has made me
Full heir to all this island.—Scotland is mine,
And England will come to me or to the child
I hope to have. It's this that makes my marriage
A matter of moment.—And this—with your good
pardon—
Will be the last for today.

   [*She goes into her study*]

Moray. Morton, I warned you
  To leave all speech to Lethington.

Morton. She sits on that throne
  Only so long as we want her there, no longer.

Bothwell. If my lord of Morton
  Would care to lose those black feathers from his crest
  I await his pleasure.

   [*He goes out*]

Moray. I'm for that, too. Settle it between you,
  And may you both win. We'll all be the better for it.

   [LIVINGSTONE *enters from the right*]

Livingstone. Lord Throgmorton is here from England
  With embassies for the queen.

Maitland. She's gone to her study.
  She'll wish to admit him.

Livingstone. Yes.

    [*She goes to the queen's study.* MORTON *goes out the other door*]

Maitland. We get no further

  Today then,

    [*He goes to the door*]

Huntley. No. Erskine, a word with you.

    [ERSKINE *and* HUNTLEY *go out.* THROGMORTON *enters*]

Maitland. Come in, Lord Throgmorton. You've been announced within.

Throgmorton. Greetings, my lord, fair greetings.

Maitland. We can have speech later.

Throgmorton. We shall.

    [MAITLAND *goes out.* THROGMORTON *and* MORAY *are alone*]

  Greetings also to my Lord James Stuart,

  In fine, the best of greetings.

Moray. From Elizabeth?

Throgmorton. I'm burdened with them—and more to you

  than any.

Moray. May I know the drift?

Throgmorton. This is hardly the place for that,

  But this much for now: Elizabeth has determined

  That you are to reign in Scotland, if not as king,

  Then as regent again.

Moray. Well, that's news.

Throgmorton. She bids me to tell you

  As if from herself, you are not to be disturbed

If her policy seems at variance with her mind.
It's a wide arc of intrigue, but she carries
These schemes in her head like a gambit, and she means
To play it to the end. Your sister Mary
Is not acceptable to her.

Moray. But this scheme of hers?

Throgmorton. Later, later. You're a silent man, I know.
No word.

Moray. None.

    [MARY *enters*]

Mary. Lord Throgmorton?

Throgmorton. Your Majesty.

    [*He kneels. She comes to him and gives him her hand to kiss*]
From one great queen to another, happiness.

Mary. A courtier in the grand style.

Throgmorton. Nay, Majesty,
A plain man of business.

Mary. Let us to business, then.

    [*She motions him to rise, and he does so*]
My brother, did you wish further word with me?

Moray. No, madame, only that I may see you tomorrow.

Mary.

    [*Goes to her chair*]
At your own time.

    [MORAY *bows low and goes out*]
You had more to say?

Throgmorton. Much more. My poor brain's taxed with re-
    membering.
But to begin, Queen Elizabeth sends her love
To her cousin of Scotland, wishes her well, and a reign
Both long and easy, and proffers to that end
Whatever friendship and amity between thrones
Your Majesty will accept.

Mary. Tell Elizabeth
She will not find me niggard of friendship or love.

Throgmorton. I shall report Your Majesty so. Then, further,
I'm bid to say, what Elizabeth most desires
Is that all briars of discord that have grown
Between this city and England, be wed away,
And leave a path for peace.

Mary. I desire that, too.
Does she put a name to these briars?

Throgmorton. Your Majesty, I am
Permitted to speak quite frankly?

Mary. I beg you to.

Throgmorton. You are next heir to the throne of England,
    and you
Are a Catholic. This is a danger to you
As well as Elizabeth. Were you to turn Protestant
Elizabeth would at once recognize in you
Next heir to her succession.

Mary. I should think she might,
Since I am next heir.

Throgmorton. Forgive me for speaking plainly.

Mary. Oh, forgive me!

Throgmorton. If this seems difficult, I am bid to remind you
  That Elizabeth was a Catholic, but became
  A Protestant for political reasons.

Mary. That
  I could never do. Nor do I see that one's faith
  Should be touched by politics.

Throgmorton. Why, not politics,
  My gracious queen! God forbid me that I should bring
  That word into such a context! We know, of course,
  How one clings, shall we say for sentimental reasons,
  To the rituals of his youth! Aye, and even a prince,
  We admit, would rather say his pater nosters
  The way he learned them when he was a child. And yet
  Must we take these childish things so gravely now,
  When war or peace hangs on them? There are Catholics
  In England still. They still plot against our queen.
  Were she struck down by one of them you'd take
  Her throne and rule us. It follows that your faith
  Is a challenge to her—yes, if your Grace will pardon
  The word—a defiance.

Mary. You were bid to say this to me?

Throgmorton. Madame, it was said so smoothly by my
    queen
  There was no offense in it, but I have no gift
  Of language. I must say things out.

Mary. Your manner
  Is packed with the most magniloquent impudence
  That's come my way. Do you or your queenly mistress

Deem me an inferior, to be given orders blithely,
With a high hand?

Throgmorton. No, madame.

Mary. Say three words more
In this cavalier offensive style of yours
And you'll find yourself in the courtyard.

Throgmorton. Madame, I—

Mary. Come down to earth, and speak without swaggering.

Throgmorton. I've been in the wrong.

Mary. That's better.

Throgmorton. It's true that I'd
Rehearsed my song and dance. Your wit is quicker
Than's been supposed in London.

Mary. Quick enough
To perceive an insult, I hope.

Throgmorton. Your Majesty,
There was none intended, but I might have spoken
more wisely
Had I known your mettle. Elizabeth is concerned,
As I have said, with the differences that are certain
To arise over your religion. Further than that,
What arrangements may be made to avert a breach
In the present concord, if we may discuss these things
Frankly, and you will make frank replies, I have
No other mission.

Mary. Now you talk sense. And frankly.
I will not change my faith.

Throgmorton. And, frankly again,
   There was little hope that you would. There is some
      hope,
   However, that when Your Majesty seeks a consort
   You will not do so to bolster up your claim
   To the English crown, which is strong enough already
   To cause us uneasiness in London.

Mary. That
   Had not occurred to me.

Throgmorton. But surely your choice in marriage
   Will imply your attitude?

Mary. I have no intention
   Of plighting my troth at once, but if I had
   I've received advice already on that point,
   A mort of it—and I'm tender.

Throgmorton. Say no more,
   Madame, and I'll say no more.

Mary. Oh, out with it now,
   Give the advice. I won't take it.

Throgmorton. Why, it's only this:
   If Your Majesty were to marry a Protestant lord
   Of no royal pretensions, it would indicate
   That you meant no danger to our Elizabeth.

Mary. She has chosen for me, I daresay? She has some lord
   Of the sort in mind?

Throgmorton. You embarrass me to go on.
   She mentioned a name.

Mary. Yes?

Throgmorton. Madame, The Earl of Leicester.

Mary. I hope her ears burn now. Leicester? Her cast-off!—
Her favorite—the one she's dangled? This is an affront—
She named Lord Leicester?

Throgmorton. Nay, nay—only to show you
What it was she had in mind. The kind of match.

Mary. I would hope so.

Throgmorton. For, you see, Your Majesty,
She had a fear of this—the young Lord Darnley
Has come north against her will. Why he's here we don't
know.
Nor whether by invitation, nor what your plans
Might be concerning him.

Mary. I have none.

Throgmorton. Then, if you will,
Forget what I've said. It was only that this Darnley
Combines to exactness what Elizabeth dreads
In case you marry. After you he's next to her throne,
And he's a Catholic. Should you marry Lord Darnley
And call up Catholic Europe to your back—
Well, we'd be ringed in steel.

Mary. I have offered your queen
My friendship and love. I meant that offer.

Throgmorton. But even
If there were no quarrel, and you should marry Darnley
And have a son by him—he'd be heir to England—
And I think the plain fact is that Elizabeth
Would rather choose her own heir.

Mary. Now God forgive me!—
I am heir to the throne of England, and after me
Whatever children I have—unless by some chance
The virgin queen should bear sons! Is it part of her love
To cut me off from my right?

Throgmorton. It must be remembered
That England is Protestant, and it might come hard
To accept a Romish sovereign. In brief, my queen
Has wished that you might choose Bothwell, or perhaps
some other
Of Protestant persuasion!

Mary. And that's the message.
We're down to it at last. My lord Throgmorton,
I marry where I please—whether now or later,
And I abate not one jot of my good blood's lien
On the English throne. Nay, knowing now the gist
Of Elizabeth's polity toward that claim, I shall rather
Strengthen it if I can. The least worthy sovereign
Has a duty toward his blood, not to weaken it
Nor let it decline in place.

Throgmorton. This will hardly please.

Mary. I could hardly expect it would. But I too am a
power,
And it matters what pleases me. This was all?

Throgmorton. This was all
I'm commissioned with.

Mary. I shall see to your safe-conduct.

Throgmorton. I thank your Majesty.

> [*He goes out.* Mary *is alone a moment, brooding.* Rizzio
> *enters*]

Mary. Oh, Rizzio, Rizzio,
They make a mock of me! It was as you predicted
To the utter syllable.

Rizzio. A warning, then.

Mary. We'll expect no friendship from England.
She cuts me off, me and my line.

Rizzio. May I say that this
Is only her wish, not accomplished?

Mary. Aye, and not to be.
I'd have stood her friend, Rizzio, meant to be her friend,
But now—this is not to be borne! Go and find Lord
Darnley.

Rizzio. Your Majesty—you have made a decision?

Mary. Yes.

Rizzio. Now I thank you. Now, God helping us, we'll win.
She'll not stamp you out.

Mary. So I think. And now find him.

Rizzio. Yes.

> [Mary Beaton *comes to the outer door*]

Beaton. Will your Majesty see a gentleman calling himself
Lord Bothwell?

> [Bothwell *comes to the door*]

Mary. He's in again?

Beaton. There's no keeping him out.

Bothwell.

    [*Entering*]

The doxy invited me in herself. She's a slut.
This Beaton of yours.

    [Rizzio *goes out the outer door*]

Mary. Oh, I know.

Beaton, May I put in a word
    For this gentleman, madame? Of all who come calling
    on you
He's the most ill-favored. It may be that he's honest,
I hope so, to go with that face. You're not afraid
To be left alone with him?

Mary. You may go, Beaton.

Beaton. Yes, Majesty.

    [*She curtseys hurriedly, and goes out*]

Bothwell. Now, what an inexperienced queen you are
    To surround yourself with such taking bitches!

Mary. My lord,
    I have heard from England.

Bothwell. Mary, my queen what you heard
    I could have guessed. She's your demon. She bodes you
    ill.

Mary. I believe it now.

Bothwell. And moreover, between the two,
    This cormorant brother of yours, and that English harpy
    They'll have the heart out of you, and share it. Trust

Not one word they say to you, trust not even the anger
Their words rouse in you. They calculate effects.

Mary. Where is Lord Morton?

Bothwell. Lord Morton is not well.
[*He is very serious*]
A sudden indisposition.

Mary. Bothwell, Bothwell—
You've fought with him!

Bothwell. A mere puncture. What men think
I cannot punish, nor what they say elsewhere but when
I hear them, by Christ, they'll learn manners.

Mary. I forbade it.

Bothwell. Forbade it! My dear, not God nor the holy angels
Forbid me when I'm angry.

Mary. I say I forbade it
It's I who's responsible for my kingdom—not you—
You were bound to keep the peace!

Bothwell. When my lady's slandered?
I'll teach them to hold their peace where you're con-
cerned.
Or find their sweet peace in heaven.

Mary. Would God I'd been born
Deep somewhere in the Highlands, and there met
you—
A maid in your path, and you but a Highland bowman
Who needed me.

Bothwell. Why, if you love me, Marie,
   You're my maid and I your soldier.

Mary. And it won't be.

Bothwell. Aye, it will be.

Mary. For, hear me, my lord of Bothwell.
   I too have a will—a will as strong as your own,
   And enemies of my own, and my long revenges
   To carry through. I will have my way in my time
   Though it burn my heart out and yours. The gods set us
      tasks,
   My lord, what we must do.

Bothwell. Let me understand you.
   The gods, supposing there are such, have thrown us
      together
   Somewhat, of late.

Mary. Look, Bothwell. I am a sovereign,
   And you obey no one. Were I married to you I'd be
   Your woman to sleep with. You'd be king here in
      Edinburgh,
   And I'd have no mind to your ruling.

Bothwell. They'll beat you alone.
   Together we could cope them.

Mary. Love you I may—
   Love you I have—but not now, and no more. It's for me
   To rule, not you. I'll deliver up no land
   To such a hot-head. If you'd been born to the blood
   I'd say, aye, take it, the heavens had a meaning in this,
   But the royal blood's in me.—It's to me they turn

To keep the peace, patch up old quarrels, bring home
Old exiles, make a truce to anarchy. Escape it I cannot.
Delegate it I cannot. The blame's my own
For whatever's done in my name.—I will have no master

[BOTHWELL *is silent when she pauses*]

Nay, I am jealous of this my Stuart blood.
Jealous of what it has meant in Scotland, jealous
Of what it may mean. They've attacked that blood, and
    I'm angry.
They'll meet more anger than they know.

Bothwell. And who
Has angered you? Not I?

Mary. Elizabeth.

Bothwell. I thought so.
She's afraid, if I'm half a prophet,
That you'll marry me.

Mary. Her fears run the other way.
She's afraid I'll marry a Catholic and threaten her
    throne!
She threatens disinheritance! Offers me Leicester!
Her leavings!

Bothwell. Yes, by God, that's a cold potato.

Mary. And means to choose another heir for her throne!
I may never sit on it, but the Stuart line
Shall not suffer by me!

Bothwell. Will you tell me what that means?

Mary. I mean if I have a son he'll govern England.

Bothwell. And so he might, if he were mine, too.

Mary. Nay, might—
　But it must be!
　She dares to threaten my heritage!

Bothwell. Does that mean Lord Darnley
　[*She is silent*]
　Aye, lady, will you stoop so low to choose
　A weapon? This is not worthy of the girl
　I've known. Am I to be ousted by a papejay
　Who drinks in the morning and cannot carry his drink?
　An end of mouldy string? You take too much
　On yourself of the future. Think of us, and the hours
　Close on us here we might have together. Leave some-
　　thing
　To the gods in heaven! They look after lovers!

Mary. Oh, what's a little love, a trick of the eyes,
　A liking, to be set beside the name
　You'll have forever, or your son will have?

Bothwell. Well, it's been nibbling at you this long while,
　And now it's got you, the blight of Charlemagne—
　The itch to conquer.

Mary. I have an itch to conquer?

Bothwell. It goes deep, too, that itch. It eats out the brain.

Mary. Well, and my love for you, how worthy is that?
　It's my body wants you. Something I've fought against
　Comes out in me when you're near. You've not held it
　　sacred,

You've taken others. I've known. And then come
wooing.
It would happen again.

Bothwell. It's a man's way. I've loved you
None the less.

Mary. You don't offer enough, Lord Bothwell.
You're not true in it, and I'm not true to myself
In what I feel for you.

Bothwell. I'm no lute-player,
To languish and write sonnets when my lady
Says me nay. Faith, I've lived rough on the border.
And cut some throats I don't forgive myself
Too easily, when I look back, but I tell you
If I give my pledge to you it's an honest pledge,
And I'll keep it. Yes, and when the tug begins
Around your throne, you'll be lost without me. Try
No threats toward England.—It will tax a hardy man
All his time to hold what you have.

Mary. We differ there, too.
What I have I'll defend for myself.

Bothwell. If you marry this Darnley
I take away my hand.

Mary. Before God, he believes
He's held me up so far, and I'd fall without him!

Bothwell. I believe it, and it's true! Darnley, sweet Christ!
No miracle could make him a king! He's a punk,
And he'll rule like a punk!

Mary. We shall see, Lord Bothwell.

Bothwell. Well I'm sped. My suit's cold. But, dod, lady—
Darnley—
He sticks in my craw—I can't go him. You'll find few
that can.
Think twice about that. Let him not cross my way,
Or he'll lose his plumes like Morton!

Mary. Will you learn, Lord Bothwell,
That this is not your palace, but mine? Or must you
Be taught that lesson?

Bothwell. There's been a bond between us
We'll find it hard to forget.

Mary. You may. Not I.
I've set my face where I'm going.

[RIZZIO *enters.* DARNLEY *is seen behind him*]

Rizzio. Lord Darnley is here,
Your Majesty.

Mary. Let him enter.

[DARNLEY *enters from the doorway*]

Bothwell. Lass, lass, God fend thee.
You've seen the last of me.

Mary. I've given no leave
For departure, Lord Bothwell

Bothwell. I need no leave, nor leave-taking.
You see no more of me.

[*He goes out.* RIZZIO *bows and follows him.* MARY *crosses the
room away from* DARNLEY *and looks for a moment in
the fire. Then she turns to him*]

Mary. I have sent for you.
   Lord Darnley, to tell you your suit has prospered.
    You've asked
   My hand in marriage, and I grant it.

Darnley. Your Majesty—
   I hardly hoped—I haven't dared—this is fortune
   To take one's breath!
      [*He comes forward and falls to one knee*]
   I shall love you, keep you, defend you!

Mary. We shall face troubled times.

Darnley. We'll meet them bravely.
   This is some dream—or a jest. It can't be.

Mary. Aye. I feel that.
   And yet it's true.

Darnley. I'm to hold you in my arms!

Mary. Not yet. And yet, if you like, come, kiss me.

Darnley. They say
   A kiss seals the bargain!
      [*He rises, staggering slightly*]

Mary. I've heard so.
      [*He crosses to her*]
   You've drunk too much.

Darnley. Nay, only a morning cup. Oh, Lady, lady—
   When you're kind the whole world's kind!

Mary
      [*She faces him, then draws back a step in repulsion*]
   You're a boy, a child.

Darnley. Older than you, though.
  It's a bargain, then?

Mary. Yes.
  [*He puts out his arms to her. Her eyes hold him off*]
  Let the kissing go. Let it go till the bond's sealed.

Darnley. Aye, madame.
  [*He drops his arms. They stand looking at each other*]

CURTAIN

MARY OF SCOTLAND
ACT TWO

ACT TWO
Scene I

SCENE: *The hall in the palace. Evening.* MARY *and the* FOUR MARY'S-IN-WAITING *are sitting near the fire, listening as* RIZZIO *sings to his lute.*

Rizzio. My heart's in the north,
  And my life's in the south
  False I've pledged with my hand,
  False I've kissed with my mouth.

  Oh, would we might lie
  Where we lay by the firth,
  With one cloak about us,
  To keep us from earth,

  With hand caught to hand
  And the rain driving blind,
  As the new years have driven
  Old love out of mind.

Mary. What is the line, False I've pledged with my hand?

Rizzio. False I've pledged with my hand,
  False I've kissed with my mouth.

Mary. Where did you come by the song?

Rizzio. It's one I made.

Mary. I thought so. Well, it's too true—and past time for crying.

Beaton. These poets make much of false pledges and false kisses—but they often turn out quiet as well.

Mary. Nay, they turn out badly. If you should love, Beaton, give yourself where you love.

Beaton. There's one of these silly hackbuteers I could have a mind to but I gather he has his penny a day and no more.

Mary. Then if I were you I'd take him.

Livingstone And live on a penny a day?

Mary. Or anything.

Rizzio. My lady, I shall never forgive myself.

Mary. It was my own doing.

Rizzio. My counsel weighed with you. I favored Darnley because he was of my faith. And he's our weakness, not our strength.

Mary. None could have known that.

Rizzio. I should have known. Bothwell would have been better.

Livingstone. Bothwell!

Rizzio. Aye, Bothwell. He'd have held them off. There's no trifling with him.

Livingstone. We do well enough without him.

Rizzio. Well enough perhaps.

Mary. Let's have no talk of Bothwell.

Livingstone. He's better away. The country's been much quieter since he left it. Hasn't it, madame?

Mary. Much quieter.

Fleming. You will have a child, your Majesty. You will have an heir, and then you will be happier.

Mary. With Darnley's child?

Fleming. He will change, too. The man changes when there are children.

Mary. We must hope so.

Seton. His Majesty will return tomorrow?

Mary. He was to have returned three days since. But the hunting may have been delayed.

Beaton. The hunting! He does his hunting o' nights.

Mary. Nay, Beaton.

Beaton. Nor do I take much joy in hearing him called His Majesty.

Seton. But it's the correct address. Lord Darnley has been crowned.

Beaton. Is that a reason for giving him any deference among ourselves? He's a baby, and a spoilt one, and it would give me small pain if I never saw his foolish face again.

Seton. I think that's very treacherous talk!

Mary. It is, too.

Beaton. I'm true to my queen, and I'll be true to none else.
[*She goes to* MARY *and leans her head against her knee*]

Mary. Not even your hackbuteer?

Beaton. Not even him.

Rizzio. Your Majesty, I have a request which you have denied before, but which I must make again. It is necessary for me to leave Scotland.

Mary. David, David!

Rizzio. I grow lonely for Italy.

Mary. And who will write my letters?

Rizzio. There are many who could write letters.

Mary. Can you name one—both efficient and to be trusted?

Rizzio. Maitland.

Mary. Would you trust him?

Rizzio. I think I should go, Your Majesty.

Mary. We know why, David, and I won't have it. I won't have my friends driven from me.

Rizzio. I think it's best.

Mary. Has His Majesty spoken to you?

Rizzio. Only by the way.—I'm not wanted here—you know that.

Mary. The king is full of these whims and fancies, my dear Rizzio. If I gave way to one I should have to humor him in all. You and I know that I am quite innocent with you, and you with me. And I can't spare you.

Rizzio. God knows you are innocent, madame, and I too unless it be a crime to love you. I do love you, I can't deny that.

Mary. Nor do I hold it a crime.

Rizzio. Majesty, I tell you honestly it's torture to speak of going away—and yet—oh, I want no harm to come to you through me!

Mary. And none will. The king is jealous, of everyone, my Rizzio, everyone, I see or have seen. It's a brainsick notion. I know that he has acted and spoken foolishly in many such matters. But as for danger, there is none.

Rizzio. I hope there is none.

[*There is a clatter of armor in the hall to the right*]

Mary. Say no more of going.

Rizzio. My queen, I am too easy to convince in this! Too much of me cries out to stay—and yet—say no more and let me go!

Mary. Why, very well.

Rizzio. But not angrily—not in anger.

Mary. Not in anger.

Rizzio. I thank your Majesty.

[*A* PORTER *comes to the door at the right*]

Porter. Master Rizzio?

Rizzio. Yes.

Porter. Lord Maitland of Lethington and Master John Knox are here.

Mary. They are to come in.

[RIZZIO *makes a gesture to the* PORTER *who goes out. The* QUEEN *rises.* RIZZIO *goes to the door and ushers in* MAITLAND *and* KNOX, *then goes out.* KNOX *stands at the door*]

Maitland. Ah, Your Majesty—I was to bring Master
Knox—

Mary. Yes, I remember.

Maitland.

   [*Looking about*]

   I gather that he wishes to speak with you in private.

Mary. I doubt that we shall find the subject makes it
necessary. Master Knox, will you come closer to the fire?

Knox. I am very well here, I thank your Majesty.

Mary. You come—was it the word?—to make a protest?

Knox. Would it be convenient that I speak with you alone?

Mary. When we last spoke alone, sir, there was some talk
to the effect that I had used arts on you. I could wish
to avoid a repetition of that.

Knox. Why, then, I have but one thing to say and I shall
make shift to say it quickly. You are a Catholic queen
in a Protestant land, your Majesty—

Mary. Only in part Protestant.

Knox. Protestant in great majority—

Mary. Yes.

Knox. You have taken a Catholic husband and set him on
the throne beside you, giving him what is called in
the courts of this world the crown matrimonial. You
have also set up an altar in this your palace, where
the mass and other idolatrous rites are said for you.
In these ways you encourage Lord Huntley and the

Highland Catholics of the north in their heathenish practices, and in so doing bring grave dissension among your people. I come to warn you.

Mary. To warn me of what, Master Knox?

Knox. That the forms and appurtenances of the Romish faith cannot be thrust upon us. That this will not be borne by the defenders of the Lord's word and church.

Mary. I ask no one to subscribe to my faith, sir. But it has been mine from a child, and I keep it.

Knox. You seek to gain it a foothold here, and build it up about you. I wish no evil to you nor to this kingdom and I say the celebration of the mass must cease, for there are those among us to whom it is abhorrent. And though it cost civil war and the slaughter of brother by brother it will not be borne.

Mary. And are you among those who will not bear it?

Knox. I am.

Mary. Do you find it written that all men must worship in one fashion?

Knox. There is but one true faith and one true fashion of worship.

Mary. And would you enforce it with the sword?

Knox. There is no tolerance for the idolator nor the adulterer. They are to be weeded out—and even now—before they come to the great pit and are given over to his unending fire—a fire not to be quenched nor remedied nor appeased.

Mary. I understand your attitude toward the idolator, Master Knox, but do you consider it apposite to bring adulterers also into this conversation?

Knox. The idolator, the adulterer, the priests of Baal, they shall be uprooted, seed and seedling, and cast into the burning—

Mary. But Master Knox, Master Knox, let us have a meeting of minds! An idolator is not the same as an adulterer. Confine yourself to some meaning!

Knox. They come among us in one person—the priests of the flesh and the worshippers of the flesh—

Mary. If you would but leave off prophesying for a moment and speak sense! Who is the idolator here?

Knox. Have you not set up an altar?

Mary. A very little one, sir. Nothing to what I could wish. And does that make me an idolator?

Knox. Will you deny it?

Mary. I do deny it. And now tell me who is the adulterer.

Knox. Let them search in their hearts who came from France.

Mary. I have searched in mine, and find no adultery there. And shall not those who live in Scotland search in their hearts also?

Maitland. Your Majesty, I have brought Master Knox here only because I am convinced that he voices an attitude which must be seriously considered.

Mary. But I try to take him seriously and he speaks in parables. I ask him to define his words and he talks of a great fire. To him a priest is a priest of Baal, an idolator is the same as an adulterer, and those who come from France run especial danger of damnation. What can one say to such a man? Master Knox, I believe you mean well, but can you not see that I also mean well, and that there might be more than one opinion concerning the worship of Our Lord?

Knox. There will be but one opinion held in that last day— when he comes with his armies, and driveth before him those who are not his children!

Mary. Look, what can one say to him? You ask him a question—and he threatens you with the Last Judgment! You see, Master Knox, you are not the judge who will sit over us in the Last Judgment! You are instead an elderly gentleman of provincial learning and fanatical beliefs, lately married to a niece of your own some forty years your junior, and one who conducts his conversations almost exclusively in quotation from the Old Testament. If you will talk sensibly with me I shall talk sensibly with you, but if you come here to frighten me I shall regard you as a most ridiculous antediluvian figure, and find you very funny. Which shall it be?

Knox. Well I know you hold the Lord God as a jest and a mockery!

Mary. Do not confuse yourself with Lord God again! There's a difference!

Knox. I am His spokesman.

[RIZZIO *comes to the door*]

Mary. Indeed. Will you show me your commission?

Knox. I call ruin to fall on this house, the shelter of the great beast—!

Mary. And there again! Maitland, can you, by any stretch of the imagination, look upon me as the great beast?

Rizzio. Your Majesty, Lord Huntley is here

Mary. Come in, Lord Huntley!

[HUNTLEY *enters*]

Sir, I have just heard myself likened to the great beast of Revelations. Can you see any similarity there?

Huntley. Why, lass, I'd say at the least it's an exaggeration.

Maitland. If Your Majesty wishes to give audience to Lord Huntley—

[*He starts to withdraw*]

Mary. Nay, why should you go? And why should John Knox and Lord Huntley not meet face to face in one room? I am aware that Master Knox is a Protestant and that Huntley is a Catholic, but they dwell in the same small kingdom, and it would be well if they understood each other.

Knox. I am loath to say it, but I am of a mind that there can be no understanding between him and me, no, nor between myself and Your Majesty, lest I betray my Lord.

Huntley. Madame, it's my opinion we understand each other dom well. Too dom well.

Mary. But since you must both live in this kingdom and one must be Catholic and one Protestant, surely it were wiser to be amiable over small matters, Maitland?

Maitland. Aye, it would be wiser.

Knox. Not for what you have said to me or of my person, for that unto seventy times seven those who follow him forgive, but because the air of this house is offensive in his nostrils, I call ruin on it! Nor will I commune in it further, neither with those who make their beds here nor with those who come here for counsel! Yea, if there are any here who would avoid the wrath, let them turn now, for it is upon you and your servants!

Mary. Well—it would seem there's little to be done about that. You are dismissed if you wish to go.

[MAITLAND *and* KNOX *turn to leave*]

Maitland. I offer my apologies, Your Majesty.

Mary. Oh, surely.

Knox. Yea, those who breed and take their ease in the places of the annointed, turn, turn now, before the axe fall quickly and be followed by silence! For now it is not too late, but no man knows when he cometh, nor of the wings of what morning!

[MAITLAND *and* KNOX *go out.* RIZZIO *rejoins the group at the fire*]

Mary. You are duly impressed by this talk, sir?

Beaton. Why, the solemn ass! He should have been booted!

Huntley. My dear, you've been too easy with him, and if you continue to be easy we'll pay for it.

Mary. And in what way, sir.

Huntley. You and I are alone here, Your Majesty, so far as Catholicism's concerned. My Highlanders are Catholic, it's true, and there's a plenty of them, and they're tough, but the rest are all against us, every noble and man of note. They're John Knox's men, and you heard yourself what he said.

Beaton. He with the persimmon-colored whiskers?

Huntley. Aye, he. And he means it.

Mary. What does he mean?

Huntley. Ruin to this house.

Mary. Is this a house to be blown down with windy talk?

Huntley. My birdie—I canna call you Ye're Majesty and all that—

Mary. You need not.

Huntley. Then, my bird, they draw their nets tight about us. I told you before, and it's coming.

Mary. And who draws the net?

Huntley.
   [*Looking at the others*]
   Lady—

Mary. These five know my secret heart. They'll say nothing.

Huntley. Lady, there's only one defence. Attack them first. And there's but one proper place for John Knox. He should be in Edinburgh Castle—and all those with him who are of his mind.

Mary. You'd imprison him?

Huntley. He and some twenty others.

Mary. And then?

Huntley. Then you can go to work. You're not safe here and I'm not safe here while a sect of Protestant lords divide your dominion with you. You rule by sufferance only.

Mary. They are here by my sufferance, Huntley.

Huntley. You have heard of the sheep nursed the wolf-pups till they tore her to pieces.

Mary. But we're not sheep and wolves, my lord. There's room for all of us here, and for whatever faiths we may choose to have.

Huntley. Never think it, my bird, never believe it! It's never yet happened that a state survived with two religions in it. Never. Elizabeth knows that. She's behind this Knox. He'd never dare be so bold if she weren't behind him.

Mary. But it's my thought that in Scotland, though it be the first time in the world, we shall all believe as we please and worship as we list. And Elizabeth may take it as she sees fit.

Huntley. She uses it against you, my dear, and uses John

Knox against you. Ladybird, I'm willing to beg it of you,
take heed of me now or we're both done!

Mary. Rizzio?

Rizzio. You know my mind. I'm with Lord Huntley in this.

Mary. But how can I bring myself to imprison men for no
wrong they've done, on suspicion only, imprison them
for their faith—?

Huntley. It's more than faith. It's works. You heard John
Knox!

Mary. It cuts athwart every right instinct I have, my lord!
Every fibre I have that's royal shrinks at such penny-
wise petty doings! And John Knox—a doddering imbecile, drooling prophecy!

Huntley. He threatened you, lady.

Mary. No, no, I can't. Even if it were wisdom to do it, and
it's not.

[*The right-hand door opens suddenly and* DARNLEY *stands in
it.* MARY *turns toward him*]

My lord!

[DARNLEY *walks slowly to the middle of the room and lays a
hand on the table*]

Darnley. I'm unexpected, perhaps? Too early? A thought
Too early? I'll retire. Come when I'm wanted.

Mary. No,
My lord, you've been long expected, and more than
welcome.

Darnley. Why, a pretty wife, a huswife with her maids;
A pretty sight, and maybe a cavalier

Or two, for the maids' company. Dod, sit down all!
Damn me if I'll intrude!

Mary. Will you speak to Lord Huntley?

Darnley.

[*Focussing on* HUNTLEY]

Right. That's right. Lord Huntley, give me your hand.
I thank you for watching over the pretty wife here.
I've been away.

Huntley.

[*Turning*]

Your Majesty, you've a wife
Such as I wish I'd had when I was young.

Darnley. Right—You have right. They all say that. I'd say
it myself.
Only I know her better.

[*He turns to the door*]

I know her too well,
And not well enough. She wouldn't care to hear it.
Not from me.

Mary. Darnley.

Darnley. She sleeps alone.
At least as far as I know.

Huntley. I'll take my leave,
My lady.

Mary. Yes.

Darnley. Stay, stay, I'm going. I only
Tell you she sleeps alone as far as I know.

A pretty wife. These women—they get with child,
You never know how—and then they won't sleep with
you.

[HUNTLEY *bows to* MARY, *turns deliberately, and goes out the
door to the right, closing it*]

What's the matter with him? He's an old married man.
He knows these things.

Mary. You're tired, my lord. Will you wish
Some service, something to eat and drink?

Darnley. She sends me
Off to bed, you note. You note it, Rizzio?
There's a service she could do me, but I doubt
She'll offer it. And I'm a king, by God, a king,
And you're a clark by office!

Mary. My lord, I hoped
You'd have some other word for me when you
Returned.

Darnley. My pink, if I gave you the word you've earned
The room would smell. I've been at the hunting. We
had
Something to drink. Alban! Alban! Allons!

Mary. You call someone?

Darnley. Alban! God's right! St. Andrew! Alban!
I'm drunk, you see.

Mary. I think not.

Darnley. Yes, but I am.
Alban! Christ his sonties, am I left
Alone here! God and St. Andrew!

[*The right hand door opens and* RUTHVEN *enters in full armor*]

Mary. What is this?
   [*To* Ruthven]
   You will retire, sir. Who are you?

Darnley. My good friend Ruthven.

Mary. Is this a place for armor? I will receive
   Lord Ruthven another time.

Darnley. The callant's there,
   Ruthven.

Ruthven. Aye.

Mary. I had heard that Lord Ruthven was ill,
   And thought to go to him, not to see him here.

Ruthven. I am ill, and it's mortal, but I've sworn to be
   mortal
   To another first.

Mary. This is my apartment, sir,
   And I ask you to go.
   [Douglas *appears behind* Ruthven]

Mary. I demand little courtesy,
   But that little I must have. Are these your friends?
   If so, take them elsewhere.

Darnley. Aye, I'm to have my friends
   In my apartment—and you're to have yours here.
   I say no—they're to mingle.—
   [*He points to* Rizzio]
   You see that grig
   With the kinked hair there? He with the lady's hands

And feet? Where does he sleep nights? That's he, that's
    the one
We have in question!

Mary. My lord, when you've been drinking
    I have little taste for your company, and tonight
    Less, perhaps, than ever.

Darnley. He, he, I tell you!
    That Italian spawn!
        [Rizzio, *trembling, steps back toward the queen's study*]

Mary.
        [*Stepping in front of* Rizzio]
    Go into my study.
        [Lord Morton *enters*]
    Lord Morton,
    Whatever you have in hand here, put no faith
    In this king I've crowned and set beside me! His word
    Is a paper shield.

Darnley. I'm king in this country, mistress—
    And I know my rights.

Mary. Beaton, why were these men
    Not stopped at my door?

Darnley. They came with me.
        [*Facing* Morton]
    Will you tell me
    What you want with the queen?

Morton.
        [*His dagger drawn*]

Damme, do you want this bodkin
Through that bodice of yours?

[*She shrinks back.* RIZZIO, *having reached the study step by step, opens it and reveals a* GUARD, *a drawn claymore in his hand*]

Rizzio. Let me pass!

The Guard. Nay, lad.

Fleming. Your Majesty,
They've broken into your rooms

[MARY *turns and sees the guard*]

Mary. Lord Darnley, was that
By your order?

Rizzio.

[*Hardly able to speak for fear*]

Save me, my queen, save me!

Mary. Aye, Rizzio.

[*The five women retreat before the armed men, covering* RIZZIO *from them*]

Morton. Look to the women-folk, Darnley. We'll care for him.

[RIZZIO *turns suddenly and leaps behind the heavy drapes of the high window down-stage.* MORTON, DOUGLAS *and* RUTHVEN *follow him*, DOUGLAS *with his dagger raised*]

Mary. Douglas, I'll remember this!

[*A fall is heard behind the curtains, but no cry.* MARY *runs toward the window, but is met by* RUTHVEN, *sheathing his dagger*]

You've murdered him!
You pack of filthy cowards!

Ruthven. Yea, and done well.

Mary. Done well! Oh, fools and cowards!

[*She runs to the curtain and with* MARY BEATON *pulls it back
from* RIZZIO, *then bends over him and draws back again.
in terror*]

Oh, David, David,
It was I wouldn't let you go!

Darnley.

[*Looking away*]
You might cover that sight.

Mary. Is he dead, Beaton?

Beaton. Yes, madame.

Mary. Oh, you do well, you do well.
All of you!

[*She conquers her repulsion, and tries to loosen* RIZZIO's *ruff.*
FLEMING *comes to help her*]

We'll help him if we can,
Fleming.

Fleming. Yes.

Mary. You were too gentle for them,
David. They couldn't bear it—these boors and swine—
Your kerchief, Fleming! He bleeds so—

Fleming. It's useless, Madame.

Mary.

[*Rising*]
Yes.

[*To the lords*]

To take him unarmed, and poniard him—
One who had never hurt you!

Ruthven.

    [*Sinking to a chair*]
Well, the work's done,
And my queen's wiped clear of him.

Mary. Wiped clear! You believed
I was guilty with him!

Ruthven. Were you not?

Mary. No!

Ruthven. I'd be sorry
If you were not. I struck him down for that.

Mary. I was not guilty. But will you tell me now
Who'll believe me innocent? You've branded me deep
With this murder, and you've killed a guiltless man!
Why do you sit in my presence?

Ruthven. Because I'm ill
And dying. I should be sorry if this thing
I've done were in error—for it's the last I'll do.

Mary. You'll stand in my presence! Whose order was it?

Ruthven. Why, ask His Majesty that—
And Morton there, and Moray.

    [*He rises with difficulty*]

Mary. Moray too?

Ruthven. Yea, your brother. For me— let me go home.

Mary. Go. Morton and Douglas, I give you three days
To leave this kingdom.

Morton. And the king? I have the king's seal
  For what I've done.

Mary. Is that true?

Darnley. Aye.

Mary. The worse for you.
  The worse for you all.

Darnley. My lady, this long while past
  You've denied me your chamber, and when I've seen you
    there's been
  This Rizzio with you.

Mary. Never again while I live
  Will you see me alone. I bear your child in me
  Or you'd answer for this!

Darnley. There'll be no answering!
  We know what we know about you!

Mary. I would I knew
  In what strange dark chamber of your oafish brain
  You found reasons for Rizzio's death. If I saw you
    seldom
  Remember how often you drank yourself imbecile
  Before you came to me. You've slain your last friend, sir.
  It was Rizzio's counsel put you where you are
  And kept you there. These are not your friends, these
    three,
  Nor Moray. They wanted Rizzio out of the way,
  And they wanted to drag you down, and drag me
    down,
  And you play into their hands. I've never been

Unfaithful to you, but we're at an end, we two.
From this time forward if I touch your hand
May God blight me and my child!

Darnley. I wanted you!
You kept away from me, and it drove me mad!

Mary. You won't mend it now. Look, young Rizzio's dead.
You've blackened me, blackened yourself, thrown a
black doubt
On the child who'll be your heir. The lords look on
And smile, knowing they've trapped you. You'll never
climb
From the pit where you've fallen, and I may fall with
you. Lord Moray
Weaves his web round us. You've helped him.

Darnley. God knows I wanted
Only my right.

Mary. You pitiful dolt! To think
Such a calf should rule, and at my choosing! God
May forgive you—not I. Nor forgive myself.—And
Rizzio.—
Take yourselves out! You pollute the dead to stand
there!
He wanted to go to Italy.

Fleming. Yes.

Mary. Will you go?

[MORTON *beckons the guards, and they cross from the study to
the outer door*]

Ruthven.

[*At the door*]

You'll want some help, mayhap.

Mary. None of yours. I've noticed
It's men that kill, but women that wash the corpse
And weep for it. May none ever weep for you.

Ruthven. None will. I've been in the wrong.

Mary. I'm sorry, Lord Ruthven.
It's an ill thing to have on your heart when you die.

Ruthven. Aye, is it.

[*He goes out, and the men follow him.* DARNLEY *looks back as if he wished to speak to the queen, but goes silently*]

Mary. And now we're alone. The lords have shown their
hand.
Rizzio's gone—and Darnley, what there was to go.
We've been not long in Scotland, but time enough
To show I can lose it, have lost it in their minds
Already. We must lay the poor lad somewhere.
Could we lift him together?

Seton. Oh, madame, I'm afraid?

Mary. Of what?

Seton. I've never seen one dead before.
I've not known it was like this.

Mary. It's poor Rizzio.
No one to hurt us. And you and I will lie
Sometime like this, and folk will be afraid
Because we lie so still. How strange it is

That he should frighten us who wished us well,
And would still if he lived. We must take him up
And lay him on my bed. I'll sleep with Beaton
Tonight.

    [*She takes a step toward* Rizzio]

Beaton. Madame, the blood will stain your dress.

Mary. If that were all. This will bring more blood after.
Now I see it. Before I reign here clearly
There will be many men lie so for me
Slain in needless quarrel. Slain, and each one
With blood to spill but once, like his. And yet
One steps on into it—steps from life to life
Till there are thousands dead, and goes on still
Till the heart faints and sickens, and still goes on
And must go on.

    [*An iron gate clangs outside.* Beaton *parts the curtains to look out*]

I tell you, Fleming, my soul
Is aghast at this blood spilled for me, and yet
It hardens me, too. These are their manners, this
Is the way they go to work. I shall work on them,
And not too lightly. They think of me as a girl,
Afraid of them. They shall see.—And yet my mind
Believes nothing of what I say; I'm weak as grief,
Stripped and wept out before them. They press me close,
And I have no one to send.

    [*There is a rattle of staves in the courtyard*]

Beaton.

    [*Turning back*]

It's the provost, madame,

I heard them call his name.

Mary. He's not to enter.
Let no one enter.

[BEATON *goes out right*]

No one. In all this kingdom
I can trust only five, and one's myself,
And we're women, all of us.—If they go scot-free
After this indignity I'm no queen. For Ruthven
He'll pay his own score. He's dying. Morton and Douglas
Must die too.

Fleming. They were under Lord Darnley's orders.

Mary. He was under theirs. It won't save them.

Fleming. Your Majesty,
They've left the city by now. They should have been
taken
While they were in your hands.

Mary. I know. It's true.
They've fled to raise troops. When next we find them
they'll meet us
With culverins.

[BEATON *enters*]

He's gone?

Beaton. Yes. But there's one
Below from France—says he has news.

Mary. From France?
Tomorrow, though. I wish I were still in France
And had never seen these stone walls.

Livingstone. And so do I.

Mary. What is his name?

Beaton. He gave me
This token for you, no name. It's a crow's feather.

Mary.

   [Takes the feather, then pauses]
Tell my Lord Bothwell I have no wish to see him
Now or later.

Beaton. Madame, you'll see him? I brought him
Along with me.

Mary. No. Not now. Not ever.
There's nothing to say between us now.

Beaton. He came
From France to see you.

Mary. Tell him.

   *[*Lord Bothwell *is seen standing in the doorway]*

Bothwell. Your Majesty,
You've had unwelcome company this hour,
If I've heard aright, and I care not to be another,
But I come to make an offer I made before—
To be your soldier.

Mary. I have no time to talk,
Lord Bothwell. Nor do I wish to see you. The time's
Gone by.

Bothwell. My queen, my queen, turn not away
Your friends. You've few enough, too few it seems
To prevent what's happened.

Mary. Go.

Bothwell. Does he still lie here?
I'll lay the poor boy away for you at least,
And then I'll go, since you wish it.
[*He crosses to* RIZZIO]
Aye, they made sure,
Lad—and their dirks were sharp. Shall I place him
within?

Mary. Yes.
[BOTHWELL *picks up* RIZZIO *and carries him into Mary's
chamber*]
Must you betray me, too?

Beaton. I wished only—
If you'd but follow your heart!

Mary. We two must twain,
My Beaton. You take too much on you. Lord Bothwell,
May be your friend, not mine.

Beaton. Forgive me.

Mary. What warrant
Have you been given to vouch for my heart, or judge
Whether I should follow it?

Beaton. None.

Mary. Oh, God, this vice
Of women, crying and tears! To weep, weep now
When I need my anger! Say my farewells for me,
I've gone to my study.
[*She turns.* BOTHWELL *enters*]

Bothwell. Goodnight, my queen.

Mary. Goodnight.
   I'm not unkind. But I'm cut off from you.
   You know that.

Bothwell. Yes. There's no need to hide your weeping.
   He was over-young to die.

Mary. It's not for him.
   No, it's for all I wanted my life to be,
   And is not.

Bothwell. Majesty, you have a fortunate star.
   It will come well yet.

Mary. If I have a star at all
   It's an evil one. To violate my room,
   Kill my servant before my eyes—How I must be hated!

Bothwell. They'll pay for that.

Mary. Perhaps.

Bothwell. I've taken an oath
   They'll pay for it. Your Majesty, I wearied
   Of France and exile, wearied of sun and wine,
   And looked north over the water, longing for fog
   And heather and my own country. Further, the news
   Was none too happy from Scotland. They want your
      throne
   And plan to have it. But I mean to live in this land
   And mean you to be queen of it. The Earl of Bothwell
   Is home, and spoiling for a fight. Before
   Day dawns they'll hear from me.

Mary. My lord, I thank you—

Bothwell. Give me no thanks. I like a fight too well
   To pretend it's a virtue. Moreover, if I'm to live here
   I'd rather you were my liege than Moray. I'm none
   So fond of your half-brother. This night's work
   Should show you he's what I knew him, half-bred, half-
      faced
And double-tongued.

Mary. You have no army.

Bothwell. I have
   My border men. Lord Huntley's joined with me
   With his Highland kilties. If you'd call your clans
   We could drive them to the wall.

Mary. It's a war then.

Bothwell. It's war,
   Already. They've turned your Darnley against you.
      They'll use him
   As long as they need his seal. Once they've got you out
   They'll set Moray up as regent. They fear one chance:
   That you and I should league together and balk them.
   I've come back in time, not too soon.

Mary. I think you have.
   My lord, I had no heart to face you. The fault
   Was mine when we parted.

Bothwell. It's not too late. I've come
   Only just in time, but in time.

Mary. It is too late—
   For you and me. These faults we commit have lives
   Of their own, and bind us to them.

Bothwell.

[*Pointing toward her bedroom*]
Yon was Darnley's work.
Are you still his?

Mary. Am I not?

[BEATON *gathers up the three others with a look and goes into
the queen's study with them silently*]
I'm to bear his child.
I cannot hate my child.

Bothwell. It's in the wind
This Darnley's not to live long.

Mary. I'd have no hand
In that—nor you!

Bothwell. It happens he's a pawn
In the game the lords are playing. They'll sacrifice him
When the time comes. It's no plot of mine.

Mary. But he lives
And I'm his wife, and my babe is his. I must drink
My cup down to the rinse. It was I that filled it,
And if there's grief at the bottom it's mine. I'll name you
My officer, but only if you can pledge
No harm will come through you to Darnley.

Bothwell. Lady,
I need you, and you need me, but I'll be damned
If Darnley's needed on this earth. I have
No project against him, but I'll give no pledge
To block me if I should have. There be men
Who wear their welcome out in this world early
And Darnley's one of them.

Mary. You have never yet
Learned how to take an order.

Bothwell. And never will—
From man or woman living, sovereign or knave,
Judge or vicegerent. I have not been conquered
And will not be. But I offer you my fealty,
And it's worth the more for that.

Mary. You must make your own terms—
I'm but a beggar here.

Bothwell. Nay, nay, it's I
That sue, a beggar for what's impossible,
With this Darnley standing between us.
     [*She pauses again*]

Mary. You shall be
My Lord Admiral and act for me. Yes, and to that
Let me add how my breath caught when I knew you
     here,
Hoping I know not what, things not to be,
Hopes I must strangle down. Oh, Bothwell, Bothwell!
I was wrong! I loved you all the time, and denied you!
Forgive me—even too late!

Bothwell. I tell you we
Shall be happy yet.

Mary. No, for I think I've been
At the top of what I'll have, and all the rest
Is going down. It's as if a queen should stand
High up, at the head of a stair—I see this now
As in a dream—and she in her dream should step

From level to level downward, all this while knowing
She should mount and not descend—till at last she walks
An outcast in the courtyard—bayed at by dogs
That were her hunters—walks there in harsh morning
And the dream's done.

Bothwell.

    [*Stepping toward her*]

You're weary. You've borne too much.
They shall pay for this.

Mary. Come no nearer, my lord. It's not ours
To have. Go now.

Bothwell. Yes, your Majesty.

    [*He turns*]

Yet
I tell you we shall be happy. And there will be nothing
Not ours to have.

    [*He goes out*]

CURTAIN

ACT TWO
Scene II

Scene: *Elizabeth's study at Whitehall.* Burghley *and* Elizabeth *are seated across a table.* A Third Figure *approaches from the side.*

Burghley. This will be Lord Throgmorton.

Elizabeth. You're early, sir.

Throgmorton. Madame, I rode all night.—I've news from the north.
Darnley's been murdered.

Elizabeth. How?

Throgmorton. Kirk o' Field was blown up.
The castle's in ruins.

Elizabeth. Now that was a waste of powder—
And of castles too. But he's dead—

Throgmorton. Yes, madame—they found him
It was no accident. He'd been strangled.

Elizabeth. So there's no more king in Scotland.
Who took this trouble?

Throgmorton. Moray, and Morton, no doubt—perhaps Maitland—

Elizabeth. Not Bothwell?—

Throgmorton. No—though he must have known of it—

Elizabeth. And the queen—
The queen weeps for her Darnley?

102

Throgmorton. Madame—

Elizabeth. Ah, yes—
  She'll weep and wear black—it becomes her. A second
  time
  She's a widow now. And she's borne a child. She begins
  To wear a little, no doubt? She must ponder now
  What costumes may become her?

Throgmorton. Nay, truly, your Grace,
  I'd say she charms as ever.

Elizabeth. Would you say so?
  But she weeps and puts on mourning?

Throgmorton. No, madame, Bothwell
  And the queen are friends again—or more than that.
  They'd be married already, I think, only Moray's
  against it
  And the earls behind him.

Elizabeth. Now in my day and time
  I have known fools and blockheads, but never, I swear,
  In such numbers as among these Scotch earls. Moray's
  against it?
  Against the queen's marriage with Bothwell?

Burghley. Your Majesty—
  If she were to marry Bothwell—we've opposed that, too,
  And even prevented it.

Elizabeth. Aye, times have changed,
  And we change along with them. She loves this Both-
  well?
  It's a great love—a queen's love?

Throgmorton. It is indeed.
A madness, almost.

Elizabeth. Yes, yes—and it's well sometimes
To be mad with love, and let the world burn down
In your own white flame. One reads this in romances—
Such a love smokes with incense; oh, and it's grateful
In the nostrils of the gods! Now who would part them
For considerations of earth? Let them have this love
This little while—let them bed and board together—
Drink it deep, be happy—aye—

Burghley. Madame, this Bothwell's
No man to play with. If they marry she'll crown him
king—

Elizabeth. You did well to ride fast, Throgmorton! Turn
now
And ride as fast back again; you can sleep later
When we're old and the years are empty.—And tell my
lord Moray
If he'd keep me a friend, let his sister marry Bothwell—
Tell him to favor it—hurry it.

Burghley. And with Bothwell king
Do you think to conquer Mary?

Elizabeth. Send next to John Knox,
But do this cleverly, giving Knox evidence
That Bothwell slew Darnley with the queen's con-
nivance
And they bed together in blood. Have you wit enough
To see this well done?

Throgmorton. I think so, Majesty.

Elizabeth. See to it.
　Who will deny that Bothwell murdered Darnley
　When he lives with the queen, and enjoys the fruits? Or
　　who
　Will credit Bothwell's denial? Your brain, my Burghley!
　Where do you wear it, or what has it hardened into
　That you're so easily gulled?

Burghley. But is it wise
　To make a false accusation? This project hangs
　By a thread. Make but one error and we shall lose
　Whatever we've gained.

Elizabeth. Go and do these things—
　They are to marry—we sanction it—let none oppose it—
　She refused him before when he could have saved her—
　She'll take him now when it's fatal—Let her have this
　　love
　This little while—we grant her that—then raise
　The winds against them—rouse the clans, cry vengeance
　On their guilty sleep and love—I say within
　This year at the very farthest, there's no more queen
　Than king in Scotland!

CURTAIN

ACT TWO
Scene III

Scene: *A hall in Dunbar Castle.* A Sentinel *is at his post near the outer gate, another at the guard-room door. There is a step on the cobbles outside. The* First Sentinel *swings round to the gate.*

Jamie.
  [*Outside*]
  Drop your point, man. Ye ken me.

First Sentinel. Eh, Jamie. What is it?

Jamie. I'm late. It was tough getting through. The queen's taken prisoner. Her army's gone.

First Sentinel. Nay! And Bothwell?

Jamie. Bothwell's free yet. Free and able to fight. We're to put the castle in posture of defense. Where's the sergeant?

First Sentinel. Call Graeme.

Second Sentinel. Graeme!—I told you this was no lucky battle to be in.

First Sentinel. Says John Knox!
  [Graeme *enters*]

Jamie. I've orders for the guard. We're to man the walls and be ready on the gates.

Graeme. It goes that way?
  [Beaton *enters from the stair*]

Jamie. That way and worse.
  [*They turn toward the gate*]

106

Beaton. Jamie, what brings you?

Jamie. Orders, lass.

Beaton. Quick, tell me!

Jamie. It goes badly with us, lass.

[LORD HUNTLEY *enters*]

Beaton. My lord—

Huntley. There's to be a parley here. Make ready for it.

Jamie. Watch that outer post.

[*The* SENTINELS *go out*]

Beaton. A parley—the battle's over?

Huntley. Aye, over and done. This is Moray's kingdom now.

Beaton. And the queen?

Huntley. The queen's a prisoner, lass. My men have deserted, her own men turned against her.

Beaton. My lord, you'll forgive me, but how could that be?

Huntley. This was John Knox's battle, lady. The auld limmer took a stance on a hill some half-mile to windward and there he stood haranguing like the angel Gabriel, swearing Bothwell killed Darnley to have the queen. And the queen's men listened to him, the psalm-singing red-beards, and then turned and made her prisoner and delivered her up to Lord Moray.

Graeme. Bothwell's returning.

Jamie. Upstairs with you, lass.

[BEATON *goes up the lower stair*]

Graeme. Shall I set the guard?

Huntley. Wait a moment.

    [Bothwell *enters*]

Bothwell. We're not through yet, my lord. You'll stand by
    me?

Huntley. Aye,
    If it's any use. One may rally an army flying.
    But one that flies toward the enemy and makes friends—

Bothwell. Who spoke of rallying? They won by treachery,
    And we'll treat them some of the same!

    [*To* Jamie]

    There were ninety men
    Left to guard the castle! They're here still?

Jamie. Aye sir.

Bothwell. They're under
    Lord Huntley's orders while this parley's on.
    Tell them to be ready. He'll join you.

Jamie. Aye.

    [*He goes into the guard-room*]

Bothwell. Sergeant, take the men you need and guard that
    arch—
    Let no one enter but the lords themselves.

Graeme. Aye, my lord.

    [*He goes out by the arch*]

Bothwell. I'll talk with these lords, and if they listen to
    reason
    They may keep their mangy lives, but if they refuse

'To release the queen and give her back her kingdom
Then hell's their home! Watch my arm, and hark
For my sword on steel. They're outnumbered three to
   one

Huntley. Kill them?

Bothwell. Cut their throats
   If you like that better.

Huntley. That's plain murder.

Bothwell. Right,
   And if they say no they've earned it.

Huntley. And we'd die, too.

Bothwell. Why, it might be we would. But I'd stake more
   On our living long with them dead. If the queen's
      deposed
   Then I've lived long enough, and so have you.
   Will you gamble with me?

Huntley. I will.
   [*They shake hands. A trumpet sounds outside*]

Bothwell. Wait for the signal.
   My sword on steel.
      [HUNTLEY *goes into the guard-room. The voices of the Lords are
         heard outside*]

Morton.
   [*Outside*]
   Go carefully now. Not too fast.

Moray. Aye, you're the man to say that.

Morton. Let Maitland speak.

    [*They enter; one or two bow ironically*]

Bothwell. You may drop these scrapings. We know what we
    think of each other!

Morton. And that's true too!

Moray. We have little to gain, Lord Bothwell,
    By a conference with you. The battle is ours. The queen
    Is prisoner to us. But to spare ourselves further blood-
      shed
    And spare you bloodshed, we grant this respite, and ask
    That you surrender without conditions.

Bothwell. No.
    No, I thank you. Moreover if your tongue's
    To be foremost in this council, we'll stop now
    And argue the matter outside.

Maitland. Be patient, Lord Moray.
    We're here to make terms, as you are, Bothwell.
      The queen
    And you have been defeated. We made war on you
    Because you two were married, and because she planned
    To make you king.

Bothwell. You make war on us
    Like the pack of lying hounds you are, by swearing
    In public and in court that we killed Darnley
    So that we might marry! You know where that guilt lies.

Moray. Who killed Darnley
    We care not. Let the courts decide it.

Bothwell. It was you that killed him!
And you fight us bearing false witness!

Moray. You wanted him dead.

Bothwell. I grant it. I wanted him dead. You killed him and managed
To shift the weight on me. You've won with that lie,
May your mouths rot out with it! And now what do you want—
What do you ask of us?

Maitland. First, that you leave Scotland.

Bothwell. That's easily said;
What else?

Maitland. Why, next that the queen should delegate
Her powers to the lords of the council, those you see
Before you—

Bothwell. Aye, I see them.

Maitland. And bind herself
To act with our consent only.

Bothwell. No more?

Maitland. No more.

Bothwell. Then here are my conditions; I will leave,
And trouble you no more, if you pledge your word
That the queen's to keep her throne and her power intact,
Without prejudice to her rights. But if you dare
Encroach one inch on her sovereignty, guard your gates,
For I'll be at them!

Morton. Aye, you make your terms!

Bothwell. Aye, I make mine; defeated, I still make mine—
And you'll do well to heed them. I shall want leave also
To see the queen for a moment.

Moray. You know our answer.

Bothwell. Then look to yourselves!
[*He lays a hand on his sword*]

Maitland. Look now, Bothwell.
It's you I rebel against. I'd lend no hand
In this company, if the queen were to rule alone,
And I've said as much to Lord Moray.

Morton. I speak for myself,
And say no to it.

Moray. And I.

Bothwell. You've wanted my earldom,
Lord Moray. Well, you may have it. I'll make it over.
You shall choose a new earl of Bothwell. I'll disband my
army.
And threaten you no more. But on condition
The queen reigns here as before.

Moray. We'll made our conditions—
We have no time for yours.

Bothwell. My lines are not broken.
I'll try conclusions yet, and you'll not sleep easy
While I'm within these borders!

Maitland. Take his terms,
My Moray.

Moray. Are we to fight a war and win
And toss the spoils away?

Bothwell. Find some agreement,
For I'm in haste, and if you say no to me
I've other plans!

Erskine. Bothwell's been our one weapon
Against the queen, Lord Moray. I believe it's wisdom
To banish him, but remember the queen's a queen
And it's dangerous to touch her. When he's gone
You'll have no cause against her.

Moray. Why, damn you all!

Morton. Let him go, and leave her the throne.

Moray. And even Morton.

Morton. Gad, I want no long wars,
I'm a married man. Send him on his way!
He leaves his earldom.

Bothwell. Then this sword stays in the scabbard
And lucky for all of you. Do you give your pledge?

Maitland. I give my pledge, Lord Bothwell, for all her
present.
We have not rebelled against the queen, and will not
If you are banished.

Bothwell. Then give me leave to speak
Alone with her.

Maitland. With the queen?

Bothwell. Aye, for a moment.

Moray. No.

Maitland. There's no harm in that, Moray.

Erskine. We'll wait in the courtyard.
It's day and we have orders to give.

Morton. Gordon and Douglas,
You won't be needed. Intercept Lord Huntley's men
While there's yet time.

Maitland. The queen is here, Lord Bothwell,
And will be free to see you.

> [*The Lords go out. After a moment's pause,* QUEEN MARY
> *comes to the door—a soldier on either side. The guards
> retire, leaving* MARY *and* BOTHWELL *alone*]

Mary. Thank God you're safe!

Bothwell. And you are safe, my queen, safe and set free
And may keep your kingdom.

Mary. At what price?

Bothwell. They've made
A bargain with me. God knows whether they'll keep it,
But I think they will, for Maitland gave his word,
And he's been honest.

Mary. What bargain? You've sacrificed
Yourself for this. What have you offered?

Bothwell. Nothing
To weigh against what you'll keep. I've given my earl-
dom—
That's a trifle to what we save.

Mary. You shall have it back,
And more to put with it.

Bothwell. No. I've accepted exile.
I'm to leave the kingdom.

Mary. Why, then, I'm exiled too.
I'm your wife and I love you, Bothwell.

Bothwell. The bargain's made.
You may keep your crown without me but not with me.
Do you abdicate your throne? What's left?

Mary. Call in
The men of your guard, cut our way through and ride!
They'll never head us! We can rouse the north,
Ask help from France and England, return with an army
They dare not meet!

Bothwell. You'd raise no army, Marie.
You forget what a drag I am on you. The north
Is sullen as the south toward you and me.
What's left we must do apart.

Mary. What if we lost?
At the worst we'd have each other.

Bothwell. And do you vision the end of that?
A woman who was a queen, a man who was
The earl, her husband, but fugitives, put to it
To ask for food and lodging, enemies
On every road; they weary, heartsick, turning,
At last on each other with reproaches, she saying:
I was a queen, would be one now but for you,
And he, I have lost my earldom.

Mary. I betrayed you once
  And betrayed my love, but I learned by that; I swear
  Though it cost my kingdom, not again!

Bothwell. If you wish
  To thrive, break that oath, betray me, betray your love,
  Give me up forever—for you know as I know
  We lose together. God knows what we'll ever win
  Apart.

Mary. Nothing. Oh, Bothwell, the earth goes empty.
  What worse could happen than parting?

Bothwell. Can I stay?
  This once for the last I can save you from yourself,
  And me. There's something wills it. I go alone.
  This is your kingdom. Rule it.

Mary. You must not surrender
  They'd serve you as they served Darnley.

Bothwell. I'll not surrender.
  I'll see to my own banishment, find my guard,
  Force my way out, and go.

Mary. We must say goodbye?

Bothwell. Aye, girl, we've spent what time we had,
  And I know not when I'll see you. Let's have no pretense
  Unworthy of us. It's likely, we'll not meet again
  On this same star.

Mary. God help me and all women
  Here in this world, and all men. Fair fall all chances
  The heart can long for—and let all women and men
  Drink deep while they can their happiness. It goes fast

And never comes again. Mine goes with you,
Youth, and the fund of dreams, and to lie a while
Trusted, in arms you trust. We're alone, alone,
Alone—even while we lie there we're alone,
For it's false. It will end. Each one dies alone.

Bothwell. I'll come
If I can. We've loved well, lass, could love better.
We've had but the broken fragment of a year
And whenever I've touched you, something that broods
    above us
Has made that touch disaster. This is not my choice.
Lest I bring you utter ruin we must wait,
Wait better times and luck. I'll come again
If I can.

Mary. Yes, if you can. Aye, among all tides
And driftings of air and water it may be
Some dust that once was mine will touch again
Dust that was yours. I'll not bear it! Oh, God, I'll not
    bear it!
Take me with you! Let us be slaves and pick
Our keep from kitchen middens and leavings! Let us
Quarrel over clouts and fragments, but not apart—
Bothwell, that much we could have!

Bothwell. Is there refuge in this world for you
And me together? Go far as we could, is there one
Turfed roof where we'd not be reminded of good days
And end in bitterness? Face these lords like a queen
And rule like a queen. I'd help you if I could
But I'm no help You must meet them now.

Mary. Yes I'll meet them
Can you break your way through? They're watching!

Bothwell. It's a chance.
Huntley! Huntley!

Huntley.
   [*Outside*]
I'm here.

Bothwell. We ride at once
For Stirling. Be ready for a fight.

Huntley. We're ready.

Bothwell. I must take my moment.

Mary. I know.

Bothwell. Goodbye, sweet, but if they wrong you—if you
   ever need me,
Look for me back.
   [*He kisses her, and goes*]

Mary. Goodbye. To our two worlds.
   [*There is a cry beyond the guard-room:* "BOTHWELL, *it's*
   BOTHWELL!" *The alarm is taken up by the men at the
   gate, who call:* "On guard there! Pistol him! Mount
   and after him! Ride, you devils! On guard! Drop the
   portcullis! He's gone!" *There is a sound of running
   feet from the gate to the other side of the stage.* MARY
   stands facing the guard-room door. GORDON *and*
   DOUGLAS *run in through the arch*]

Douglas. Through the guard-room!

Gordon. He'll be over the wall—

Douglas. Out of the way, madam—

Gordon. Nay, it's the queen—

Douglas. Will you let us pass?

Mary. I guard this door, Lord Douglas.
   You'll go the long way round!

Gordon. Your pardon, your majesty.
   [*He bows.* BEATON *appears on the stairway.* LORDS MORTON,
       MORAY *and* MAITLAND *enter*]

Morton. This was hardly well done, your majesty.

Mary. Take care whom you question, sir.

Moray. You've sent Bothwell off!
   That was your ruse!

Mary. Lord Bothwell will leave Scotland.
   That was what you wanted.
       [*Enter* LORD ERSKINE]

Moray. He's gone?

Erskine. Clean away!

Maitland. Madame, there was some understanding
   You two would remain here.

Mary. None that I know of.

Morton. Eh, God, he'll wish he had.
       [JOHN KNOX *appears in the archway*]

Mary. Remove that man from my presence! Is every
   stranger
   Free to enter my courts?

Knox. Though you be a queen
   And have faith in thy gods and idols, yet in this day

It will not staunch nor avail! Bid the sea remove
From the castle front, and gnaw it no more, as soon
Will it obey thee. Pluck down the whore! Pluck her
  down,
This contamination of men!

Mary. Maitland, if there's to be counsel here, send out
This preacher and his ravings!

Maitland. He may stay, for me.

Moray. Madame, collect what necessities you require.
You will change your residence.

Mary. That is at my will, I think.

Morton. Do you think so?

Maitland. You are to be lodged
In Holyroodhouse for the time.

Mary. I am to be lodged—
And your faith? You pledged your faith and word,—
  all of you—
To leave my power untouched, leave me my throne
If Bothwell and I were parted.

Maitland. We'll keep it
When Lord Bothwell's surrendered to us.

Mary. Go out and take him!
Take him if you can! But for your queen,
I warn you, never since there were kings and queens
In Scotland, has a liegeman laid his hand
On my line without regret!

Morton. We'll take care of that.

Mary. My lords, if I go with you, expect no pardon,
No clemency; I have friends, this farce will end.
Once more, then, leave me in peace
I have used you royally. Use me so.

Maitland. What you need,
Gather it quickly.

Mary. This is betrayal at once
Of your word and sovereign.

Morton. We know that.

[*A pause*]

Mary. I need nothing.
I am a prisoner, Beaton. Come after me
To Holyroodhouse. I may have my own rooms there,
perhaps?

Maitland. Yes, Madame.

Mary. You show great courtesy. For a liar and traitor.
You lied to us, a black and level lie!
Blackest and craftiest! It was you we believed!

Moray. Aye, sister. It was that we counted on.

Mary. Aye, brother.

[MARY *turns from* MAITLAND *to* MORAY, *then walks to the
archway and goes out*]

CURTAIN

MARY OF SCOTLAND
ACT THREE

ACT THREE

Scene: *A room in Carlisle Castle, in England. There are two windows at the right, both barred, a door at the rear and another, the hall-door, at the left. It is a prison room, but furnished scantily now for the queen's habitation. It is evening, but still light.*

Mary *sits at one of the windows, leaning her head against the bars.*

Beaton *is leaning over a table where* Fleming *has unrolled a map.*

Fleming. We came this way, through Cockermouth, and then took hired horses.

Beaton. If I had a thousand maps, I couldna tell you how I came. Jamie's acquent wi' the drovers and all the back ways. Seton and Livingstone, poor things, they're pining away back in Edinburgh Town.

Fleming. We might be as well off in Edinburgh ourselves, as it turns out. We'd looked forward to England for a free country, and strained toward it till our shoulders ached, trying to help the boat through the water. And here we are, and there's bars on the windows.

Beaton. But whose prisoners are we, Fleming?

Fleming. I would I knew. It's been a month now, and all I can tell you is we're prisoners, for we cannot leave.

Beaton. There's some mistake, Fleming.

Fleming. Aye, if it was a mistake, like, would it last a month? It's heartbreaking to escape one jailer and walk into the arms of another.

Mary. When does the guard change, Fleming?

Fleming. At ten, madame.

Mary. You're certain Jamie will come?

Beaton. Unless he's taken or dead, Your Majesty. He's true as one can have in a lad.

Mary. But they may unmask him.

Beaton. It's true, they may.

Fleming. Ye've more friends than a few in this castle, madame. They'd let us know if summat went wrong.

Mary. What friends?

Fleming. The two guards that go on for evening watch.

Mary. I fear they can't help much.

Fleming. They can always bring us news.

Beaton. And you've more friends than that, Your Majesty. Here and everywhere. As I came through the back roads I heard talk of you everywhere. I think they love their queen better now than before, now that she's shut away unjustly.

Mary. Do you think so?

Beaton. From what I heard I'd say the lords had worked their own ruin when they first betrayed you. If they could hear the buzzing against them they'd sleep badly there nights. And who rules Scotland now? Moray has no right to it, and nobody can give him the right save your own self.

Mary. Aye, that's so. He'll come begging yet.

Beaton. And for what he'll never have.

Mary. They've taken my son from me, though. If I have friends I would they'd hurry.

[*She turns toward the window*]

God know what Elizabeth means.

Fleming. You'll hear from Bothwell tonight, madame, or hear of him. I'm certain of it.

[A WATCHMAN *calls outside*]

Watchman. Ten o'clock, and all well. All well.

Beaton. Ten o'clock and still light.

Fleming. The days grow longer and longer.

Mary. They've grown so long that each is the whole time between a birth and a death—and yet they go so fast, too, that I catch at them with my hand. So fast that I watch the even light jealously, like a last candle burning. This is life, too, Beaton, here in this prison, and it goes from us quite as much as though we were free. We shall never see these same days again.

Fleming. And little will I want to.

Mary. But suppose you were to spend all your life in prisons? Might not one grow to love even prison-days— as better than none?

Beaton. We shall have better, though. These are the worst we shall have, and I think the last of them.

[*There is a rasping at the door*]

Your hear?—the signal—

[*There is a silence*]

Fleming. Nay, not yet.

> [*Another pause*]

Beaton. It's ten, and more.

Fleming. If we must wait again, then we must wait. He'll come at the latest, tomorrow.

'*Mary.*

> [*Rising and pacing near her window*]

But what could Elizabeth mean? What could she mean? She is my friend—over and over she writes she is my friend, I am her dear cousin, her sister sovereign, that she suffers when I suffer, that she would confine me on no pretext if it were not to secure me against my own enemies! Enemies! What enemies have I in her kingdom? What right has she to imprison a sovereign who takes sanctuary in England?

Fleming. Has anyone ever known Elizabeth's mind on any subject?

Mary. Writes, too, that she will come to see me, writes again to put it off, writes to say she cannot bear the week to pass without reassuring me of her good love.

Beaton. And yet I believe if all else fails Elizabeth will be found a friend and a good one at the end. If only for her own interest.

Mary. It may still be that she goes, in her own muddled and devious way, about the business of aiding me. It still may be.

> [*There is a rasping at the door again*]

Beaton. Yes?

[*The door opens a crack, a chain clanging*]

Jamie.

[*Outside*]

I may enter?

Beaton. Aye, come in.

[JAMIE *steps in, closing the door*]

Jamie.

[*Bonnet in hand*]

Your Majesty!

Mary. Good evening, Jamie.

Jamie. Ye'll forgive me. I was not sure I could jouk in, for the captain loitered about. However, the lad Mark keeps a look-out, and warns me if there's footsteps.

Beaton. Was there a messenger through, Jamie?

Jamie. Aye, I'll be quick, for I must, though a man hates to be quick wi' ill news. There's been a messenger, true enough, coming down wi' the drovers, as we cam'—and his tale is there was a battle at the Little Minch. Ma'am, it went badly for Bothwell, if the man says sooth, for he was defeated and taken.

Mary. Bothwell taken?

Jamie. Aye, madame. Aye, but there's some good, too. Kirkaldy of Grange has come over to Your Majesty's side and makes his threats against Moray.

Mary. But Bothwell, Bothwell was taken? How?

Jamie. That's the bare sum of it, madame. Just that he
was prisoner to the lords. Only Kirkaldy has said Bothwell should be freed, and that he will see to it.

Mary. It's little comfort.

Jamie. Aye, so I feared. Though Kirkaldy was their best
general, and they'll miss him.

Mary. I could have used him once.

Jamie. And now, if you'll pardon me, I must go. I had
little liking to come—it's sore bad manners to leave
folk wi' heavy hearts—

Mary. Nay, run no risk—only come again if there's any
tidings.

Jamie. Yes, Your Majesty, and I pray God they be better.
  [*He turns*]

Beaton. Jamie.
  [*There is a sharp rap at the door*]

Jamie. Aye?
  [BEATON *goes up to him*]
Nay, lass, it's good just to see thee, but we'll not kiss
afore Her Majesty.
  [*The rap again*]
It's for me. Keep thee, and all here.
  [*He opens the door and goes out, closing it softly. The chain
  clanks. There is silence*]

Mary. It's this that drives one mad, Beaton, to know
That on one certain day, at a certain hour,
If one had but chosen well, he'd have stood beside me

In a land all mine and his. Choosing wrong, I bring him
To fight a long war for me, and lose, bow his shoulders
To a castle keep.

Fleming. They'll not hold him long.

Mary. And that's
To remember too. He's not a man to hold
Easily, no, nor hold at all. I've seen him
When they thought him trapped, and well caught. His
     face goes cold,
Stern, and morgue under his morion. While he lives
And I live, they'll not jail us two apart,
Nor keep our due from us. Aye, it's something to love,
Even late, even bitterly, where it's deserved. Kirkaldy
Throws his weight on our side. There'll be others, too.
     Oh, Bothwell,
You've been my one hope! Bring me back to mind,
Now, as I bring you back!

> [*The chains of the door are undone, and the door opens.* A
> GUARD *steps in*]

Guard. Your Majesty,
Lord Ruthven desires to see you.

Mary. Lord Ruthven's in Scotland.

Guard. No, Madame, he's here.

Mary. Why, I will see Lord Ruthven.
Yes, let him come in.

> [*The door swings wider and* YOUNG RUTHVEN *enters. He bows*]

Sir, there've been days,
Not so far back when I'd have shifted somehow

To do without your face, or any visage
Among a certain congeries of lords
Of which you're one. Perhaps I'm tamed a trace
Sitting mewed at my window, for I'd accept
Any visitor from Scotland, bailiffs and hang-men
Not excluded, I'm that lonely.

Ruthven. Madame,
You hold against me much that was not my own.
I'm of a party, and one must swim or go down
With those of his interest.

Mary. Do you come now to see me
In your own person, then, or as representing
Those sharks you swam with last?

Ruthven. Why, Your Majesty,
It may be we're sharks. My mind's not made up. But
    I've come,
If you'll pardon me—and this is more truth, I think,
Than I'm supposed to say—because the lords
Who now hold Scotland had more hope you'd see me
Than any the others.

Mary. That's frank.

Ruthven. And I lend myself
To the embassy because, as things drift at home,
We verge on the rocks there. You are still queen of
    Scotland,
Yet you don't rule, and can't rule, being here,
A prisoner—and the upshot is we're not ruled.
There's anarchy in the air. It's necessary

That some approach be made between you and your
  brother
Before there's anarchy in the streets.

Beaton. We were saying
  That he'd come begging.

Mary. What does my brother ask—
  This good brother of mine?

Ruthven. That goes beyond
  My mission. To be frank still, I'm sent before
  To ask whether you will see him.

Mary. Let him ask my jailers
  Whether I may be seen.

Ruthven. He has asked already, madame.
  The request is granted.

Mary. Lord Moray is with you?

Ruthven. He is waiting.

Mary. Why, this is an honor. And others too, no doubt?
  A shoal of them?

Ruthven. Madame, as you have supposed
  They are all here.

Mary. It will please me vastly to view them,
  If only to know from them who gave permission
  To see me. For I swear, I guess not so far
  Whose prisoner I am, or who keeps my jail. I've moith-
  ered
  Over this a good deal.

Ruthven. I may call them?

Mary. If you'll be so good.

> [RUTHVEN *bows and goes out past the* GUARD]
> Is it you, sir, who chain my door
> So assiduously at night?

Guard. No, madame, the turn-key
Goes the rounds at twelve.

Mary. Will you ask him, then.
To make a thought less jangling if he can?
We try to sleep, you see, and these chimes at midnight
Are not conducive to slumber.

Guard. He shall be told;
I'm very sorry, Your Majesty.

Mary. Thank you.

> [MORTON *and* MORAY *come in, and behind them* MAITLAND
> *and* DOUGLAS. RUTHVEN *re-enters with* THROG-
> MORTON]

Gentlemen,
I greet you. You are all here, I see, the whole
Blood-thirsty race. But we lack John Knox. Now, surely,
John Knox should be with you.

Moray. Have your jest, my sister. For us
We're not here for jesting.

Mary. Oh, I'd have sworn you weren't.
You're no harbinger of merriment, my brother,
Nor of good fortune. The corbies from the wood
Presage more of that. And here's the Lord Throgmorton
Presses in among you! It should be a good day
When I'm crossed by this constellation!

Throgmorton. We pray it will,
  Your Majesty, and that things may be ironed out clean
  That have grieved us all.

Mary. Oh, do you know of grief,
  You who may take your meals in your own widehalls
  And walk in the rainy air? I had thought that grieving
  Was something found behind bars.

Maitland. This has lasted too long,
  This imprisonment, Your Majesty, and was never
  To any purpose. We come to offer you
  Release, and speedily.

Mary. The diplomat always, Maitland.
  Always the secret thought glancing behind
  The quick-silver tongue. You come to ask for much
  And give little for it, as ever.

Moray. We come to ask
  For what we have.

Mary. There, now it's brutally said,
  In my brother's plain-Scotch way, spoken plainly out of
  His plain Scotch face. He comes to ask, he says,
  For what he has, and he makes no doubt he'll get it.
  What is it you have, dear brother, and if you have it
  Why ask for it?

Maitland. Will Your Majesty give me leave
  To rehearse a brief history that may weary you
  Since you know it?

Mary. It will weary me, but go on.

Maitland. Forgive me: Your Majesty broke from prison
 in Scotland
And fled to England. This action was tantamount
To abandoning your throne.

Mary. Indeed it was not.
I came here for aid against you.

Maitland. We will pass that point.

Mary. Do. There's nothing gives me more pleasure, Lord
 Maitland,
Than passing a point.

Maitland. Then am I delighted to render
Your Majesty pleasure. Your wit is sharper than mine.
But to proceed: You were taken prisoner in England—

Mary. By whom, Lord Maitland—will you tell me that?
Who holds me here?

Maitland. That I'm not free to answer.
It remains that you're a prisoner, and that your realm
Is governed only by makeshift. Your son, the prince
 James—

Mary. Aye, what of him? My lords, I beg of you,
Whatever you must do, or think you must do,
To secure yourselves, he's but a babe, remember.
I can stand up and fight you for myself,
But use my child more kindly.

Maitland. The prince James,
Is well, and well cared for, and will be. The succession
Depends on him. We plan to make him king.
Your absence makes this necessary.

Mary. My absence
   Is not permanent, I hope. I am queen of Scotland
   And have not abdicated, nor do I intend
   To abdicate.

Morton. Will you tell us what you think
   To find, should you return?

Mary. If I return
   As I intend, I shall not find you there,
   Lord Morton, if you're wise. The country's fickle.
   For you, as it was for me. Now they've pushed their
      queen
   Aside, they begin to wonder if they were not wrong.
   And wonder too if they profit by the exchange,
   And give you side-long looks.

Maitland. If it's still in your mind
   That you might win your throne back, ponder on this:
   The lord of the isles has given you up, the north
   Is solidly with us, Bothwell has broken faith—

Mary. Aye?

Maitland. For the good of the kingdom, to secure your son
   His right to the throne, we ask you tonight to sign
   Your abdication, let us take it back with us.

Mary. Yes,
   But I catch you in two lies. Kirkaldy of Grange
   Has come over to me; you have taken Bothwell prisoner,
   But before he fights on your side you'll rot in the damp
   Under Edinburgh castle, and he'll see you do it!

Maitland. Madame,
   You've been misinformed.

Mary. I've been lied to and by you
   Specifically! Let me rehearse for you
   A history you may recall, you that stand before me:
   It was you killed Rizzio, and made capital of it
   To throw discredit on me. It was you
   Killed Darnley, and then threw the weight of that
   On Bothwell, saying through John Knox that I lived
   With my husband's murderer. It was you that promised
   To give me fealty if Bothwell and I were parted,
   And then cast me into prison! I escaped,
   As the truth will escape about you, and when it's known
   My people will drive you out. What you ask of me
   I refuse it, finally! I will not abdicate,
   Not to this off-scum that's boiled up around
   My throne to dirty me! Not now and not ever!
   [*The Lords are silent for a moment, and then* MORAY *nods an
      assent to* MAITLAND]

Maitland. Your Majesty, you asked me a moment since
   Who held you prisoner here. I cannot answer
   Still, but say there's another and higher judge
   Must pass on these charges of yours.

Mary. Nay, I know that.

Maitland. Oh, an earthly judge, Your Majesty, and yet
   High enough, I think. We wish you goodnight.

Mary. Goodnight.
   [*The Lords go out.* MARY *stands unmoving, watching the door.
      After a pause the* GUARD *pushes the door back and with-*

draws. ELIZABETH *comes to the doorway.* MARY *looks
at her questioningly*]

I have seen but a poor likeness, and yet I believe
This is Elizabeth.

Elizabeth. I am Elizabeth.
May we be alone together?

[*At a sign from* MARY *the* MAIDS *go out the rear door.* ELIZA-
BETH *enters and the hall-door swings to behind her*]

Mary. I had hoped to see you.
When last you wrote you were not sure.

Elizabeth. If I've come
So doubtfully and tardigrade, my dear,
And break thus in upon you, it's not for lack
Of thinking of you. Rather because I've thought
Too long, perhaps, and carefully. Then at last
It seemed if I saw you near, and we talked as sisters
Over these poor realms of ours, some light might break
That we'd never see apart.

Mary. Have I been so much
A problem?

Elizabeth. Have you not? When the winds blow down
The houses, and there's a running and arming of men,
And a great cry of praise and blame, and the center
Of all this storm's a queen, she beautiful—
As I see you are—

Mary. Nay—

Elizabeth. Aye, with the Stuart mouth
And the high forehead and French ways and thoughts—

Well, we must look to it.—Not since that Helen
We read of in dead Troy, has a woman's face
Stirred such a confluence of air and waters
To beat against the bastions. I'd thought you taller,
But truly, since that Helen, I think there's been
No queen so fair to look on.

Mary. You flatter me.

Elizabeth. It's more likely envy. You see this line
Drawn down between my brows? No wash or ointments
Nor wearing of straight plasters in the night
Will take that line away. Yet I'm not much older
Than you, and had looks, too, once.

Mary. I had wished myself
For a more regal beauty such as yours,
More fitting for a queen.

Elizabeth. Were there not two verses
In a play I remember:
    Brightness falls from the air;
    Queens have died young and fair—?
They must die young if they'd die fair, my cousin,
Brightness falls from them, but not from you yet; be‑
    lieve me,
It's envy, not flattery.

Mary. Can it be—as I've hoped—
Can it be that you come to me as a friend—
Meaning me well?

Elizabeth. Would you have me an enemy?

Mary. I have plenty to choose among as enemies—
And sometimes, as your word reached out to me

Through embassies, entangled with men's tongues,
It has seemed you judged me harshly, even denying
My right to a place beside you. But now you are here,
And a woman like myself, fearing as I do,
With the little dark fears of a woman, the creeping of age
On a young face, I see truer—I think I see truer,
And that this may be someone to whom I can reach a
    hand
And feel a clasp, and trust it. A woman's hand,
Stronger than mine in this hour, willing to help.
If that were so—

Elizabeth. Aye.

Mary. Oh, if that were so,
    I have great power to love! Let them buzz forever
    Between us, these men with messages and lies,
    You'll find me still there, and smiling, and open-hearted,
    Unchanging while the cusped hills wear down!

Elizabeth.
    [*Smiling*]
    Nay, pledge
    Not too much, my dear, for in these uncertain times
    It's slippery going for all of us. I, who seem now
    So firm in my footing, well I know one mis-step
    Could make me a most unchancy friend. If you'd keep
    Your place on this rolling ball, let the mountains slide
    And slip to the valleys. Put no hand to them
    Or they'll pull you after.

Mary. But does this mean you can lend
    No hand to me, or I'll pull you down?

Elizabeth. I say it
   Recalling how I came to my throne as you did,
   Some five or six years before, beset as you were
   With angry factions—and came there young, loving
     truth,
   As you did. This was many centuries since,
   Or seems so to me, I'm so old by now
   In shuffling tricks and the huckstering of souls
   For lands and pensions. I learned to play it young,
   Must learn it or die.—It's thus if you would rule;
   Give up good faith, the word that goes with the heart,
   The heart that clings where it loves. Give these up, and
     love
   Where your interest lies, and should your interest change
   Let your love follow it quickly. This is queen's porridge,
   And however little stomach she has for it
   A queen must eat it.

Mary. I, too, Elizabeth,
   Have read my Machiavelli. His is a text-book
   Much studied in the French court. Are you serious
   To rede me this lesson?

Elizabeth. You have too loving a heart,
   I fear, and too bright a face to be a queen.

Mary. That's not what's charged against me. When I've
     lost
   So far it's been because my people believed
   I was more crafty than I am. I've been
   Traduced as a murderess and adulteress
   And nothing I could have said, and nothing done

Would have warded the blow. What I seek now is only
My freedom, so that I may return and prove
In open court, and before my witnesses,
That I am guiltless. You are the queen of England,
And I am held prisoner in England. Why am I held,
And who is it holds me?

Elizabeth. It was to my interest, child,
To protect you, lest violence be offered to a princess
And set a precedent. Is there anyone in England
Who could hold you against my will?

Mary. Then I ask as a sovereign,
Speaking to you as an equal, that I be allowed
To go, and fight my own battles.

Elizabeth. It would be madness.

Mary. May I not judge of that?

Elizabeth. See, here is our love!

Mary. If you wish my love and good-will you shall have it
freely
When I am free.

Elizabeth. You will never govern, Mary. If I let you go
There will be long broils again in Scotland, dangers,
And ripe ones, to my peace at home. To be fair
To my own people, this must not be.

Mary. Now speak once
What your will is, and what behind it! You wish me here,
You wish me in prison—have we come to that?

Elizabeth. It's safer.

Mary. Who do you wish to rule in Scotland,
  If not my Stuart line?

Elizabeth. Have I said, my dear,
  That I'd bar the Stuarts from Scotland, or bar your reign
  If you were there, and reigned there? I say only
  You went the left way about it, and since it's so
  And has fallen out so, it were better for both our king-
    doms
  If you remained my guest.

Mary. For how long?

Elizabeth. Until
  The world is quieter.

Mary. And who will rule in my place?

Elizabeth. Why, who rules now? Your brother.

Mary. He rules by stealth—

Elizabeth. But all this could be arranged,
  Or so I'm told, if your son were to be crowned king,
  And Moray made regent.

Mary. My son in Moray's hands—
  Moray in power—

Elizabeth. Is there any other way?
  [*A pause*]

Mary. Elizabeth—I have been here a long while
  Already—it seems so. If it's your policy
  To keep me—shut me up—. I can argue no more—
  No—I beg now. There's one I love in the north,
  You know that—and my life's there, my throne's there,
    my name

To be defended—and I must lie here darkened
From news and from the sun—lie here impaled
On a brain's agony—wondering even sometimes
If I were what they said me—a carrion-thing
In my desires—can you understand this?—I speak it
Too brokenly to be understood, but I beg you
As you are a woman and I am—and our brightness falls
Soon enough at best—let me go, let me have my life
Once more—and my dear health of mind again—
For I rot away here in my mind—in what
I think of myself—some death-tinge falls over one
In prisons—

Elizabeth. It will grow worse, not better. I've known
Strong men shut up alone for years—it's not
Their hair turns white only; they sicken within
And scourge themselves. If you would think like a queen
This is no place for you. The brain taints here
Till all desires are alike. Be advised and sign
The abdication.

Mary. Stay now a moment. I begin to glimpse
Behind this basilisk mask of yours. It was this
You've wanted from the first.

Elizabeth. This that I wanted?

Mary. It was you sent Lord Throgmorton long ago
When first I'd have married Bothwell. All this while
Some evil's touched my life at every turn.
To cripple what I'd do. And now—why now—
Looking on you—I see it incarnate before me—
It was your hand that touched me. Reaching out

In little ways—here a word, there an action—this
Was what you wanted. I thought perhaps a star—
Wildly I thought it—perhaps a star might ride
Astray—or a crone that burned an image down
In wax—filling the air with curses on me
And slander; the murder of Rizzio, Moray in that
And you behind Moray—the murder of Darnley, Throg-
    morton
Behind that too, you with them—and that winged
    scandal
You threw at us when we were married. Proof I have
    none
But I've felt it—would know it anywhere—in your
    eyes—
There—before me.

Elizabeth. What may become a queen
Is to rule her kingdom. Had you ruled yours I'd say
She has her ways, I mine. Live and let live
And a merry world for those who have it. But now
I must think this over—sadness has touched your brain.
I'm no witch to charm you, make no incantations;
You came here by your own road.

Mary. I see how I came.
Back, back, each step the wrong way, and each sign
    followed
As you'd have me go, till the skein picks up and we stand
Face to face here. It was you forced Bothwell from me—
You there, and always. Oh, I'm to blame in this, too!
I should have seen your hand!

Elizabeth. It has not been my use
  To speak much or spend my time—

Mary. How could I have been
  Mistaken in you for an instant?

Elizabeth. You were not mistaken.
  I am all women I must be. One's a young girl,
  Young and harrowed as you are—one who could weep
  To see you here—and one's a bitterness
  At what I have lost and can never have, and one's
  The basilisk you saw. This last stands guard
  And I obey it. Lady, you came to Scotland
  A fixed and subtle enemy, more dangerous
  To me than you've ever known. This could not be borne,
  And I set myself to cull you out and down,
  And down you are.

Mary. When was I your enemy?

Elizabeth. Your life was a threat to mine, your throne to
    my throne,
  Your policy a threat.

Mary. How? Why?

Elizabeth. It was you
  Or I. Do you know that? The one of us must win
  And I must always win. Suppose one lad
  With a knife in his hand, a Romish lad who planted
  That knife between my shoulders—my kingdom was
    yours.
  It was too easy. You might not have wished it.
  But you'd take it if it came.

Mary. And you'd take my life
And love to avoid this threat?

Elizabeth. Nay, keep your life.
And your love, too. The lords have brought a parchment
For you to sign. Sign it and live.

Mary. If I sign it
Do I live where I please? Go free?

Elizabeth. Nay, I would you might,
But you'd go to Bothwell, and between you two
You might be too much for Moray. You'll live with me
In London. There are other loves, my dear.
You'll find amusement there in the court. I assure you
It's better than a cell.

Mary. And if I will not sign
This abdication?

Elizabeth. You've tasted prison. Try
A diet of it.

Mary. And so I will.

Elizabeth. I can wait.

Mary. And I can wait. I can better wait than you.
Bothwell will fight free again. Kirkaldy
Will fight beside him, and others will spring up
From these dragon's teeth you've sown. Each week that
     passes
I'll be stronger, and Moray weaker.

Elizabeth. And do you fancy
They'll rescue you from an English prison? Why,
Let them try it.

Mary. Even that they may do. I wait for Bothwell—
And wait for him here.

Elizabeth. Where you will wait, bear in mind,
Is for me to say. Give up Bothwell, give up your throne
If you'd have a life worth living.

Mary. I will not.

Elizabeth. I can wait.

Mary. And will not because you play to lose. This trespass
Against God's right will be known. The nations will
    know it,
Mine and yours. They will see you as I see you
And pull you down.

Elizabeth. Child, child, I've studied this gambit
Before I play it. I will send each year
This paper to you. Not signing, you will step
From one cell to another, step lower always,
Till you reach the last, forgotten, forgotten of men,
Forgotten among causes, a wraith that cries
To fallen gods in another generation
That's lost your name. Wait then for Bothwell's rescue.
It will never come.

Mary. I may never see him?

Elizabeth. Never.
It would not be wise.

Mary. And suppose indeed you won
Within our life-time, still looking down from the heavens
And up from men around us, God's spies that watch

The fall of great and little, they will find you out—
I will wait for that, wait longer than a life,
Till men and the times unscroll you, study the tricks
You play, and laugh, as I shall laugh, being known
Your better, haunted by your demon, driven
To death, or exile by you, unjustly. Why,
When all's done, it's my name I care for, my name and
    heart,
To keep them clean. Win now, take your triumph now,
For I'll win men's hearts in the end—though the sifting
    takes
This hundred years—or a thousand.

Elizabeth. Child, child, are you gulled
    By what men write in histories, this or that,
    And never true? I am careful of my name
    As you are, for this day and longer. It's not what hap-
        pens
    That matters, no, not even what happens that's true,
    But what men believe to have happened. They will be-
        lieve
    The worst of you, the best of me, and that
    Will be true of you and me. I have seen to this.
    What will be said about us in after-years
    By men to come, I control that, being who I am.
    It will be said of me that I governed well,
    And wisely, but of you, cousin, that your life,
    Shot through with ill-loves, battened on lechery, made
        you
    An ensign of evil, that men tore down and trampled.
    Shall I call for the lord's parchment?

Mary. This will be said—?
But who will say it? It's a lie—will be known as a lie!

Elizabeth. You lived with Bothwell before Darnley died,
You and Bothwell murdered Darnley.

Mary. And that's a lie!

Elizabeth. Your letters, my dear. Your letters to Bothwell
prove it.
We have those letters.

Mary. Then they're forged and false!
For I never wrote them!

Elizabeth. It may be they were forged.
But will that matter, Mary, if they're believed?
All history is forged.

Mary. You would do this?

Elizabeth. It is already done.

Mary. And still I win.
A demon has no children, and you have none,
Will have none, can have none, perhaps. This crooked
track
You've drawn me on, cover it, let it not be believed
That a woman was a fiend. Yes, cover it deep,
And heap my infamy over it, lest men peer
And catch sight of you as you were and are. In myself
I know you to be an eater of dust. Leave me here
And set me lower this year by year, as you promise,
Till the last is an oubliette, and my name inscribed
On the four winds. Still, STILL I win! I have been
A woman, and I have loved as a woman loves,

Lost as a woman loses. I have borne a son,
And he will rule Scotland—and England. You have no
    heir!
A devil has no children.

Elizabeth. By God, you shall suffer
For this, but slowly.

Mary. And that I can do. A woman
Can do that. Come, turn the key. I have a hell
For you in mind, where you will burn and feel it,
Live where you like, and softly.

Elizabeth. Once more I ask you,
And patiently. Give up your throne.

Mary. No, devil.
My pride is stronger than yours, and my heart beats
    blood
Such as yours has never known. And in this dungeon,
I win here, alone.

Elizabeth.
    [*Turning*]
Goodnight, then.

Mary. Aye, goodnight.
    [ELIZABETH *goes to the door, which opens before her. She goes
        out slowly. As the door begins to close upon her* MARY
        calls]
Beaton:

Elizabeth.
    [*Turning*]
You will not see your maids again,
I think. It's said they bring you news from the north.

Mary. I thank you for all kindness.

> [ELIZABETH *goes out.* MARY *stands for a moment in thought, then walks to the wall and lays her hand against the stone, pushing outward. The stone is cold, and she shudders. Going to the window she sits again in her old place and looks out into the darkness*]

CURTAIN

Winterset

CHARACTERS

TROCK	CARR
SHADOW	HERMAN
GARTH	LUCIA
MIRIAMNE	PINY
ESDRAS	A SAILOR
THE HOBO	STREET URCHIN
1st GIRL	POLICEMAN
2nd GIRL	RADICAL
JUDGE GAUNT	SERGEANT
MIO	

Non-speaking

URCHINS

TWO MEN IN BLUE SERGE

ACT ONE

Scene I

Scene: *The scene is the bank of a river under a bridgehead. A gigantic span starts from the rear of the stage and appears to lift over the heads of the audience and out to the left. At the right rear is a wall of solid supporting masonry. To the left an apartment building abuts against the bridge and forms the left wall of the stage with a dark basement window and a door in the brick wall. To the right, and in the foreground, an outcropping of original rock makes a barricade behind which one may enter through a cleft. To the rear, against the masonry, two sheds have been built by waifs and strays for shelter. The river bank, in the foreground, is black rock worn smooth by years of trampling. There is room for exit and entrance to the left around the apartment house, also around the rock to the right. A single street lamp is seen at the left—and a glimmer of apartment lights in the background beyond. It is an early, dark December morning.*

Two Young Men in Serge *lean against the masonry, matching bills.* Trock Estrella *and* Shadow *come in from the left.*

Trock. Go back and watch the car.

[*The* Two Young Men *go out.* Trock *walks to the corner and looks toward the city*]

You roost of punks and gulls! Sleep, sleep it off,
whatever you had last night, get down in warm,
one big ham-fat against another—sleep,
cling, sleep and rot! Rot out your pasty guts
with diddling, you had no brain to begin. If you had
there'd be no need for us to sleep on iron
who had too much brains for you.

3

Shadow. Now look, Trock, look,
   what would the warden say to talk like that?

Trock. May they die as I die!
   By God, what life they've left me
   they shall keep me well! I'll have that out of them—
   these pismires that walk like men!

Shadow. Because, look, chief,
   it's all against science and penology
   for you to get out and begin to cuss that way
   before your prison vittles are out of you. Hell,
   you're supposed to leave the pen full of high thought,
   kind of noble-like, loving toward all mankind,
   ready to kiss their feet—or whatever parts
   they stick out toward you. Look at me!

Trock. I see you.
   And even you may not live as long as you think.
   You think too many things are funny. Well, laugh.
   But it's not so funny.

Shadow. Come on, Trock, you know me.
   Anything you say goes, but give me leave
   to kid a little.

Trock. Then laugh at somebody else!
   It's a lot safer! They've soaked me once too often
   in that vat of poisoned hell they keep up-state
   to soak men in, and I'm rotten inside, I'm all
   one liquid puke inside where I had lungs
   once, like yourself! And now they want to get me
   and stir me in again—and that'd kill me—

and that's fine for them. But before that happens to me
a lot of these healthy boys'll know what it's like
when you try to breathe and have no place to put air—
they'll learn it from me!

Shadow. They've got nothing on you, chief.

Trock. I don't know yet. That's what I'm here to find out.
If they've got what they might have
it's not a year this time—
no, nor ten. It's screwed down under a lid.—
I can die quick enough, without help.

Shadow. You're the skinny kind
that lives forever.

Trock. He gave me a half a year,
the doc at the gate.

Shadow. Jesus.

Trock. Six months I get,
and the rest's dirt, six feet.

> [LUCIA, *the street-piano man, comes in right from behind the
> rock and goes to the shed where he keeps his piano.*
> PINY, *the apple-woman, follows and stands in the en-
> trance.* LUCIA *speaks to Estrella, who still stands facing
> Shadow*]

Lucia. Morning.

> [TROCK *and* SHADOW *go out round the apartment house without
> speaking*]

Piny. Now what would you call them?

Lucia. Maybe someting da river washed up.

Piny. Nothing ever washed him—that black one.

Lucia. Maybe not, maybe so. More like his pa and ma raise-a heem in da cellar.

[*He wheels out the piano*]

Piny. He certainly gave me a turn.

[*She lays a hand on the rock*]

Lucia. You don' live-a right, ol' gal. Take heem easy. Look on da bright-a side. Never say-a die. Me, every day in every way I getta be da regular heller.

[*He starts out*]

CURTAIN

ACT ONE

Scene II

Scene: *A cellar apartment under the apartment building, floored with cement and roofed with huge boa constrictor pipes that run slantwise from left to right, dwarfing the room. An outside door opens to the left and a door at the right rear leads to the interior of the place. A low squat window to the left. A table at the rear and a few chairs and books make up the furniture. Garth, son of Esdras, sits alone, holding a violin upside down to inspect a crack at its base. He lays the bow on the floor and runs his fingers over the joint. Miriamne enters from the rear, a girl of fifteen. Garth looks up, then down again.*

Miriamne. Garth—

Garth. The glue lets go. It's the steam, I guess.
It splits the hair on your head.

Miriamne. It can't be mended?

Garth. I can't mend it.
No doubt there are fellows somewhere
who'd mend it for a dollar—and glad to do it.
That is if I had a dollar.—Got a dollar?
No, I thought not.

Miriamne. Garth, you've sat at home here
three days now. You haven't gone out at all.
Something frightens you.

Garth. Yes?

Miriamne. And father's frightened.
He reads without knowing where. When a shadow falls

7

across the page he waits for a blow to follow
after the shadow. Then in a little while
he puts his book down softly and goes out
to see who passed.

Garth.   A bill collector, maybe.
We haven't paid the rent.

Miriamne. No.

Garth. You're a bright girl, sis.—
You see too much. You run along and cook.
Why don't you go to school?

Miriamne. I don't like school.
They whisper behind my back.

Garth. Yes? About what?

Miriamne. What did the lawyer mean
that wrote to you?

Garth.

    [*Rising*]
What lawyer?

Miriamne. I found a letter
on the floor of your room. He said, "Don't get me wrong,
but stay in out of the rain the next few days,
just for instance."

Garth. I thought I burned that letter.

Miriamne. Afterward you did. And then what was printed
about the Estrella gang—you hid it from me,
you and father. What is it—about this murder—?

Garth. Will you shut up, you fool!

Miriamne. But if you know
why don't you tell them, Garth?
If it's true—what they say—
you knew all the time Romagna wasn't guilty,
and could have said so—

Garth. Everybody knew
Romagna wasn't guilty! But they weren't listening
to evidence in his favor. They didn't want it.
They don't want it now.

Miriamne. But was that why
they never called on you?—

Garth. So far as I know
they never'd heard of me—and I can assure you
I knew nothing about it—

Miriamne. But something's wrong—
and it worries father—

Garth. What could be wrong?

Miriamne. I don't know.

   [*A pause*]

Garth. And I don't know. You're a good kid, Miriamne,
but you see too many movies. I wasn't mixed up
in any murder, and I don't mean to be.
If I had a dollar to get my fiddle fixed
and another to hire a hall, by God I'd fiddle
some of the prodigies back into Sunday School
where they belong, but I won't get either, and so

I sit here and bite my nails—but if you hoped
I had some criminal romantic past
you'll have to look again!

Miriamne. Oh, Garth, forgive me—
But I want you to be so far above such things
nothing could frighten you. When you seem to shrink
and be afraid, and you're the brother I love,
I want to run there and cry, if there's any question
they care to ask, you'll be quick and glad to answer,
for there's nothing to conceal!

Garth. And that's all true—

Miriamne. But then I remember—
how you dim the lights—
and we go early to bed—and speak in whispers—
and I could think there's a death somewhere behind us—
an evil death—

Garth.

   [*Hearing a step*]

Now for God's sake, be quiet!

   [ESDRAS, *an old rabbi with a kindly face, enters from the outside. He is hurried and troubled*]

Esdras. I wish to speak alone with someone here
if I may have this room. Miriamne—

Miriamne.

   [*Turning to go*]

Yes, father.

   [*The outer door is suddenly thrown open.* TROCK *appears*]

Trock.

   [*After a pause*]

You'll excuse me for not knocking.

   [Shadow *follows Trock in*]

Sometimes it's best to come in quiet. Sometimes
it's a good way to go out. Garth's home, I see.
He might not have been here if I made a point
of knocking at doors.

Garth. How are you, Trock?

Trock. I guess
you can see how I am.

   [*To Miriamne*]

   Stay here. Stay where you are.
We'd like to make your acquaintance.
—If you want the facts
I'm no better than usual, thanks. Not enough sun,
my physician tells me. Too much close confinement.
A lack of exercise and an overplus
of beans in the diet. You've done well, no doubt?

Garth. I don't know what makes you think so.

Trock. Who's the family?

Garth. My father and my sister.

Trock. Happy to meet you.
Step inside a minute. The boy and I
have something to talk about.

Esdras. No, no—he's said nothing—
nothing, sir, nothing!

Trock. When I say go out, you go—

Esdras.

[*Pointing to the door*]

Miriamne—

Garth. Go on out, both of you!

Esdras. Oh, sir—I'm old—
old and unhappy—

Garth. Go on!

[MIRIAMNE *and* ESDRAS *go inside*]

Trock. And if you listen
I'll riddle that door!

[SHADOW *shuts the door behind them and stands against it*]

I just got out, you see,
and I pay my first call on you.

Garth. Maybe you think
I'm not in the same jam you are.

Trock. That's what I do think.
Who started looking this up?

Garth. I wish I knew,
and I wish he was in hell! Some damned professor
with nothing else to do. If you saw his stuff
you know as much as I do.

Trock. It wasn't you
turning state's evidence?

Garth. Hell, Trock, use your brain!
The case was closed. They burned Romagna for it
and that finished it. Why should I look for trouble
and maybe get burned myself?

Trock. Boy, I don't know,
but I just thought I'd find out.

Garth. I'm going straight, Trock.
I can play this thing, and I'm trying to make a living.
I haven't talked and nobody's talked to me.
Christ—it's the last thing I'd want!

Trock. Your old man knows.

Garth. That's where I got the money that last time
when you needed it. He had a little saved up,
but I had to tell him to get it. He's as safe
as Shadow there.

Trock.

[*Looking at Shadow*]

There could be people safer
than that son-of-a-bitch.

Shadow. Who?

Trock. You'd be safer dead
along with some other gorillas.

Shadow. It's beginning to look
as if you'd feel safer with everybody dead,
the whole god-damn world.

Trock. I would. These Jesus-bitten
　　professors! Looking up their half-ass cases!
　　We've got enough without that.

Garth. There's no evidence
　　to reopen the thing.

Trock. And suppose they called on you
　　and asked you to testify?

Garth. Why then I'd tell 'em
　　that all I know is what I read in the papers.
　　And I'd stick to that.

Trock. How much does your sister know?

Garth. I'm honest with you, Trock. She read my name
　　in the professor's pamphlet, and she was scared
　　the way anybody would be. She got nothing
　　from me, and anyway she'd go to the chair
　　herself before she'd send me there.

Trock. Like hell.

Garth. Besides, who wants to go to trial again
　　except the radicals?—You and I won't spill
　　and unless we did there's nothing to take to court
　　as far as I know. Let the radicals go on howling
　　about getting a dirty deal. They always howl
　　and nobody gives a damn. This professor's red—
　　everybody knows it.

Trock. You're forgetting the judge.
　　Where's the damn judge?

Garth. What judge?

Trock. Read the morning papers.
It says Judge Gaunt's gone off his nut. He's got
that damn trial on his mind, and been going round
proving to everybody he was right all the time
and the radicals were guilty—stopping people
in the street to prove it—and now he's nuts entirely
and nobody knows where he is.

Garth. Why don't they know?

Trock. Because he's on the loose somewhere! They've got
the police of three cities looking for him.

Garth. Judge Gaunt?

Trock. Yes. Judge Gaunt.

Shadow. Why should that worry you?
He's crazy, ain't he? And even if he wasn't
he's arguing on your side. You're jittery, chief.
God, all the judges are looney. You've got the jitters,
and you'll damn well give yourself away some time
peeing yourself in public.

> [TROCK *half turns toward Shadow in anger*]

Don't jump the gun now,
I've got pockets in my clothes, too.

> [*His hand is in his coat pocket*]

Trock. All right. Take it easy.

> [*He takes his hand from his pocket, and* SHADOW *does the same*]
> [*To Garth*]

Maybe you're lying to me and maybe you're not.
Stay at home a few days.

Garth. Sure thing. Why not?

Trock. And when I say stay home I mean stay home.
If I have to go looking for you you'll stay a long time
wherever I find you.

[*To Shadow*]

Come on. We'll get out of here.

[*To Garth*]

Be seeing you.

[SHADOW *and* TROCK *go out. After a pause* GARTH *walks over
to his chair and picks up the violin. Then he puts it
down and goes to the inside door, which he opens*]

Garth. He's gone.

[MIRIAMNE *enters,* ESDRAS *behind her*]

Miriamne.

[*Going up to Garth*]

Let's not stay here.

[*She puts her hands on his arms*]

I thought he'd come for something—horrible.
Is he coming back?

Garth. I don't know.

Miriamne. Who is he, Garth?

Garth. He'd kill me if I told you who he is,
that is, if he knew.

Miriamne. Then don't say it—

Garth. Yes, and I'll say it! I was with a gang one time
that robbed a pay roll. I saw a murder done,
and Trock Estrella did it. If that got out
I'd go to the chair and so would he—that's why
he was here today—

Miriamne. But that's not true—

Esdras. He says it
to frighten you, child.

Garth. Oh, no I don't! I say it
because I've held it in too long! I'm damned
if I sit here forever, and look at the door,
waiting for Trock with his sub-machine gun, waiting
for police with a warrant!—I say I'm damned, and I am,
no matter what I do! These piddling scales
on a violin—first position, third, fifth,
arpeggios in E—and what I'm thinking
is Romagna dead for the murder—dead while I sat here
dying inside—dead for the thing Trock did
while I looked on—and I could have saved him, yes—
but I sat here and let him die instead of me
because I wanted to live! Well, it's no life,
and it doesn't matter who I tell, because
I mean to get it over!

Miriamne. Garth, it's not true!

Garth. I'd take some scum down with me if I died—
that'd be one good deed—

Esdras. Son, son, you're mad—
someone will hear—

Garth. Then let them hear! I've lived
with ghosts too long, and lied too long. God damn you
if you keep me from the truth!—

[*He turns away*]

Oh, God damn the world!
I don't want to die!

[*He throws himself down*]

Esdras. I should have known.
I thought you hard and sullen,
Garth, my son. And you were a child, and hurt
with a wound that might be healed.
—All men have crimes,
and most of them are hidden, and many are heavy
as yours must be to you.

[GARTH *sobs*]

They walk the streets
to buy and sell, but a spreading crimson stain
tinges the inner vestments, touches flesh,
and burns the quick. You're not alone.

Garth. I'm alone
in this.

Esdras. Yes, if you hold with the world that only
those who die suddenly should be revenged.
But those whose hearts are cancered, drop by drop
in small ways, little by little, till they've borne
all they can bear, and die—these deaths will go
unpunished now as always. When we're young
we have faith in what is seen, but when we're old

we know that what is seen is traced in air
and built on water. There's no guilt under heaven,
just as there's no heaven, till men believe it—
no earth, till men have seen it, and have a word
to say this is the earth.

Garth. Well, I say there's an earth,
and I say I'm guilty on it, guilty as hell.

Esdras. Yet till it's known you bear no guilt at all—
unless you wish. The days go by like film,
like a long written scroll, a figured veil
unrolling out of darkness into fire
and utterly consumed. And on this veil,
running in sounds and symbols of men's minds
reflected back, life flickers and is shadow
going toward flame. Only what men can see
exists in that shadow. Why must you rise and cry out:
That was I, there in the ravelled tapestry,
there, in that pistol flash, when the man was killed.
I was there, and was one, and am bloodstained!
Let the wind
and fire take that hour to ashes out of time
and out of mind! This thing that men call justice,
this blind snake that strikes men down in the dark,
mindless with fury, keep your hand back from it,
pass by in silence—let it be forgotten, forgotten!—
Oh, my son, my son—have pity!

Miriamne. But if it was true
and someone died—then it was more than shadow—
and it doesn't blow away—

Garth. Well, it was true.

Esdras. Say it if you must. If you have heart to die,
say it, and let them take what's left—there was little
to keep, even before—

Garth. Oh, I'm a coward—
I always was. I'll be quiet and live. I'll live
even if I have to crawl. I know.

[*He gets up and goes into the inner room*]

Miriamne. Is it better
to tell a lie and live?

Esdras. Yes, child. It's better.

Miriamne. But if I had to do it—
I think I'd die.

Esdras. Yes, child. Because you're young.

Miriamne. Is that the only reason?

Esdras. The only reason.

CURTAIN

ACT ONE

Scene III

SCENE: *Under the bridge, evening of the same day. When the curtain rises* MIRIAMNE *is sitting alone on the ledge at the rear of the apartment house. A spray of light falls on her from a street lamp above. She shivers a little in her thin coat, but sits still as if heedless of the weather. Through the rocks on the other side a* TRAMP *comes down to the river bank, hunting a place to sleep. He goes softly to the apple-woman's hut and looks in, then turns away, evidently not daring to preëmpt it. He looks at Miriamne doubtfully. The door of the street-piano man is shut. The vagabond passes it and picks carefully among some rags and shavings to the right.* MIRIAMNE *looks up and sees him but makes no sign. She looks down again, and the man curls himself up in a makeshift bed in the corner, pulling a piece of sacking over his shoulders.* TWO GIRLS *come in from round the apartment house.*

1st Girl. Honest, I never heard of anything so romantic. Because you never liked him.

2nd Girl. I certainly never did.

1st Girl. You've got to tell me how it happened. You've got to.

2nd Girl. I couldn't. As long as I live I couldn't. Honest, it was terrible. It was terrible.

1st Girl. What was so terrible?

2nd Girl. The way it happened.

1st Girl. Oh, please—not to a soul, never.

21

2nd Girl. Well, you know how I hated him because he had such a big mouth. So he reached over and grabbed me, and I began all falling to pieces inside, the way you do— and I said, "Oh no you don't mister," and started screaming and kicked a hole through the windshield and lost a shoe, and he let go and was cursing and growling because he borrowed the car and didn't have money to pay for the windshield, and he started to cry, and I got so sorry for him I let him, and now he wants to marry me.

1st Girl. Honest, I never heard of anything so romantic!

[*She sees the sleeping Tramp*]

My God, what you won't see!

[*They give the Tramp a wide berth, and go out right. The* TRAMP *sits up looking about him.* JUDGE GAUNT, *an elderly, quiet man, well dressed but in clothes that have seen some weather, comes in uncertainly from the left. He holds a small clipping in his hand and goes up to the Hobo*]

Gaunt.

[*Tentatively*]

Your pardon, sir. Your pardon, but perhaps you **can** tell me the name of this street.

Hobo. Huh?

Gaunt. The name of this street?

Hobo. This ain't no street.

Gaunt. There, where the street lamps are.

Hobo. That's the alley.

Gaunt. Thank you. It has a name, no doubt?

Hobo. That's the alley.

Gaunt. I see. I won't trouble you. You wonder why I ask, I daresay.—I'm a stranger.—Why do you look at me?

[*He steps back*]

I—I'm not the man you think. You've mistaken me, sir.

Hobo. Huh?

Judge. Perhaps misled by a resemblance. But you're mistaken—I had an errand in this city. It's only by accident that I'm here—

Hobo.

[*Muttering*]

You go to hell.

Judge.

[*Going nearer to him, bending over him*]

Yet why should I deceive you? Before God, I held the proofs in my hands. I hold them still. I tell you the defense was cunning beyond belief, and unscrupulous in its use of propaganda—they gagged at nothing—not even—

[*He rises*]

No, no—I'm sorry—this will hardly interest you. I'm sorry. I have an errand.

[*He looks toward the street.* ESDRAS *enters from the basement and goes to Miriamne. The* JUDGE *steps back into the shadows*]

Esdras. Come in, my daughter. You'll be cold here.

Miriamne. After a while.

Esdras. You'll be cold. There's a storm coming.

Miriamne. I didn't want him to see me crying. That was all.

Esdras. I know.

Miriamne. I'll come soon.

> [ESDRAS *turns reluctantly and goes out the way he came.* MIRIAMNE *rises to go in, pausing to dry her eyes.* MIO *and* CARR, *road boys of seventeen or so, come round the apartment house. The Judge has disappeared*]

Carr. Thought you said you were never coming east again.

Mio. Yeah, but—I heard something changed my mind.

Carr. Same old business?

Mio. Yes. Just as soon not talk about it.

Carr. Where did you go from Portland?

Mio. Fishing—I went fishing. God's truth.

Carr. Right after I left?

Mio. Fell in with a fisherman's family on the coast and went after the beautiful mackerel fish that swim in the beautiful sea. Family of Greeks—Aristides Marinos was his lovely name. He sang while he fished. Made the pea-green Pacific ring with his bastard Greek chanties. Then I went to Hollywood High School for a while.

Carr. I'll bet that's a seat of learning.

Mio. It's the hind end of all wisdom. They kicked me out after a time.

Carr. For cause?

Mio. Because I had no permanent address, you see. That means nobody's paying school taxes for you, so out you go.
[*To Miriamne*]
What's the matter, kid?

Mariamne. Nothing.
[*She looks up at him, and they pause for a moment*]
Nothing.

Mio. I'm sorry.

Miriamne. It's all right.
[*She withdraws her eyes from his and goes out past him. He turns and looks after her*]

Carr. Control your chivalry.

Mio. A pretty kid.

Carr. A baby.

Mio. Wait for me.

Carr. Be a long wait?
[Mio *steps swiftly out after Miriamne, then returns*]
Yeah?

Mio. She's gone.

Carr. Think of that.

Mio. No, but I mean—vanished. Presto—into nothing—prodigioso.

Carr. Damn good thing, if you ask me. The homely ones are bad enough, but the lookers are fatal.

Mio. You exaggerate, Carr.

Carr. I doubt it.

Mio. Well, let her go. This river bank's loaded with typhus rats, too. Might as well die one death as another.

Carr. They say chronic alcoholism is nice but expensive. You can always starve to death.

Mio. Not always. I tried it. After the second day I walked thirty miles to Niagara Falls and made a tour of the plant to get the sample of shredded wheat biscuit on the way out.

Carr. Last time I saw you you couldn't think of anything you wanted to do except curse God and pass out. Still feeling low?

Mio. Not much different.

[*He turns away, then comes back*]

Talk about the lost generation, I'm the only one fits that title. When the State executes your father, and your mother dies of grief, and you know damn well he was innocent, and the authorities of your home town politely inform you they'd consider it a favor if you lived somewhere else—that cuts you off from the world—with a meat-axe.

Carr. They asked you to move?

Mio. It came to that.

Carr. God, that was white of them.

Mio. It probably gave them a headache just to see me after all that agitation. They knew as well as I did my father never staged a holdup. Anyway, I've got a new interest in life now.

Carr. Yes—I saw her.

Mio. I don't mean the skirt.—No, I got wind of something, out west, some college professor investigating the trial and turning up new evidence. Couldn't find anything he'd written out there, so I beat it east and arrived on this blessed island just in time to find the bums holing up in the public library for the winter. I know now what the unemployed have been doing since the depression started. They've been catching up on their reading in the main reference room. Man, what a stench! Maybe I stank, too, but a hobo has the stench of ten because his shoes are poor.

Carr. Tennyson.

Mio. Right. Jeez, I'm glad we met up again! Never knew anybody else that could track me through the driven snow of Victorian literature.

Carr. Now you're cribbing from some half-forgotten criticism of Ben Jonson's Roman plagiarisms.

Mio. Where did you get your education, sap?

Carr. Not in the public library, sap. My father kept a news-stand.

Mio. Well, you're right again.

[*There is a faint rumble of thunder*]

What's that? Winter thunder?

Carr. Or Mister God, beating on His little tocsin. Maybe announcing the advent of a new social order.

Mio. Or maybe it's going to rain coffee and doughnuts.

Carr. Or maybe it's going to rain.

Mio. Seems more likely.

[*Lowering his voice*]

Anyhow, I found Professor Hobhouse's discussion of the Romagna case. I think he has something. It occurred to me I might follow it up by doing a little sleuthing on my own account.

Carr. Yes?

Mio. I have done a little. And it leads me to somewhere in that tenement house that backs up against the bridge. That's how I happen to be here.

Carr. They'll never let you get anywhere with it, Mio. I told you that before.

Mio. I know you did.

Carr. The State can't afford to admit it was wrong, you see. Not when there's been that much of a row kicked up over it. So for all practical purposes the State was right and your father robbed the pay roll.

Mio. There's still such a thing as evidence.

Carr. It's something you can buy. In fact, at the moment
I don't think of anything you can't buy, including life,
honor, virtue, glory, public office, conjugal affection and
all kinds of justice, from the traffic court to the immortal
nine. Go out and make yourself a pot of money and you
can buy all the justice you want. Convictions obtained,
convictions averted. Lowest rates in years.

Mio. I know all that.

Carr. Sure.

Mio. This thing didn't happen to you.
They've left you your name
and whatever place you can take. For my heritage
they've left me one thing only, and that's to be
my father's voice crying up out of the earth
and quicklime where they stuck him. Electrocution
doesn't kill, you know. They eviscerate them
with a turn of the knife in the dissecting room.
The blood spurts out. The man was alive. Then into
the lime pit, leave no trace. Make it short shrift
and chemical dissolution. That's what they thought
of the man that was my father. Then my mother—
I tell you these county burials are swift
and cheap and run for profit! Out of the house
and into the ground, you wife of a dead dog. Wait,
here's some Romagna spawn left.
Something crawls here—
something they called a son. Why couldn't he die
along with his mother? Well, ease him out of town,

ease him out, boys, and see you're not too gentle.
He might come back. And, by their own living Jesus,
I will go back, and hang the carrion
around their necks that made it!
Maybe I can sleep then.
Or even live.

Carr. You have to try it?

Mio. Yes.
Yes. It won't let me alone. I've tried to live
and forget it—but I was birthmarked with hot iron
into the entrails. I've got to find out who did it
and make them see it till it scalds their eyes
and make them admit it till their tongues are blistered
with saying how black they lied!

[HERMAN, *a gawky shoe salesman, enters from the left*]

Herman. Hello. Did you see a couple of girls go this way?

Carr. Couple of girls? Did we see a couple of girls?

Mio. No.

Carr. No. No girls.

[HERMAN *hesitates, then goes out right.* LUCIA *comes in from
    the left, trundling his piano.* PINY *follows him, weeping*]

Piny. They've got no right to do it—

Lucia. All right, hell what, no matter, I got to put him
away, I got to put him away, that's what the hell!

[Two STREET URCHINS *follow him in*]

Piny. They want everybody on the relief rolls and nobody
making a living?

Lucia. The cops, they do what the big boss says. The big boss, that's the mayor, he says he heard it once too often, the sextette—

Piny. They want graft, that's all. It's a new way to get graft—

Lucia. Oh, no, no, no! He's a good man, the mayor. He's just don't care for music, that's all.

Piny. Why shouldn't you make a living on the street? The National Biscuit Company ropes off Eighth Avenue—and does the mayor do anything? No, the police hit you over the head if you try to go through!

Lucia. You got the big dough, you get the pull, fine. No big dough, no pull, what the hell, get off the city property! Tomorrow I start cooking chestnuts . . .

[*He strokes the piano fondly. The* Two Girls *and* Herman *come back from the right*]

She's a good little machine, this baby. Cost plenty—and two new records I only played twice. See, this one.

[*He starts turning the crank, talking while he plays*]

Two weeks since they play this one in a picture house.

[*A* Sailor *wanders in from the left. One of the* Street Urchins *begins suddenly to dance a wild rumba, the others watch*]

Good boy—see, it's a lulu—it itches in the feet!

[Herman, *standing with his girl, tosses the boy a penny. He bows and goes on dancing; the other* Urchin *joins him. The* Sailor *tosses a coin*]

Sailor. Go it, Cuba! Go it!

[Lucia *turns the crank, beaming*]

2nd Girl. Oh, Herman!

[*She throws her arms round Herman and they dance*]

1st Urchin. Hey, pipe the professionals!

1st Girl. Do your glide, Shirley! Do your glide!

Lucia. Maybe we can't play in front, maybe we can play behind!

[*The* Hobo *gets up from his nest and comes over to watch.* A Young Radical *wanders in*]

Maybe you don't know, folks! Tonight we play good-bye to the piano! Good-bye forever! No more piano on the streets! No more music! No more money for the music-man! Last time, folks! Good-bye to the piano— good-bye forever!

[Miriamne *comes out the rear door of the apartment and stands watching. The* Sailor *goes over to the 1st Girl and they dance together*]

Maybe you don't know, folks! Tomorrow will be sad as hell, tonight we dance! Tomorrow no more Verdi, no more rumba, no more good time! Tonight we play good-bye to the piano, good-bye forever!

[*The* Radical *edges up to Miriamne, and asks her to dance. She shakes her head and he goes to Piny, who dances with him. The* Hobo *begins to do a few lonely curvets on the side above*]

Hoy! Hoy! Pick 'em up and take 'em around! Use the head, use the feet! Last time forever!

[*He begins to sing to the air*]

Mio. Wait for me, will you?

Carr. Now's your chance.

[MIO *goes over to Miriamne and holds out a hand, smiling. She stands for a moment uncertain, then dances with him.* ESDRAS *comes out to watch.* JUDGE GAUNT *comes in from the left. There is a rumble of thunder*]

Lucia. Hoy! Hoy! Maybe it rains tonight, maybe it snows tomorrow! Tonight we dance good-bye.

[*He sings the air lustily.* A POLICEMAN *comes in from the left and looks on.* TWO OR THREE PEDESTRIANS *follow him*]

Policeman. Hey you!

[LUCIA *goes on singing*]

Hey, you!

Lucia.

[*Still playing*]

What you want?

Policeman. Sign off!

Lucia. What you mean? I get off the street!

Policeman. Sign off!

Lucia.

[*Still playing*]

What you mean?

[*The* POLICEMAN *walks over to him.* LUCIA *stops playing and the* DANCERS *pause*]

Policeman. Cut it.

Lucia. Is this a street?

Policeman. I say cut it out.

[*The* Hobo *goes back to his nest and sits in it, watching*]

Lucia. It's the last time. We dance good-bye to the piano.

Policeman. You'll dance good-bye to something else if I catch you cranking that thing again.

Lucia. All right.

Piny. I'll bet you don't say that to the National Biscuit Company!

Policeman. Lady, you've been selling apples on my beat for some time now, and I said nothing about it—

Piny. Selling apples is allowed—

Policeman. You watch yourself—

[*He takes a short walk around the place and comes upon the Hobo*]

What are you doing here?

[*The* Hobo *opens his mouth, points to it, and shakes his head*]

Oh, you are, are you?

[*He comes back to Lucia*]

So you trundle your so-called musical instrument to wherever you keep it, and don't let me hear it again.

[*The* Radical *leaps on the base of the rock at right. The* 1st Girl *turns away from the Sailor toward the 2nd Girl and Herman*]

Sailor. Hey, captain, what's the matter with the music?

Policeman. Not a thing, admiral.

Sailor. Well, we had a little party going here—

Policeman. I'll say you did.

2nd Girl. Please, officer, we want to dance.

Policeman. Go ahead. Dance.

2nd Girl. But we want music!

Policeman.
   [*Turning to go*]
   Sorry. Can't help you.

Radical. And there you see it, the perfect example of capi-
talistic oppression! In a land where music should be free
as air and the arts should be encouraged, a uniformed
minion of the rich, a guardian myrmidon of the Park
Avenue pleasure hunters, steps in and puts a limit on
the innocent enjoyments of the poor! We don't go to
theatres! Why not? We can't afford it! We don't go to
night clubs, where women dance naked and the music
drips from saxophones and leaks out of Rudy Vallee—
we can't afford that either!—But we might at least dance
on the river bank to the strains of a barrel organ—!
   [GARTH *comes out of the apartment and listens*]

Policeman. It's against the law!

Radical. What law? I challenge you to tell me what law of
God or man—what ordinance—is violated by this
spontaneous diversion? None! I say none! An official
whim of the masters who should be our servants!—

Policeman. Get down! Get down and shut up!

Radical. By what law, by what ordinance do you order me to be quiet?

Policeman. Speaking without a flag. You know it.

Radical.

[*Pulling out a small American flag*]

There's my flag! There's the flag of this United States which used to guarantee the rights of man—the rights of man now violated by every third statute of the commonweal—

Policeman. Don't try to pull tricks on me! I've seen you before! You're not making any speech, and you're climbing down—

Judge Gaunt.

[*Who has come quietly forward*]

One moment, officer. There is some difference of opinion even on the bench as to the elasticity of police power when applied in minor emergencies to preserve civil order. But the weight of authority would certainly favor the defendant in any equable court, and he would be upheld in his demand to be heard.

Policeman. Who are you?

Judge Gaunt. Sir, I am not accustomed to answer that question.

Policeman. I don't know you.

Gaunt. I am a judge of some standing, not in your city but in another with similar statutes. You are aware, of

course, that the bill of rights is not to be set aside lightly
by the officers of any municipality—

Policeman.

   [*Looking over Gaunt's somewhat bedraggled costume*]

Maybe they understand you better in the town you come
from, but I don't get your drift.—

   [*To the Radical*]

I don't want any trouble, but if you ask for it you'll
get plenty. Get down!

Radical. I'm not asking for trouble, but I'm staying right
here.

   [*The* POLICEMAN *moves toward him*]

Gaunt.

   [*Taking the policeman's arm, but shaken off roughly*]

I ask this for yourself, truly, not for the dignity of the
law nor the maintenance of precedent. Be gentle with
them when their threats are childish—be tolerant while
you can—for your least harsh word will return on you
in the night—return in a storm of cries!—

   [*He takes the Policeman's arm again*]

Whatever they may have said or done, let them disperse
in peace! It is better that they go softly, lest when they
are dead you see their eyes pleading, and their out-
stretched hands touch you, fingering cold on your heart!
—I have been harsher than you. I have sent men down
that long corridor into blinding light and blind darkness!

   [*He suddenly draws himself erect and speaks defiantly*]

And it was well that I did so! I have been an upright judge! They are all liars! Liars!

Policeman.

[*Shaking* GAUNT *off so that he falls*]

Why, you fool, you're crazy!

Gaunt. Yes, and there are liars on the force! They came to me with their shifty lies!

[*He catches at the* POLICEMAN, *who pushes him away with his foot*]

Policeman. You think I've got nothing better to do **than** listen to a crazy fool?

1st Girl. Shame, shame!

Policeman. What have I got to be ashamed of? And what's going on here, anyway? Where in hell did you all **come** from?

Radical. Tread on him! That's right! Tread down the poor and the innocent!

[*There is a protesting murmur in the crowd*]

Sailor.

[*Moving in a little*]

Say, big boy, you don't have to step on the guy.

Policeman.

[*Facing them, stepping back*]

What's the matter with you? I haven't stepped on any-body!

Mio.

[*At the right, across from the Policeman*]

Listen now, fellows, give the badge a chance.
He's doing his job, what he gets paid to do,
the same as any of you. They're all picked men,
these metropolitan police, hand picked
for loyalty and a fine up-standing pair
of shoulders on their legs—it's not so easy
to represent the law. Think what he does
for all of us, stamping out crime!
Do you want to be robbed and murdered in your beds?

Sailor. What's eating you?

Radical. He must be a capitalist.

Mio. They pluck them fresh
from Ireland, and a paucity of headpiece
is a prime prerequisite. You from Ireland, buddy?

Policeman.

[*Surly*]

Where are you from?

Mio. Buddy, I tell you flat
I wish I was from Ireland, and could boast
some Tammany connections. There's only one drawback
about working on the force. It infects the brain,
it eats the cerebrum. There've been cases known,
fine specimens of manhood, too, where autopsies,
conducted in approved scientific fashion,
revealed conditions quite incredible

in policemen's upper layers. In some, a trace,
in others, when they've swung a stick too long,
there was nothing there!—but nothing! Oh, my friends,
this fine athletic figure of a man
that stands so grim before us, what will they find
when they saw his skull for the last inspection?
I fear me a little puffball dust will blow away
rejoining earth, our mother—and this same dust,
this smoke, this ash on the wind, will represent
all he had left to think with!

The Hobo. Hooray!

> [*The* POLICEMAN *turns on his heel and looks hard at the* HOBO, *who slinks away*]

Policeman. Oh, yeah?

Mio. My theme
gives ears to the deaf and voice to the dumb! But now
forgive me if I say you were most unkind
in troubling the officer. He's a simple man
of simple tastes, and easily confused
when faced with complex issues. He may reflect
on returning home, that is, so far as he
is capable of reflection, and conclude
that he was kidded out of his uniform pants,
and in his fury when this dawns on him
may smack his wife down!

Policeman. That'll be about enough from you, too, professor!

Mio. May I say that I think you have managed this whole
situation rather badly, from the beginning?—

Policeman. You may not!

> [TROCK *slips in from the background. The* TWO YOUNG MEN
> IN SERGE *come with him*]

Mio. Oh, but your pardon, sir! It's apparent to the least
competent among us that you should have gone about
your task more subtly—the glove of velvet, the hand of
iron, and all that sort of thing—

Policeman. Shut that hole in your face!

Mio. Sir, for that remark I shall be satisfied with nothing
less than an unconditional apology! I have an old score
to settle with policemen, brother, because they're fools
and fat-heads, and you're one of the most fatuous fat-
heads that ever walked his feet flat collecting graft! Tell
that to your sergeant back in the booby-hatch.

Policeman. Oh, you want an apology, do you? You'll get an
apology out of the other side of your mouth!

> [*He steps toward Mio.* CARR *suddenly stands in his path*]

Get out of my way!

> [*He pauses and looks round him; the crowd looks less and less
> friendly. He lays a hand on his gun and backs to a
> position where there is nobody behind him*]

Get out of here, all of you! Get out! What are you trying
to do—start a riot?

Mio. There now, that's better! That's in the best police
tradition. Incite a riot yourself and then accuse the
crowd.

Policeman. It won't be pleasant if I decide to let somebody
have it! Get out!

[*The onlookers begin to melt away. The* SAILOR *goes out left with the* GIRLS *and* HERMAN. CARR *and* MIO *go out right,* CARR *whistling "The Star Spangled Banner." The* HOBO *follows them. The* RADICAL *walks past with his head in the air.* PINY *and* LUCIA *leave the piano where it stands and slip away to the left. At the end the* POLICE-MAN *is left standing in the center, the* JUDGE *near him.* ESDRAS *stands in the doorway.* MIRIAMNE *is left sitting half in shadow and unseen by* ESDRAS]

Judge Gaunt.

[*To the Policeman*]

Yes, but should a man die, should it be necessary that one man die for the good of many, make not yourself the instrument of death, lest you sleep to wake sobbing! Nay, it avails nothing that you are the law—this delicate ganglion that is the brain, it will not bear these things—!

[*The* POLICEMAN *gives the Judge the once-over, shrugs, decides to leave him there and starts out left.* GARTH *goes to his father—a fine sleet begins to fall through the street lights.* TROCK *is still visible*]

Garth. Get him in here, quick.

Esdras. Who, son?

Garth. The Judge, damn him!

Esdras. Is it Judge Gaunt?

Garth. Who did you think it was? He's crazy as a bedbug and telling the world. Get him inside!

[*He looks round*]

Esdras.

[*Going up to Gaunt*]

Will you come in, sir?

Gaunt. You will understand, sir. We old men know how softly we must proceed with these things.

Esdras. Yes, surely, sir.

Gaunt. It was always my practice—always. They will tell you that of me where I am known. Yet even I am not free of regret—even I. Would you believe it?

Esdras. I believe we are none of us free of regret.

Gaunt. None of us? I would it were true. I would I thought it were true.

Esdras. Shall we go in, sir? This is sleet that's falling.

Gaunt. Yes. Let us go in.

> [ESDRAS, GAUNT *and* GARTH *enter the basement and shut the door.* TROCK *goes out with his men. After a pause* MIO *comes back from the right, alone. He stands at a little distance from Miriamne*]

Mio. Looks like rain.

> [*She is silent*]

You live around here?

> [*She nods gravely*]

I guess
you thought I meant it—about waiting here to meet me.

> [*She nods again*]

I'd forgotten about it till I got that winter
across the face. You'd better go inside.

I'm not your kind. I'm nobody's kind but my own.
I'm waiting for this to blow over.

[*She rises*]

　I lied. I meant it—
I meant it when I said it—but there's too much black
whirling inside me—for any girl to know.
So go on in. You're somebody's angel child
and they're waiting for you.

Miriamne. Yes. I'll go.

[*She turns*]

Mio. And tell them
when you get inside where it's warm,
and you love each other,
and mother comes to kiss her darling, tell them
to hang on to it while they can, believe while they can
it's a warm safe world, and Jesus finds his lambs
and carries them in his bosom.—I've seen some lambs
that Jesus missed. If they ever want the truth
tell them that nothing's guaranteed in this climate
except it gets cold in winter, nor on this earth
except you die sometime.

[*He turns away*]

Miriamne. I have no mother.
And my people are Jews.

Mio. Then you know something about it.

Miriamne. Yes.

Mio. Do you have enough to eat?

Miriamne. Not always.

Mio. What do you believe in?

Miriamne. Nothing.

Mio. Why?

Miriamne. How can one?

Mio. It's easy if you're a fool. You see the words
in books. Honor, it says there, chivalry, freedom,
heroism, enduring love—and these
are words on paper. It's something to have them there.
You'll get them nowhere else.

Miriamne. What hurts you?

Mio. Just that.
You'll get them nowhere else.

Miriamne. Why should you want them?

Mio. I'm alone, that's why. You see those lights,
along the river, cutting across the rain—?
those are the hearths of Brooklyn, and up this way
the love-nests of Manhattan—they turn their points
like knives against me—outcast of the world,
snake in the streets.—I don't want a hand-out.
I sleep and eat.

Miriamne. Do you want me to go with you?

Mio. Where?

Miriamne. Where you go.

    [*A pause. He goes nearer to her*]

Mio. Why, you god-damned little fool—
what made you say that?

Miriamne. I don't know.

Mio. If you have a home
stay in it. I ask for nothing. I've schooled myself
to ask for nothing, and take what I can get,
and get along. If I fell for you, that's my look-out,
and I'll starve it down.

Miriamne. Wherever you go, I'd go.

Mio. What do you know about loving?
How could you know?
Have you ever had a man?

Miriamne.

[*After a slight pause*]

No. But I know.
Tell me your name.

Mio. Mio. What's yours?

Miriamne. Miriamne.

Mio. There's no such name.

Miriamne. But there's no such name as Mio!
M.I.O. It's no name.

Mio. It's for Bartolomeo.

Miriamne. My mother's name was Miriam,
so they called me Miriamne.

Mio. Meaning little Miriam?

Miriamne. Yes.

Mio. So now little Miriamne will go in
and take up quietly where she dropped them all
her small housewifely cares.—When I first saw you,
not a half-hour ago, I heard myself saying,
this is the face that launches ships for me—
and if I owned a dream—yes, half a dream—
we'd share it. But I have no dream. This earth
came tumbling down from chaos, fire and rock,
and bred up worms, blind worms that sting each other
here in the dark. These blind worms of the earth
took out my father—and killed him, and set a sign
on me—the heir of the serpent—and he was a man
such as men might be if the gods were men—
but they killed him—
as they'll kill all others like him
till the sun cools down to the stabler molecules,
yes, till men spin their tent-worm webs to the stars
and what they think is done, even in the thinking,
and they are the gods, and immortal, and constellations
turn for them all like mill wheels—still as they are
they will be, worms and blind. Enduring love,
oh gods and worms, what mockery!—And yet
I have blood enough in my veins. It goes like music,
singing, because you're here. My body turns
as if you were the sun, and warm. This men called love
in happier times, before the Freudians taught us
to blame it on the glands. Only go in
before you breathe too much of my atmosphere
and catch death from me.

Miriamne. I will take my hands
and weave them to a little house, and there
you shall keep a dream—

Mio. God knows I could use a dream
and even a house.

Miriamne. You're laughing at me, Mio!

Mio. The worms are laughing.
I tell you there's death about me
and you're a child! And I'm alone and half mad
with hate and longing. I shall let you love me
and love you in return, and then, why then
God knows what happens!

Miriamne. Something most unpleasant?

Mio. Love in a box car—love among the children.
I've seen too much of it. Are we to live
in this same house you make with your two hands
mystically, out of air?

Miriamne. No roof, no mortgage!
Well, I shall marry a baker out in Flatbush,
it gives hot bread in the morning! Oh, Mio, Mio,
in all the unwanted places and waste lands
that roll up into the darkness out of sun
and into sun out of dark, there should be one empty
for you and me.

Mio. No.

Miriamne. Then go now and leave me.
I'm only a girl you saw in the tenements,
and there's been nothing said.

Mio. Miriamne.

[*She takes a step toward him*]

Miriamne. Yes.

[*He kisses her lips lightly*]

Mio. Why, girl, the transfiguration on the mount
was nothing to your face. It lights from within—
a white chalice holding fire, a flower in flame,
this is your face.

Miriamne. And you shall drink the flame
and never lessen it. And round your head
the aureole shall burn that burns there now,
forever. This I can give you. And so forever
the Freudians are wrong.

Mio. They're well-forgotten
at any rate.

Miriamne. Why did you speak to me
when you first saw me?

Mio. I knew then.

Miriamne. And I came back
because I must see you again. And we danced together
and my heart hurt me. Never, never, never,
though they should bind me down and tear out my eyes,
would I ever hurt you now. Take me with you, Mio,
let them look for us, whoever there is to look,
but we'll be away.

[Mio *turns away toward the tenement*]

Mio. When I was four years old
  we climbed through an iron gate, my mother and I,
  to see my father in prison. He stood in the death-cell
  and put his hand through the bars and said, My Mio,
  I have only this to leave you, that I love you,
  and will love you after I die. Love me then, Mio,
  when this hard thing comes on you, that you must live
  a man despised for your father. That night the guards,
  walking in flood-lights brighter than high noon,
  led him between them with his trousers slit
  and a shaven head for the cathodes. This sleet and rain
  that I feel cold here on my face and hands
  will find him under thirteen years of clay
  in prison ground. Lie still and rest, my father,
  for I have not forgotten. When I forget
  may I lie blind as you. No other love,
  time passing, nor the spaced light-years of suns
  shall blur your voice, or tempt me from the path
  that clears your name—
  till I have these rats in my grip
  or sleep deep where you sleep.

   [*To Miriamne*]

   I have no house,
nor home, nor love of life, nor fear of death,
nor care for what I eat, or who I sleep with,
or what color of calcimine the Government
will wash itself this year or next to lure
the sheep and feed the wolves. Love somewhere else,
and get your children in some other image
more acceptable to the State! This face of mine
is stamped for sewage!

[*She steps back, surmising*]

Miriamne. Mio—

Mio. My road is cut
in rock, and leads to one end. If I hurt you, I'm sorry.
One gets over hurts.

Miriamne. What was his name—
your father's name?

Mio. Bartolomeo Romagna.
I'm not ashamed of it.

Miriamne. Why are you here?

Mio. For the reason
I've never had a home. Because I'm a cry
out of a shallow grave, and all roads are mine
that might revenge him!

Miriamne. But Mio—why here—why here?

Mio. I can't tell you that.

Miriamne. No—but—there's someone
lives here—lives not far—and you mean to see him—
you mean to ask him—

[*She pauses*]

Mio. Who told you that?

Miriamne. His name
is Garth—Garth Esdras—

Mio.

[*After a pause, coming nearer*]

Who are you, then? You seem
to know a good deal about me.—Were you sent
to say this?

Miriamne. You said there was death about you! Yes,
but nearer than you think! Let it be as it is—
let it all be as it is, never see this place
nor think of it—forget the streets you came
when you're away and safe! Go before you're seen
or spoken to!

Mio. Will you tell me why?

Miriamne. As I love you
I can't tell you—and I can never see you—

Mio. I walk where I please—

Miriamne. Do you think it's easy for me
to send you away?

    [*She steps back as if to go*]

Mio. Where will I find you then
if I should want to see you?

Miriamne. Never—I tell you
I'd bring you death! Even now. Listen!

    [Shadow *and* Trock *enter between the bridge and the tenement
house.* Miriamne *pulls* Mio *back into the shadow of the
rock to avoid being seen*]

Trock. Why, fine.

Shadow. You watch it now—just for the record, Trock—
you're going to thank me for staying away from it
and keeping you out. I've seen men get that way,

thinking they had to plug a couple of guys
and then a few more to cover it up, and then
maybe a dozen more. You can't own all
and territory adjacent, and you can't
slough all the witnesses, because every man
you put away has friends—

Trock. I said all right.
I said fine.

Shadow. They're going to find this judge,
and if they find him dead it's just too bad,
and I don't want to know anything about it—
and you don't either.

Trock. You all through?

Shadow. Why sure.

Trock. All right.
We're through, too, you know.

Shadow. Yeah?

[*He becomes wary*]

Trock. Yeah, we're through.

Shadow. I've heard that said before, and afterwards
somebody died.

[Trock *is silent*]

Is that what you mean?

Trock. You can go.
I don't want to see you.

Shadow. Sure, I'll go.
Maybe you won't mind if I just find out
what you've got on you. Before I turn my back
I'd like to know.

[*Silently and expertly he touches Trock's pockets, extracting a
gun*]

Not that I'd distrust you,
but you know how it is.

[*He pockets the gun*]

So long, Trock.

Trock. So long.

Shadow. I won't talk.
You can be sure of that.

Trock. I know you won't.

[Shadow *turns and goes out right, past the rock and along the
bank. As he goes the* Two Young Men in Blue Serge
*enter from the left and walk slowly after Shadow. They
look toward Trock as they enter and he motions with his
thumb in the direction taken by Shadow. They follow
Shadow out without haste.* Trock *watches them dis-
appear, then slips out the way he came.* Mio *comes a
step forward, looking after the two men. Two or three
shots are heard, then silence.* Mio *starts to run after
Shadow*]

Miriamne. Mio!

Mio. What do you know about this?

Miriamne. The other way,
Mio—quick!

[Carr *slips in from the right, in haste*]

Carr. Look, somebody's just been shot.
He fell in the river. The guys that did the shooting
ran up the bank.

Mio. Come on.

> [MIO *and* CARR *run out right.* MIRIAMNE *watches uncertainly,
> then slowly turns and walks to the rear door of the
> tenement. She stands there a moment, looking after
> Mio, then goes in, closing the door.* CARR *and* MIO
> *return*]

Carr. There's a rip tide past the point. You'd never find
him.

Mio. No.

Carr. You know a man really ought to carry insurance
living around here.—God, it's easy, putting a fellow
away. I never saw it done before.

Mio.

> [*Looking at the place where Miriamne stood*]

They have it all worked out.

Carr. What are you doing now?

Mio. I have a little business to transact in this neighbor-
hood.

Carr. You'd better forget it.

Mio. No.

Carr. Need any help?

Mio. Well, if I did I'd ask you first. But I don't see how it
would do any good. So you keep out of it and take care
of yourself.

Carr. So long, then.

Mio. So long, Carr.

Carr.

> [*Looking down-stream*]

He was drifting face up. Must be halfway to the island the way the tide runs.

> [*He shivers*]

God, it's cold here. Well—

> [*He goes out to the left.* Mio *sits on the edge of the rock.* Lucia *comes stealthily back from between the bridge and the tenement, goes to the street-piano and wheels it away.* Piny *comes in. They take a look at Mio, but say nothing.* Lucia *goes into his shelter and* Piny *into hers.* Mio *rises, looks up at the tenement, and goes out to the left*]

CURTAIN

WINTERSET

ACT TWO

ACT TWO

SCENE: *The basement as in Scene 2 of Act One. The same evening.*
ESDRAS *sits at the table reading,* MIRIAMNE *is seated at the left,
listening and intent. The door of the inner room is half open
and Garth's violin is heard. He is playing the theme from the
third movement of Beethoven's Archduke Trio.* ESDRAS *looks
up.*

Esdras. I remember when I came to the end
of all the Talmud said, and the commentaries,
then I was fifty years old—and it was time
to ask what I had learned. I asked this question
and gave myself the answer. In all the Talmud
there was nothing to find but the names of things,
set down that we might call them by those names
and walk without fear among things known. Since then
I have had twenty years to read on and on
and end with Ecclesiastes. Names of names,
evanid days, evanid nights and days
and words that shift their meaning. Space is time,
that which was is now—the men of tomorrow
live, and this is their yesterday. All things
that were and are and will be, have their being
then and now and to come. If this means little
when you are young, remember it. It will return
to mean more when you are old.

Miriamne. I'm sorry—I
was listening for something.

Esdras. It doesn't matter.
It's a useless wisdom. It's all I have,

59

but useless. It may be there is no time,
but we grow old. Do you know his name?

Miriamne. Whose name?

Esdras. Why, when we're young and listen for a step
the step should have a name—

[MIRIAMNE, *not hearing, rises and goes to the window.* GARTH
*enters from within, carrying his violin and carefully
closing the door*]

Garth.

[*As* ESDRAS *looks at him*]

Asleep.

Esdras. He may
sleep on through the whole night—then in the morning
we can let them know.

Garth. We'd be wiser to say nothing—
let him find his own way back.

Esdras. How did he come here?

Garth. He's not too crazy for that. If he wakes again
we'll keep him quiet and shift him off tomorrow.
Somebody'd pick him up.

Esdras. How have I come
to this sunken end of a street, at a life's end—?

Garth. It was cheaper here—not to be transcendental—
So—we say nothing—?

Esdras. Nothing.

Miriamne. Garth, there's no place
in this whole city—not one—
where you wouldn't be safer
than here—tonight—or tomorrow.

Garth.

[*Bitterly*]

Well, that may be.
What of it?

Miriamne. If you slipped away and took
a place somewhere where Trock couldn't find you—

Garth. Yes—
using what for money? and why do you think
I've sat here so far—because I love my home
so much? No, but if I stepped round the corner
it'd be my last corner and my last step.

Miriamne. And yet—
if you're here—they'll find you here—
Trock will come again—
and there's worse to follow—

Garth. Do you want to get me killed?

Miriamne. No.

Garth. There's no way out of it. We'll wait
and take what they send us.

Esdras. Hush! You'll wake him.

Garth. I've done it.
I hear him stirring now.

[*They u ait quietly.* JUDGE GAUNT *opens the door and enters*]

Gaunt.

　　[*In the doorway*]

I beg your pardon—
no, no, be seated—keep your place—I've made
your evening difficult enough, I fear;
and I must thank you doubly for your kindness,
for I've been ill—I know it.

Esdras. You're better, sir?

Gaunt. Quite recovered, thank you. Able, I hope,
to manage nicely now. You'll be rewarded
for your hospitality—though at this moment

　　[*He smiles*]

I'm low in funds.

　　[*He inspects his billfold*]

　　Sir, my embarrassment
is great indeed—and more than monetary,
for I must own my recollection's vague
of how I came here—how we came together—
and what we may have said. My name is Gaunt,
Judge Gaunt, a name long known in the criminal courts,
and not unhonored there.

Esdras. My name is Esdras—
and this is Garth, my son. And Miriamne,
the daughter of my old age.

Gaunt. I'm glad to meet you.
Esdras. Garth Esdras.

　　[*He passes a hand over his eyes*]

It's not a usual name.
Of late it's been connected with a case—
a case I knew. But this is hardly the man.
Though it's not a usual name.

[*They are silent*]

Sir, how I came here,
as I have said, I don't well know. Such things
are sometimes not quite accident.

Esdras. We found you
outside our door and brought you in.

Gaunt. The brain
can be overworked, and weary, even when the man
would swear to his good health. Sir, on my word
I don't know why I came here, nor how, nor when,
nor what would explain it. Shall we say the machine
begins to wear? I felt no twinge of it.—
You will imagine how much more than galling
I feel it, to ask my way home—and where I am—
but I do ask you that.

Esdras. This is New York City—
or part of it.

Gaunt. Not the best part, I presume?

[*He smiles grimly*]

No, not the best.

Esdras. Not typical, no.

Gaunt. And you—

[*To Garth*]

you are Garth Esdras?

Garth. That's my name.

Gaunt. Well, sir,

[*To Esdras*]

I shall lie under the deepest obligation
if you will set an old man on his path,
for I lack the homing instinct, if the truth
were known. North, east and south mean nothing to me
here in this room.

Esdras. I can put you in your way.

Garth. Only you'd be wiser to wait a while—
if I'm any judge.—

Gaunt. It happens I'm the judge—

[*With stiff humor*]

in more ways than one. You'll forgive me if I say
I find this place and my predicament
somewhat distasteful.

[*He looks round him*]

Garth. I don't doubt you do;
but you're better off here.

Gaunt. Nor will you find it wise
to cross my word as lightly as you seem
inclined to do. You've seen me ill and shaken—
and you presume on that.

Garth. Have it your way.

Gaunt. Doubtless what information is required
we'll find nearby.

Esdras. Yes, sir—the terminal,—
if you could walk so far.

Gaunt. I've done some walking—
to look at my shoes.

[*He looks down, then puts out a hand to steady himself*]

That—that was why I came—
never mind—it was there—and it's gone.

[*To Garth*]

Professor Hobhouse—
that's the name—he wrote some trash about you
and printed it in a broadside.
—Since I'm here I can tell you
it's a pure fabrication—lacking facts
and legal import. Senseless and impudent,
written with bias—with malicious intent
to undermine the public confidence
in justice and the courts. I knew it then—
all he brings out about this testimony
you might have given. It's true I could have called you,
but the case was clear—Romagna was known guilty,
and there was nothing to add. If I've endured
some hours of torture over their attacks
upon my probity—and in this torture
have wandered from my place, wandered perhaps
in mind and body—and found my way to face you—
why, yes, it is so—I know it—I beg of you
say nothing. It's not easy to give up

a fair name after a full half century
of service to a state. It may well rock
the surest reason. Therefore I ask of you
say nothing of this visit.

Garth. I'll say nothing.

Esdras. Nor any of us.

Gaunt. Why, no—for you'd lose, too.
You'd have nothing to gain.

Esdras. Indeed we know it.

Gaunt. I'll remember you kindly. When I've returned,
there may be some mystery made of where I was—
we'll leave it a mystery?

Garth. Anything you say.

Gaunt. Why, now I go with much more peace of mind—
if I can call you friends.

Esdras. We shall be grateful
for silence on your part, Your Honor.

Gaunt. Sir—
if there were any just end to be served
by speaking out, I'd speak! There is none. No—
bear that in mind!

Esdras. We will, Your Honor.

Gaunt. Then—
I'm in some haste. If you can be my guide,
we'll set out now.

Esdras. Yes, surely.

> [*There is a knock at the door. The four look at each other with some apprehension.* MIRIAMNE *rises*]

I'll answer it.

Miriamne. Yes.

> [*She goes into the inner room and closes the door.* ESDRAS *goes to the outer door. The knock is repeated. He opens the door.* MIO *is there*]

Esdras. Yes, sir.

Mio. May I come in?

Esdras. Will you state your business, sir?
It's late—and I'm not at liberty—

Mio. Why, I might say
that I was trying to earn my tuition fees
by peddling magazines. I could say that,
or collecting old newspapers—paying cash—
highest rates—no questions asked—

> [*He looks round sharply*]

Garth. We've nothing to sell.
What do you want?

Mio. Your pardon, gentlemen.
My business is not of an ordinary kind,
and I felt the need of this slight introduction
while I might get my bearings. Your name is Esdras,
or they told me so outside.

Garth. What do you want?

Mio. Is that the name?

Garth. Yes.

Mio. I'll be quick and brief.
I'm the son of a man who died many years ago
for a pay roll robbery in New England. You
should be Garth Esdras, by what I've heard. You have
some knowledge of the crime, if one can believe
what he reads in the public prints, and it might be
that your testimony, if given, would clear my father
of any share in the murder. You may not care
whether he was guilty or not. You may not know.
But I do care—and care deeply, and I've come
to ask you face to face.

Garth. To ask me what?

Mio. What do you know of it?

Esdras. This man Romagna,
did he have a son?

Mio. Yes, sir, this man Romagna,
as you choose to call him, had a son, and I
am that son, and proud.

Esdras. Forgive me.

Mio. Had you known him,
and heard him speak, you'd know why I'm proud,
and why
he was no malefactor.

Esdras. I quite believe you.
If my son can help he will. But at this moment,
as I told you—could you, I wonder, come tomorrow,
at your own hour?

Mio. Yes.

Esdras. By coincidence
    we too of late have had this thing in mind—
    there have been comments printed, and much discussion
    which we could hardly avoid.

Mio. Could you tell me then
    in a word?—What you know—
    is it for him or against him?—
    that's all I need.

Esdras. My son knows nothing.

Garth. No.
    The picture-papers lash themselves to a fury
    over any rumor—make them up when they're short
    of bedroom slops.—This is what happened. I
    had known a few members of a gang one time
    up there—and after the murder they picked me up
    because I looked like someone that was seen
    in what they called the murder car. They held me
    a little while, but they couldn't identify me
    for the most excellent reason I wasn't there
    when the thing occurred. A dozen years later now
    a professor comes across this, and sees red
    and asks why I wasn't called on as a witness
    and yips so loud they syndicate his picture
    in all the rotos. That's all I know about it.
    I wish I could tell you more.

Esdras. Let me say too
    that I have read some words your father said,

and you were a son fortunate in your father,
whatever the verdict of the world.

Mio. There are few
who think so, but it's true, and I thank you. Then—
that's the whole story?

Garth. All I know of it.

Mio. They cover their tracks well, the inner ring
that distributes murder. I came three thousand miles
to this dead end.

Esdras. If he was innocent
and you know him so, believe it, and let the others
believe as they like.

Mio. Will you tell me how a man's
to live, and face his life, if he can't believe
that truth's like a fire,
and will burn through and be seen
though it takes all the years there are?
While I stand up and have breath in my lungs
I shall be one flame of that fire;
it's all the life I have.

Esdras. Then you must live so.
One must live as he can.

Mio. It's the only way
of life my father left me.

Esdras. Yes? Yet it's true
the ground we walk on is impacted down
and hard with blood and bones of those who died

unjustly. There's not one title to land or life,
even your own, but was built on rape and murder,
back a few years. It would take a fire indeed
to burn out all this error.

Mio. Then let it burn down,
all of it!

Esdras. We ask a great deal of the world
at first—then less—and then less.
We ask for truth
and justice. But this truth's a thing unknown
in the lightest, smallest matter—and as for justice,
who has once seen it done? You loved your father,
and I could have loved him, for every word he spoke
in his trial was sweet and tolerant, but the weight
of what men are and have, rests heavy on
the graves of those who lost. They'll not rise again,
and their causes lie there with them.

Gaunt. If you mean to say
that Bartolomeo Romagna was innocent,
you are wrong. He was guilty.
There may have been injustice
from time to time, by regrettable chance, in our courts,
but not in that case, I assure you.

Mio. Oh, you assure me!
You lie in your scrag teeth, whoever you are!
My father was murdered!

Gaunt. Romagna was found guilty
by all due process of law, and given his chance
to prove his innocence.

Mio. What chance? When a court
　panders to mob hysterics, and the jury
　comes in loaded to soak an anarchist
　and a foreigner, it may be due process of law
　but it's also murder!

Gaunt. He should have thought of that
　before he spilled blood.

Mio. He?

Gaunt. Sir, I know too well
　that he was guilty.

Mio. Who are you? How do you know?
　I've searched the records through, the trial and what
　came after, and in all that million words
　I found not one unbiased argument
　to fix the crime on him.

Gaunt. And you yourself,
　were you unprejudiced?

Mio. Who are you?

Esdras. Sir,
　this gentleman is here, as you are here,
　to ask my son, as you have asked, what ground
　there might be for this talk of new evidence
　in your father's case. We gave him the same answer
　we've given you.

Mio. I'm sorry. I'd supposed
　his cause forgotten except by myself. There's still
　a defense committee then?

Gaunt. There may be. I
   am not connected with it.

Esdras. He is my guest,
   and asks to remain unknown.

Mio.

   [*After a pause, looking at Gaunt*]
   The judge at the trial
   was younger, but he had your face. Can it be
   that you're the man?—Yes—Yes.—The jury charge—
   I sat there as a child and heard your voice,
   and watched that Brahminical mouth. I knew even then
   you meant no good to him. And now you're here
   to winnow out truth and justice—the fountain-head
   of the lies that slew him! Are you Judge Gaunt?

Gaunt. I am.

Mio. Then tell me what damnation to what inferno
   would fit the toad that sat in robes and lied
   when he gave the charge, and knew he lied! Judge that,
   and then go to your place in that hell!

Gaunt. I know and have known
   what bitterness can rise against a court
   when it must say, putting aside all weakness,
   that a man's to die. I can forgive you that,
   for you are your father's son, and you think of him
   as a son thinks of his father. Certain laws
   seem cruel in their operation; it's necessary
   that we be cruel to uphold them. This cruelty
   is kindness to those I serve.

Mio. I don't doubt that.
  I know who it is you serve.

Gaunt. Would I have chosen
  to rack myself with other men's despairs,
  stop my ears, harden my heart, and listen only
  to the voice of law and light, if I had hoped
  some private gain for serving? In all my years
  on the bench of a long-established commonwealth
  not once has my decision been in question
  save in this case. Not once before or since.
  For hope of heaven or place on earth, or power
  or gold, no man has had my voice, nor will
  while I still keep the trust that's laid on me
  to sentence and define.

Mio. Then why are you here?

Gaunt. My record's clean. I've kept it so. But suppose
  with the best intent, among the myriad tongues
  that come to testify, I had missed my way
  and followed a perjured tale to a lethal end
  till a man was forsworn to death? Could I rest or sleep
  while there was doubt of this,
  even while there was question in a layman's mind?
  For always, night and day,
  there lies on my brain like a weight, the admonition:
  see truly, let nothing sway you; among all functions
  there's but one godlike, to judge. Then see to it
  you judge as a god would judge, with clarity,
  with truth, with what mercy is found consonant
  with order and law. Without law men are beasts,

and it's a judge's task to lift and hold them
above themselves. Let a judge be once mistaken
or step aside for a friend, and a gap is made
in the dykes that hold back anarchy and chaos,
and leave men bond but free.

Mio. Then the gap's been made,
and you made it.

Gaunt. I feared that too. May you be a judge
sometime, and know in what fear,
through what nights long
in fear, I scanned and verified and compared
the transcripts of the trial.

Mio. Without prejudice,
no doubt. It was never in your mind to prove
that you'd been right.

Gaunt. And conscious of that, too—
that that might be my purpose—watchful of that,
and jealous as his own lawyer of the rights
that should hedge the defendant!
And still I found no error,
shook not one staple of the bolts that linked
the doer to the deed! Still following on
from step to step, I watched all modern comment,
and saw it centered finally on one fact—
Garth Esdras was not called. This is Garth Esdras,
and you have heard him. Would his deposition
have justified a new trial?

Mio. No. It would not.

Gaunt. And there I come, myself. If the man were still
in his cell, and waiting, I'd have no faint excuse
for another hearing.

Mio. I've told you that I read
the trial from beginning to end. Every word you spoke
was balanced carefully to keep the letter
of the law and still convict—convict, by Christ,
if it tore the seven veils! You stand here now
running cascades of casuistry, to prove
to yourself and me that no judge of rank and breeding
could burn a man out of hate! But that's what you did
under all your varnish!

Gaunt. I've sought for evidence,
and you have sought. Have you found it? Can you cite
one fresh word in defence?

Mio. The trial itself
was shot full of legerdemain, prearranged to lead
the jury astray—

Gaunt. Could you prove that?

Mio. Yes!

Gaunt. And if
the jury were led astray, remember it's
the jury, by our Anglo-Saxon custom,
that finds for guilt or innocence. The judge
is powerless in that matter.

Mio. Not you! Your charge
misled the jury more than the evidence,
accepted every biased meaning, distilled
the poison for them!

Gaunt. But if that were so
    I'd be the first, I swear it, to step down
    among all men, and hold out both my hands
    for manacles—yes, publish it in the streets,
    that all I've held most sacred was defiled
    by my own act. A judge's brain becomes
    a delicate instrument to weigh men's lives
    for good and ill—too delicate to bear
    much tampering. If he should push aside
    the weights and throw the beam, and say, this once
    the man is guilty, and I will have it so
    though his mouth cry out from the ground,
    and all the world
    revoke my word, he'd have a short way to go
    to madness. I think you'd find him in the squares,
    stopping the passers-by with arguments,—
    see, I was right, the man was guilty there—
    this was brought in against him, this—and this—
    and I was left no choice! It's no light thing
    when a long life's been dedicate to one end
    to wrench the mind awry!

Mio. By your own thesis
    you should be mad, and no doubt you are.

Gaunt. But my madness
    is only this—that I would fain look back
    on a life well spent—without one stain—one breath
    of stain to flaw the glass—not in men's minds
    nor in my own. I take my God as witness
    I meant to earn that clearness, and believe
    that I have earned it. Yet my name is clouded

with the blackest, fiercest scandal of our age
that's touched a judge. What I can do to wipe
that smutch from my fame I will. I think you know
how deeply I've been hated, for no cause
that I can find there. Can it not be—and I ask this
quite honestly—that the great injustice lies
on your side and not mine? Time and time again
men have come before me perfect in their lives,
loved by all who knew them, loved at home,
gentle, not vicious, yet caught so ripe red-handed
in some dark violence there was no denying
where the onus lay.

Mio. That was not so with my father!

Gaunt. And yet it seemed so to me. To other men
who sat in judgment on him. Can you be sure—
I ask this in humility—that you,
who were touched closest by the tragedy,
may not have lost perspective—may have brooded
day and night on one theme—till your eyes are tranced
and show you one side only?

Mio. I see well enough.

Gaunt. And would that not be part of the malady—
to look quite steadily at the drift of things
but see there what you wish—not what is there—
not what another man to whom the story
was fresh would say is there?

Mio. You think I'm crazy.
Is that what you meant to say?

Gaunt. I've seen it happen
with the best and wisest men. I but ask the question.
I can't speak for you. Is it not true wherever
you walk, through the little town where you knew him
   well,
or flying from it, inland or by the sea,
still walking at your side, and sleeping only
when you too sleep, a shadow not your own
follows, pleading and holding out its hands
to be delivered from shame?

Mio. How you know that
by God I don't know.

Gaunt. Because one spectre haunted you and me—
and haunts you still, but for me it's laid to rest
now that my mind is satisfied. He died
justly and not by error.

   [*A pause*]

Mio.

   [*Stepping forward*]

Do you care to know
you've come so near to death it's miracle
that pulse still beats in your splotchy throat?
Do you know
there's murder in me?

Gaunt. There was murder in your sire,
and it's to be expected! I say he died
justly, and he deserved it!

Mio. Yes, you'd like too well
    to have me kill you! That would prove your case
    and clear your name, and dip my father's name
    in stench forever! You'll not get that from me!
    Go home and die in bed, get it under cover,
    your lux-et-lex putrefaction of the right thing,
    you man that walks like a god!

Gaunt. Have I made you angry
    by coming too near the truth?

Mio. This sets him up,
    this venomous slug, this sets him up in a gown,
    deciding who's to walk above the earth
    and who's to lie beneath! And giving reasons!
    The cobra giving reasons; I'm a god,
    by Buddha, holy and worshipful my fang,
    and can I sink it in!

      [*He pauses, turns as if to go, then sits*]

    This is no good.
    This won't help much.

      [*The* JUDGE *and* ESDRAS *look at each other*]

Gaunt. We should be going.

Esdras. Yes.

      [*They prepare to go*]

    I'll lend you my coat.

Gaunt.

      [*Looking at it with distaste*]

    No, keep it. A little rain
    shouldn't matter to me.

Esdras. It freezes as it falls,
and you've a long way to go.

Gaunt. I'll manage, thank you.

> [GAUNT *and* ESDRAS *go out*, ESDRAS *obsequious, closing the door*]

Garth.

> [*Looking at Mio's back*]

Well?

Mio.

> [*Not moving*]

Let me sit here a moment.

> [GARTH *shrugs his shoulders and goes toward the inner door.* MIRIAMNE *opens it and comes out.* GARTH *looks at her, then at Mio, then lays his fingers on his lips. She nods.* GARTH *goes out.* MIRIAMNE *sits and watches* MIO. *After a little he turns and sees her*]

Mio. How did you come here?

Miriamne. I live here.

Mio. Here?

Miriamne. My name is Esdras. **Garth**
is my brother. The walls are thin.
I heard what was said.

Mio.

> [*Stirring wearily*]

I'm going. This is no place for me.

Miriamne. What place
would be better?

Mio. None. Only it's better to go.
Just to go.

> [*She comes over to him, puts her arm round him and kisses his
> forehead*]

Miriamne. Mio.

Mio. What do you want?
Your kisses burn me—and your arms. Don't offer
what I'm never to have! I can have nothing. They say
they'll cross the void sometime to the other planets
and men will breathe in that air.
Well, I could breathe there,
but not here now. Not on this ball of mud.
I don't want it.

Miriamne. They can take away so little
with all their words. For you're a king among them.
I heard you, and loved your voice.

Mio. I thought I'd fallen
so low there was no further, and now a pit
opens beneath. It was bad enough that he
should have died innocent, but if he were guilty—
then what's my life—what have I left to do—?
The son of a felon—and what they spat on me
was earned—and I'm drenched with the stuff.
Here on my hands
and cheeks, their spittle hanging! I liked my hands
because they were like his. I tell you I've lived

by his innocence, lived to see it flash
and blind them all—

Miriamne. Never believe them, Mio,
never.

[*She looks toward the inner door*]

Mio. But it was truth I wanted, truth—
not the lies you'd tell yourself, or tell a woman,
or a woman tells you! The judge with his cobra mouth
may have spat truth—and I may be mad! For me—
your hands are too clean to touch me. I'm to have
the scraps from hotel kitchens—and instead of love
those mottled bodies that hitch themselves through alleys
to sell for dimes or nickels. Go, keep yourself chaste
for the baker bridegroom—baker and son of a baker,
let him get his baker's dozen on you!

Miriamne. No—
say once you love me—say it once; I'll never
ask to hear it twice, nor for any kindness,
and you shall take all I have!

[GARTH *opens the inner door and comes out*]

Garth. I interrupt
a love scene, I believe. We can do without
your adolescent mawkishness.

[*To Miriamne*]

You're a child.
You'll both remember that.

Miriamne. I've said nothing to harm you—
and will say nothing.

Garth. You're my sister, though,
and I take a certain interest in you. Where
have you two met?

Miriamne. We danced together.

Garth. Then
the dance is over, I think.

Miriamne. I've always loved you
and tried to help you, Garth. And you've been kind.
Don't spoil it now.

Garth. Spoil it how?

Miriamne. Because I love him.
I didn't know it would happen. We danced together.
And the world's all changed. I see you through a mist,
and our father, too. If you brought this to nothing
I'd want to die.

Garth.

   [*To Mio*]

You'd better go.

Mio. Yes, I know.

   [*He rises. There is a trembling knock at the door.* MIRIAMNE
       goes to it. The HOBO *is there shivering*]

Hobo. Miss, could I sleep under the pipes tonight, miss?
Could I, please?

Miriamne. I think—not tonight.

Hobo. There won't be any more nights—
if I don't get warm, miss.

Miriamne. Come in.

[*The* Hobo *comes in, looks round deprecatingly, then goes to a corner beneath a huge heating pipe, which he crawls under as if he'd been there before*]

Hobo. Yes, miss, thank you.

Garth. Must we put up with that?

Miriamne. Father let him sleep there—
last winter.

Garth. Yes, God, yes.

Mio. Well, good night.

Miriamne. Where will you go?

Mio. Yes, where? As if it mattered.

Garth. Oh, sleep here, too.
We'll have a row of you under the pipes.

Mio. No, thanks.

Miriamne. Mio, I've saved a little money. It's only
some pennies, but you must take it.

[*She shakes some coins out of a box into her hand*]

Mio. No, thanks.

Miriamne. And I love you.
You've never said you love me.

Mio. Why wouldn't I love you
when you're clean and sweet,
and I've seen nothing sweet or clean

this last ten years? I love you. I leave you that
for what good it may do you. It's none to me.

Miriamne. Then kiss me.

Mio.

    [*Looking at Garth*]

With that scowling over us? No.
When it rains, some spring
on the planet Mercury, where the spring comes often,
I'll meet you there, let's say. We'll wait for that.
It may be some time till then.

    [*The outside door opens and* Esdras *enters with* Judge Gaunt,
    then, after a slight interval, Trock *follows.* Trock
    surveys the interior and its occupants one by one, care-
    fully]

Trock. I wouldn't want to cause you inconvenience,
any of you, and especially the Judge.
I think you know that. You've all got things to do—
trains to catch, and so on. But trains can wait.
Hell, nearly anything can wait, you'll find,
only I can't. I'm the only one that can't
because I've got no time. Who's all this here?
Who's that?

    [*He points to the Hobo*]

Esdras. He's a poor half-wit, sir,
that sometimes sleeps there.

Trock. Come out. I say come out,
whoever you are.

    [*The* Hobo *stirs and looks up*]

Yes, I mean you. Come out.

[*The* HOBO *emerges*]

What's your name?

Hobo. They mostly call me Oke.

Trock. What do you know?

Hobo. No, sir.

Trock. Where are you from?

Hobo. I got a piece of bread.

 [*He brings it out, trembling*]

Trock. Get back in there!

 [*The* HOBO *crawls back into his corner*]

Maybe you want to know why I'm doing this.
Well, I've been robbed, that's why—
robbed five or six times;
the police can't find a thing—so I'm out for myself—
if you want to know.

 [*To Mio*]

 Who are you?

Mio. Oh, I'm a half-wit,
came in here by mistake. The difference is
I've got no piece of bread.

Trock. What's your name?

Mio. My name?
Theophrastus Such. That's respectable.
You'll find it all the way from here to the coast

on the best police blotters.
Only the truth is we're a little touched in the head,
Oke and me. You'd better ask somebody else.

Trock. Who is he?

Esdras. His name's Romagna. He's the son.

Trock. Then what's he doing here? You said you were on
the level.

Garth. He just walked in. On account of the stuff in the
papers. We didn't ask him.

Trock. God, we are a gathering. Now if we had Shadow
we'd be all here, huh? Only I guess we won't see Shadow.
No, that's too much to ask.

Mio. Who's Shadow?

Trock. Now you're putting questions. Shadow was just
nobody, you see. He blew away. It might happen to
anyone.

[*He looks at Garth*]

Yes, anyone at all.

Mio. Why do you keep your hand in your pocket, friend?

Trock. Because I'm cold, punk. Because I've been outside
and it's cold as the tomb of Christ.

[*To Garth*]

Listen, there's a car waiting up at the street to take the
Judge home. We'll take him to the car.

Garth. That's not necessary.

Esdras. No.

Trock. I say it is, see? You wouldn't want to let the Judge walk, would you? The Judge is going to ride where he's going, with a couple of chauffeurs, and everything done in style. Don't you worry about the Judge. He'll be taken care of. For good.

Garth. I want no hand in it.

Trock. Anything happens to me happens to you too, musician.

Garth. I know that.

Trock. Keep your mouth out of it then. And you'd better keep the punk here tonight, just for luck.

> [*He turns toward the door. There is a brilliant lightning flash through the windows, followed slowly by dying thunder.* TROCK *opens the door. The rain begins to pour in sheets*]

Jesus, somebody tipped it over again!

> [*A cough racks him*]

Wait till it's over. It takes ten days off me every time I step into it.

> [*He closes the door*]

Sit down and wait.

> [*Lightning flashes again. The thunder is fainter.* ESDRAS, GARTH *and the* JUDGE *sit down*]

Gaunt. We were born too early. Even you who are young
are not of the elect. In a hundred years
man will put his finger on life itself, and then
he will live as long as he likes. For you and me

we shall die soon—one day, one year more or less, when or where, it's no matter. It's what we call an indeterminate sentence. I'm hungry.

[GARTH *looks at Miriamne*]

Miriamne. There was nothing left tonight.

Hobo. I've got a piece of bread.

[*He breaks his bread in two and hands half to the Judge*]

Gaunt. I thank you, sir.

[*He eats*]

This is not good bread.

[*He rises*]

Sir, I am used to other company. Not better, perhaps, but their clothes were different. These are what it's the fashion to call the underprivileged.

Trock. Oh, hell!

[*He turns toward the door*]

Mio.

[*To Trock*]

It would seem that you and the Judge know each other.

[TROCK *faces him*]

Trock. I've been around.

Mio. Maybe you've met before.

Trock. Maybe we have.

Mio. Will you tell me where?

Trock. How long do you want to live?

Mio. How long? Oh, I've got big ideas about that.

Trock. I thought so. Well, so far I've got nothing against you but your name, see? You keep it that way.

[*He opens the door. The rain still falls in torrents. He closes the door. As he turns from it, it opens again, and* SHADOW, *white, bloodstained and dripping, stands in the doorway.* GARTH *rises.* TROCK *turns*]

Gaunt.

[*To the Hobo*]

Yet if one were careful of his health, ate sparingly, drank not at all, used himself wisely, it might be that even an old man could live to touch immortality. They may come on the secret sooner than we dare hope. You see? It does no harm to try.

Trock.

[*Backing away from Shadow*]

By God, he's out of his grave!

Shadow.

[*Leaning against the doorway, holding a gun in his hands*]

Keep your hands where they belong, Trock.
You know me.

Trock. Don't! Don't! I had nothing to do with it!

[*He backs to the opposite wall*]

Shadow. You said the doctor gave you six months to live—
well, I don't give you that much. That's what you had,
six months, and so you start bumping off your friends
to make sure of your damn six months. I got it from you.
I know where I got it.
Because I wouldn't give it to the Judge.
So he wouldn't talk.

Trock. Honest to God—

Shadow. What God?
The one that let you put three holes in me
when I was your friend? Well, He let me get up again
and walk till I could find you. That's as far as I get,
but I got there, by God! And I can hear you
even if I can't see!

    [*He takes a staggering step forward*]

  A man needs blood
to keep going.—I got this far.—And now I can't see!
It runs out too fast—too fast—
when you've got three slugs
clean through you.
Show me where he is, you fools! He's here!
I got here!

    [*He drops the gun*]

  Help me! Help me! Oh, God! Oh, God!
I'm going to die! Where does a man lie down?
I want to lie down!

    [MIRIAMNE *starts toward Shadow.* GARTH *and* ESDRAS *help
him into the next room,* MIRIAMNE *following.* TROCK
squats in his corner, breathing hard, looking at the door.

Mio stands, watching Trock. Garth returns, wiping his hand with a handkerchief. Mio picks up and pockets the gun. Miriamne comes back and leans against the door jamb]

Gaunt. You will hear it said that an old man makes a good judge, being calm, clear-eyed, without passion. But this is not true. Only the young love truth and justice. The old are savage, wary, violent, swayed by maniac desires, cynical of friendship or love, open to bribery and the temptations of lust, corrupt and dastardly to the heart. I know these old men. What have they left to believe, what have they left to lose? Whorers of daughters, lickers of girls' shoes, contrivers of nastiness in the night, purveyors of perversion, worshippers of possession! Death is the only radical. He comes late, but he comes at last to put away the old men and give the young their places. It was time.

[*He leers*]

Here's one I heard yesterday:
    Marmaduke behind the barn
      got his sister in a fix;
    he says damn instead of darn;
      ain't he cute? He's only six!

The Hobo. He, he, he!

Gaunt.

    And the hoot-owl hoots all night,
      and the cuckoo cooks all day,
    and what with a minimum grace of God
      we pass the time away.

The Hobo. He, he, he—I got ya!

[*He makes a sign with his thumb*]

Gaunt.

[*Sings*]

> And he led her all around
> and he laid her on the ground
> and he ruffled up the feathers of her
> cuckoo's nest!

Hobo. Ho, ho, ho!

Gaunt. I am not taken with the way you laugh. You should cultivate restraint.

[ESDRAS *reënters*]

Trock. Shut the door.

Esdras. He won't come back again.

Trock. I want the door shut! He was dead, I tell you!

[*Esdras closes the door*]

And Romagna was dead, too, once! Can't they keep a man under ground?

Mio. No. No more! They don't stay under ground any more, and they don't stay under water! Why did you have him killed?

Trock. Stay away from me! I know you!

Mio. Who am I, then?

Trock. I know you, damn you! Your name's Romagna!

Mio. Yes! And Romagna was dead, too, and Shadow was dead, but the time's come when you can't keep them down, these dead men! They won't stay down! They come in with their heads shot off and their entrails dragging! Hundreds of them! One by one—all you ever had killed! Watch the door! See!—It moves!

Trock.

[*Looking, fascinated, at the door*]

Let me out of here!

[*He tries to rise*]

Mio.

[*The gun in his hand*]

Oh, no! You'll sit there and wait for them! One by one they'll come through that door, pulling their heads out of the gunny-sacks where you tied them—glauming over you with their rotten hands! They'll see without eyes and crawl over you—Shadow and the paymaster and all the rest of them—putrescent bones without eyes! Now! Look! Look! For I'm first among them!

Trock. I've done for better men than you! And I'll do for you!

Gaunt.

[*Rapping on the table*]

Order, gentlemen, order! The witness will remember that a certain decorum is essential in the court-room!

Mio. By God, he'll answer me!

Gaunt.

[*Thundering*]

Silence! Silence! Let me remind you of courtesy toward
the witness! What case is this you try?

Mio. The case of the state against Bartolomeo Romagna
for the murder of the paymaster!

Gaunt. Sir, that was disposed of long ago!

Mio. Never disposed of, never, not while I live!

Gaunt. Then we'll have done with it now! I deny the
appeal! I have denied the appeal before and I do so
again!

Hobo. He, he!—He thinks he's in the moving pictures!

[*A flash of lightning*]

Gaunt. Who set that flash! Bailiff, clear the court! This is
not Flemington, gentlemen! We are not conducting this
case to make a journalistic holiday!

[*The thunder rumbles faintly.* GARTH *opens the outside door
and faces a solid wall of rain*]

Stop that man! He's one of the defendants!

[GARTH *closes the door*]

Mio. Then put him on the stand!

Garth. What do you think you're doing?

Mio. Have you any objection?

Gaunt. The objection is not sustained. We will hear the
new evidence. Call your witness.

Mio. Garth Esdras!

Gaunt. He will take the stand!

Garth. If you want me to say what I said before I'll say it!

Mio. Call Trock Estrella then!

Gaunt. Trock Estrella to the stand!

Trock. No, by God!

Mio. Call Shadow, then! He'll talk! You thought he was
    dead, but he'll get up again and talk!

Trock.

  [*Screaming*]

  What do you want of me?

Mio. You killed the paymaster! You!

Trock. You lie! It was Shadow killed him!

Mio. And now I know! Now I know!

Gaunt. Again I remind you of courtesy toward the witness!

Mio. I know them now!
    Let me remind you of courtesy toward the dead!
    He says that Shadow killed him! If Shadow were here
    he'd say it was Trock! There were three men involved
    in the new version of the crime for which
    my father died! Shadow and Trock Estrella
    as principals in the murder—Garth as witness!—
    Why are they here together?—and you—the Judge—
    why are you here? Why, because you were all afraid

and you drew together out of that fear to arrange
a story you could tell! And Trock killed Shadow
and meant to kill the Judge out of that same fear—
to keep them quiet! This is the thing I've hunted
over the earth to find out, and I'd be blind
indeed if I missed it now!

   [To Gaunt]

   You heard what he said:
It was Shadow killed him! Now let the night conspire
with the sperm of hell! It's plain beyond denial
even to this fox of justice—and all his words
are curses on the wind! You lied! You lied!
You knew this too!

Gaunt.

   [Low]

Let me go. Let me go!

Mio. Then why
   did you let my father die?

Gaunt. Suppose it known,
   but there are things a judge must not believe
   though they should head and fester underneath
   and press in on his brain. Justice once rendered
   in a clear burst of anger, righteously,
   upon a very common laborer,
   confessed an anarchist, the verdict found
   and the precise machinery of law
   invoked to know him guilty—think what furor
   would rock the state if the court then flatly said;

all this was lies—must be reversed? It's better,
as any judge can tell you, in such cases,
holding the common good to be worth more
than small injustice, to let the record stand,
let one man die. For justice, in the main,
is governed by opinion. Communities
will have what they will have, and it's quite as well,
after all, to be rid of anarchists. Our rights
as citizens can be maintained as rights
only while we are held to be the peers
of those who live about us. A vendor of fish
is not protected as a man might be
who kept a market. I own I've sometimes wished
this was not so, but it is. The man you defend
was unfortunate—and his misfortune bore
almost as heavily on me.—I'm broken—
broken across. You're much too young to know
how bitter it is when a worn connection chars
and you can't remember—can't remember.

    [*He steps forward*]
    You
will not repeat this? It will go no further?

Mio. No.
No further than the moon takes the tides—no further
than the news went when he died—
when you found him guilty
and they flashed that round the earth. Wherever men
still breathe and think, and know what's done to them
by the powers above, they'll know. That's all I ask.
That'll be enough.

[TROCK *has risen and looks darkly at Mio*]

Gaunt. Thank you. For I've said some things
a judge should never say.

Trock. Go right on talking.
Both of you. It won't get far, I guess.

Mio. Oh, you'll see to that?

Trock. I'll see to it. Me and some others.
Maybe I lost my grip there just for a minute.
That's all right.

Mio. Then see to it! Let it rain!
What can you do to me now when the night's on fire
with this thing I know? Now I could almost wish
there was a god somewhere—I could almost think
there was a god—and he somehow brought me here
and set you down before me here in the rain
where I could wring this out of you! For it's said,
and I've heard it, and I'm free! He was as I thought him,
true and noble and upright, even when he went
to a death contrived because he was as he was
and not your kind! Let it rain! Let the night speak fire
and the city go out with the tide, for he was a man
and I know you now, and I have my day!

> [*There is a heavy knock at the outside door.* MIRIAMNE *opens
> it, at a glance from* GARTH. *The* POLICEMAN *is there in
> oilskins*]

Policeman. Evening.

> [*He steps in, followed by a* SERGEANT, *similarly dressed*]

We're looking for someone
might be here. Seen an old man around
acting a little off?

[*To Esdras*]

You know the one
I mean. You saw him out there. Jeez! You've got
a funny crowd here!

[*He looks round. The* Hobo *shrinks into his corner*]

That's the one I saw.
What do you think?

Sergeant. That's him. You mean to say
you didn't know him by his pictures?

[*He goes to Gaunt*]

Come on, old man.
You're going home.

Gaunt. Yes, sir. I've lost my way.
I think I've lost my way.

Sergeant. I'll say you have.
About three hundred miles. Now don't you worry.
We'll get you back.

Gaunt. I'm a person of some rank
in my own city.

Sergeant. We know that. One look at you
and we'd know that.

Gaunt. Yes, sir.

Policeman. If it isn't Trock!
Trock Estrella. How are you, Trock?

Trock. Pretty good,
Thanks.

Policeman. Got out yesterday again, I hear?

Trock. That's right.

Sergeant. Hi'ye, Trock?

Trock. O.K.

Sergeant. You know we got orders
to watch you pretty close. Be good now, baby,
or back you go. Don't try to pull anything,
not in my district.

Trock. No, sir.

Sergeant. No bumping off.
If you want my advice quit carrying a gun.
Try earning your living for once.

Trock. Yeah.

Sergeant. That's an idea.
Because if we find any stiffs on the river bank
we'll know who to look for.

Mio. Then look in the other room!
I accuse that man of murder! Trock Estrella!
He's a murderer!

Policeman. Hello. I remember you.

Sergeant. Well, what murder?

Mio. It was Trock Estrella
that robbed the pay roll thirteen years ago
and did the killing my father died for! You know
the Romagna case! Romagna was innocent,
and Trock Estrella guilty

Sergeant.

[*Disgusted*]

Oh, what the hell!
That's old stuff—the Romagna case.

Policeman. Hey, Sarge!

[*The* SERGEANT *and* POLICEMAN *come closer together*]

The boy's a professional kidder. He took me over
about half an hour ago. He kids the police
and then ducks out!

Sergeant. Oh, yeah?

Mio. I'm not kidding now.
You'll find a dead man there in the next room
and Estrella killed him!

Sergeant. Thirteen years ago?
And nobody smelled him yet?

Mio.

[*Pointing*]

I accuse this man
of two murders! He killed the paymaster long ago
and had Shadow killed tonight. Look, look for yourself!
He's there all right!

Policeman. Look boy. You stood out there
  and put the booby sign on the dumb police
  because they're fresh out of Ireland. Don't try it twice.

Sergeant.

  [*To Garth*]

  Any corpses here?

Garth. Not that I know of.

Sergeant. I thought so.

  [MIO *looks at Miriamne*]
  [*To Mio*]

  Think up a better one.

Mio. Have I got to drag him
  out here where you can see him?

  [*He goes toward the inner door*]

  Can't you scent a murder
  when it's under your nose? Look in!

Miriamne. No, no—there's no one—there's no one there!

Sergeant.

  [*Looking at Miriamne*]

  Take a look inside.

Policeman. Yes, sir.

  [*He goes into the inside room. The* SERGEANT *goes up to the
  door. The* POLICEMAN *returns*]

  He's kidding, Sarge. If there's a cadaver
  in here I don't see it.

Mio. You're blind then!

[*He goes into the room, the* SERGEANT *following him*]

Sergeant. What do you mean?

[*He comes out,* MIO *following him*]

When you make a charge of murder it's better to have
the corpus delicti, son. You're the kind puts in
fire alarms to see the engine!

Mio. By God, he was there!
He went in there to die.

Sergeant. I'll bet he did.
And I'm Haile Selassie's aunt! What's your name?

Mio. Romagna.

[*To Garth*]

What have you done with him?

Garth. I don't know what you mean.

Sergeant.

[*To Garth*]

What's he talking about?

Garth. I wish I could tell you.
I don't know.

Sergeant. He must have seen something.

Policeman. He's got
the Romagna case on the brain. You watch yourself,
chump, or you'll get run in.

Mio. Then they're in it together!
All of them!

   [*To Miriamne*]

     Yes, and you!

Garth. He's nuts, I say.

Miriamne.

   [*Gently*]

  You have dreamed something—isn't it true?
You've dreamed—
But truly, there was no one—

   [*Mio looks at her comprehendingly*]

Mio. You want me to say it.

   [*He pauses*]

  Yes, by God, I was dreaming.

Sergeant.

   [*To Policeman*]

  I guess you're right.
We'd better be going. Haven't you got a coat?

Gaunt. No, sir.

Sergeant. I guess I'll have to lend you mine.

   [*He puts his oilskins on Gaunt*]

  Come on, now. It's getting late.

   [Gaunt, *the* Policeman *and the* Sergeant *go out*]

Trock. They're welcome to him.
His fuse is damp. Where is that walking fool
with the three slugs in him?

Esdras. He fell in the hall beyond
and we left him there.

Trock. That's lucky for some of us. Is he out this time
or is he still butting around?

Esdras. He's dead.

Trock. That's perfect.

> [*To Mio*]

Don't try using your firearms, amigo baby,
the Sarge is outside.

> [*He turns to go*]

Better ship that carrion
back in the river! The one that walks when he's dead;
maybe he'll walk the distance for you.

Garth. Coming back?

Trock. Well, if I come back,
you'll see me. If I don't, you won't. Let the punk
go far as he likes. Turn him loose and let him go.
And may you all rot in hell.

> [*He pulls his coat around him and goes to the left.* Miriamne
> *climbs up to look out a window*]

Miriamne. He's climbing up to the street,
along the bridgehead.

> [*She turns*]

Quick, Mio! It's safe now! Quick!

Garth. Let him do as he likes.

Miriamne. What do you mean? Garth! He means to kill
him!
You know that!

Garth. I've no doubt Master Romagna
can run his own campaign.

Miriamne. But he'll be killed!

Mio. Why did you lie about Shadow?

> [*There is a pause.* GARTH *shrugs, walks across the room, and
> sits*]

You were one of the gang!

Garth. I can take a death if I have to! Go tell your story,
only watch your step, for I warn you, Trock's out gunning
and you may not walk very far. Oh, I could defend it
but it's hardly worth while.
If they get Trock they get me too.
Go tell them. You owe me nothing.

Esdras. This Trock you saw,
no one defends him. He's earned his death so often
there's nobody to regret it. But his crime,
his same crime that has dogged you, dogged us down
from what little we had, to live here among the drains,
where the waterbugs break out like a scrofula
on what we eat—and if there's lower to go
we'll go there when you've told your story. And more
that I haven't heart to speak—

Mio.

> [*To Garth*]
> My father died

in your place. And you could have saved him!
You were one of the gang!

Garth. Why, there you are.
You certainly owe me nothing.

Miriamne.

[*Moaning*]

I want to die.
I want to go away.

Mio. Yes, and you lied!
And trapped me into it!

Miriamne. But Mio, he's my brother.
I couldn't give them my brother.

Mio. No. You couldn't.
You were quite right. The gods were damned ironic
tonight, and they've worked it out.

Esdras. What will be changed
if it comes to trial again? More blood poured out
to a mythical justice, but your father lying still
where he lies now.

Mio. The bright, ironical gods!
What fun they have in heaven! When a man prays hard
for any gift, they give it, and then one more
to boot that makes it useless.

[*To Miriamne*]

You might have picked
some other stranger to dance with!

Miriamne. I know.

Mio. Or chosen
some other evening to sit outside in the rain.
But no, it had to be this. All my life long
I've wanted only one thing, to say to the world
and prove it: the man you killed was clean and true
and full of love as the twelve-year-old that stood
and taught in the temple. I can say that now
and give my proofs—and now you stick a girl's face
between me and the rites I've sworn the dead
shall have of me! You ask too much! Your brother
can take his chance! He was ready enough to let
an innocent man take certainty for him
to pay for the years he's had. That parts us, then,
but we're parted anyway, by the same dark wind
that blew us together. I shall say what I have to say.

[*He steps back*]

And I'm not welcome here.

Miriamne. But don't go now! You've stayed
too long! He'll be waiting!

Mio. Well, is this any safer?
Let the winds blow, the four winds of the world,
and take us to the four winds.

[*The three are silent before him. He turns and goes out*]

CURTAIN

WINTERSET
ACT THREE

ACT THREE

SCENE: *The river bank outside the tenement, a little before the close
of the previous act. The rain still falls through the street lamps.
The* TWO NATTY YOUNG MEN IN SERGE AND GRAY *are leaning
against the masonry in a ray of light, concentrating on a game
of chance. Each holds in his hand a packet of ten or fifteen crisp
bills. They compare the numbers on the top notes and immedi-
ately a bill changes hands. This goes on with varying fortune
until the tide begins to run toward the* 1ST GUNMAN, *who has
accumulated nearly the whole supply. They play on in complete
silence, evidently not wishing to make any noise. Occasionally
they raise their heads slightly to look carefully about. Luck
begins to favor the* 2ND GUNMAN, *and the notes come his way.
Neither evinces the slightest interest in how the game goes. They
merely play on, bored, half-absorbed. There is a slight noise at
the tenement door. They put the bills away and watch.* TROCK
*comes out, pulls the door shut and comes over to them. He says
a few words too low to be heard, and without changing expression
the* YOUNG MEN *saunter toward the right.* TROCK *goes out to
the left, and the* 2ND PLAYER, *catching that out of the corner of
his eye, lingers in a glimmer of light to go on with the game.
The* 1ST, *with an eye on the tenement door, begins to play without ado, and the bills again shift back and forth, then concen-
trate in the hands of the* 1ST GUNMAN. *The* 2ND *shrugs his
shoulders, searches his pockets, finds one bill, and playing with
it begins to win heavily. They hear the door opening, and
putting the notes away, slip out in front of the rock.* MIO
*emerges, closes the door, looks round him and walks to the left.
Near the corner of the tenement he pauses, reaches out his hand
to try the rain, looks up toward the street, and stands uncertainly a moment. He returns and leans against the tenement
wall.* MIRIAMNE *comes out.* MIO *continues to look off into
space as if unaware of her. She looks away.*

Mio. This rather takes one off his high horse.—What I

113

mean, tough weather for a hegira. You see, this is my sleeping suit, and if I get it wet—basta!

Miriamne. If you could only hide here.

Mio. Hide?

Miriamne. Lucia would take you in. The street-piano man.

Mio. At the moment I'm afflicted with claustrophobia. I prefer to die in the open, seeking air.

Miriamne. But you could stay there till daylight.

Mio. You're concerned about me.

Miriamne. Shall I ask him?

Mio. No. On the other hand there's a certain reason in your concern. I looked up the street and our old friend Trock hunches patiently under the warehouse eaves.

Miriamne. I was sure of that.

Mio. And here I am, a young man on a cold night, waiting the end of the rain. Being read my lesson by a boy, a blind boy—you know the one I mean. Knee-deep in the salt-marsh, Miriamne, bitten from within, fought.

Miriamne. Wouldn't it be better if you came back in the house?

Mio. You forget my claustrophobia.

Miriamne. Let me walk with you, then. Please. If I stay beside you he wouldn't dare.

Mio. And then again he might.—We don't speak the same language, Miriamne.

Miriamne. I betrayed you. Forgive me.

Mio. I wish I knew this region. There's probably a path along the bank.

Miriamne. Yes. Shadow went that way.

Mio. That's true, too. So here I am, a young man on a wet night, and blind in my weather eye. Stay and talk to me.

Miriamne. If it happens—it's my fault.

Mio. Not at all, sweet. You warned me to keep away. But I would have it. Now I have to find a way out. It's like a chess game. If you think long enough there's always a way out.—For one or the other.—I wonder why white always wins and black always loses in the problems. White to move and mate in three moves. But what if white were to lose—ah, what then? Why, in that case, obviously black would be white and white would be black.—As it often is.—As we often are.—Might makes white. Losers turn black. Do you think I'd have time to draw a gun?

Miriamne. No.

Mio. I'm a fair shot. Also I'm fair game.

> [*The door of the tenement opens and* GARTH *comes out to look about quickly. Seeing only Mio and Miriamne he goes in and comes out again almost immediately carrying one end of a door on which a body lies covered with a cloth. The* HOBO *carries the other end. They go out to the right with their burden*]

This is the burial of Shadow, then;
feet first he dips, and leaves the haunts of men.

Let us make mourn for Shadow, wetly lying,
in elegiac stanzas and sweet crying.
Be gentle with him, little cold waves and fishes;
nibble him not, respect his skin and tissues—

Miriamne. Must you say such things?

Mio. My dear, some requiem is fitting over the dead, even
for Shadow. But the last rhyme was bad.

Whittle him not, respect his dying wishes.

That's better. And then to conclude:

His aromatic virtues, slowly rising
will circumnamb the isle, beyond disguising.
He clung to life beyond the wont of men.
Time and his silence drink us all. Amen.

How I hate these identicals. The French allow them, but
the French have no principles anyway. You know, Miriamne, there's really nothing mysterious about human
life. It's purely mechanical, like an electric appliance.
Stop the engine that runs the generator and the current's
broken. When we think the brain gives off a small electric discharge—quite measurable, and constant within
limits. But that's not what makes your hair stand up
when frightened.

Miriamne. I think it's a mystery.

Mio. Human life? We'll have to wear veils if we're to keep
it a mystery much longer. Now if Shadow and I were
made up into sausages we'd probably make very good
sausages.

Miriamne. Don't—

Mio. I'm sorry. I speak from a high place, far off, long ago,
looking down. The cortège returns.

> [GARTH *and the* HOBO *return, carrying the door, the cloth lying
> loosely over it*]

I hope you placed an obol in his mouth to pay the ferry-
man? Even among the Greeks a little money was prerequisite to Elysium.

> [GARTH *and the* HOBO *go inside, silent*]

No? It's grim to think of Shadow lingering among lesser
shades on the hither side. For lack of a small gratuity

> [ESDRAS *comes out the open door and closes it behind him*]

Esdras. You must wait here, Mio, or go inside. I know
you don't trust me, and I haven't earned your trust
You're young enough to seek truth—
and there is no truth;
and I know that—
but I shall call the police and see that you
get safely off.

Mio. It's a little late for that.

Esdras. I shall try.

Mio. And your terms? For I daresay you make terms?

Esdras. No.

Mio. Then let me remind you what will happen.
The police will ask some questions.
When they're answered

they'll ask more, and before they're done with it
your son will be implicated.

Esdras. Must he be?

Mio. I shall not keep quiet.

[*A pause*]

Esdras. Still, I'll go.

Mio. I don't ask help, remember. I make no truce.
He's not on my conscience, and I'm not on yours.

Esdras. But you
could make it easier, so easily.
He's my only son. Let him live.

Mio. His chance of survival's
better than mine, I'd say.

Esdras. I'll go.

Mio. I don't urge it.

Esdras. No. I put my son's life in your hands.
When you're gone,
that may come to your mind.

Mio. Don't count on it.

Esdras. Oh,
I count on nothing.

[*He turns to go.* MIRIAMNE *runs over to him and silently
kisses his hands*]

Not mine, not mine, my daughter!
They're guilty hands.

[*He goes out left.* GARTH'S *violin is heard within*]

Mio. There was a war in heaven
  once, all the angels on one side, and all
  the devils on the other, and since that time
  disputes have raged among the learned, concerning
  whether the demons won, or the angels. Maybe
  the angels won, after all.

Miriamne. And again, perhaps
  there are no demons or angels.

Mio. Oh, there are none.
  But I could love your father.

Miriamne. I love him. You see,
  he's afraid because he's old. The less one has
  to lose the more he's afraid.

Mio. Suppose one had
  only a short stub end of life, or held
  a flashlight with the batteries run down
  till the bulb was dim, and knew that he could live
  while the glow lasted. Or suppose one knew
  that while he stood in a little shelter of time
  under a bridgehead, say, he could live, and then,
  from then on, nothing. Then to lie and turn
  with the earth and sun, and regard them not in the least
  when the bulb was extinguished or he stepped beyond
  his circle into the cold? How would he live
  that last dim quarter-hour, before he went,
  minus all recollection, to grow in grass
  between cobblestones?

Miriamne. Let me put my arms round you, Mio.
  Then if anything comes, it's for me, too.
    [*She puts both arms round him*]

Mio. Only suppose
this circle's charmed! To be safe until he steps
from this lighted space into dark! Time pauses here
and high eternity grows in one quarter-hour
in which to live.

Miriamne. Let me see if anyone's there—
there in the shadows.

> [*She looks toward the right*]

Mio. It might blast our eternity—
blow it to bits. No, don't go. This is forever,
here where we stand. And I ask you, Miriamne,
how does one spend a forever?

Miriamne. You're frightened?

Mio. Yes.
So much that time stands still.

Miriamne. Why didn't I speak—
tell them—when the officers were here? I failed you
in that one moment!

Mio. His life for mine? Oh, no.
I wouldn't want it, and you couldn't give it.
And if I should go on living we're cut apart
by that brother of yours.

Miriamne. Are we?

Mio. Well, think about it.
A body lies between us, buried in quicklime.
Your allegiance is on the other side of that grave
and not to me.

Miriamne. No, Mio! Mio, I love you!

Mio. I love you, too, but in case my life went on
beyond that barrier of dark—then Garth
would run his risk of dying.

Miriamne. He's punished, Mio.
His life's been torment to him. Let him go,
for my sake, Mio.

Mio. I wish I could. I wish
I'd never seen him—or you. I've steeped too long
in this thing. It's in my teeth and bones. I can't
let go or forget. And I'll not add my lie
to the lies that cumber his ground. We live our days
in a storm of lies that drifts the truth too deep
for path or shovel; but I've set my foot on a truth
for once, and I'll trail it down!

    [*A silence.* Miriamne *looks out to the right*]

Miriamne. There's someone there—
I heard—

    [Carr *comes in from the right*]

Mio. It's Carr.

Carr. That's right. No doubt about it.
Excuse me.

Mio. Glad to see you. This is Miriamne.
Carr's a friend of mine.

Carr. You're better employed
than when I saw you last.

Mio. Bow to the gentleman,
  Miriamne. That's meant for you.

Miriamne. Thank you, I'm sure.
  Should I leave you, Mio? You want to talk?

Mio. Oh, no,
  we've done our talking.

Miriamne. But—

Carr. I'm the one's out of place—
  I wandered back because I got worried about you,
  that's the truth.—Oh—those two fellows with the hats
  down this way, you know, the ones that ran
  after we heard the shooting—they're back again,
  lingering or malingering down the bank,
  revisiting the crime, I guess. They may
  mean well.

Mio. I'll try to avoid them.

Carr. I didn't care
  for the way they looked at me.—No luck, I suppose,
  with that case history? The investigation
  you had on hand?

Mio. I can't say. By the way,
  the stiff that fell in the water and we saw swirling
  down the eddy, he came trudging up, later on,
  long enough to tell his name. His name was Shadow,
  but he's back in the water now. It's all in an evening.
  These things happen here.

Carr. Good God!

Mio. I know.
I wouldn't believe it if you told it.

Carr. But—
the man was alive?

Mio. Oh, not for long! He's dunked
for good this time. That's all that's happened.

Carr. Well,
if you don't need me—

Miriamne. You had a message to send—
have you forgotten—?

Mio. I?—Yes, I had a message—
but I won't send it—not now.

Miriamne. Then I will—!

Mio. No.
Let it go the way it is! It's all arranged
another way. You've been a good scout, Carr,
the best I ever knew on the road.

Carr. That sounds
like making your will.

Mio. Not yet, but when I do
I've thought of something to leave you. It's the view
of Mt. Rainier from the Seattle jail,
snow over cloud. And the rusty chain in my pocket
from a pair of handcuffs my father wore. That's all
the worldly goods I'm seized of.

Carr. Look, Mio—hell—
if you're in trouble—

Mio. I'm not. Not at all. I have
a genius that attends me where I go,
and guards me now. I'm fine.

Carr. Well, that's good news.
He'll have his work cut out.

Mio. Oh, he's a genius.

Carr. I'll see you then.
I'll be at the Grand Street place. I'm lucky tonight,
and I can pay. I could even pay for two.

Mio. Thanks, I may take you up.

Carr. Good night.

Mio. Right, Carr.

Carr.

   [*To Miriamne*]

Good night.

Miriamne.

   [*After a pause*]

Good night.

   [CARR *goes out to the left*]

Why did you do that? He's your genius, Mio,
and you let him go.

Mio. I couldn't help it.

Miriamne. Call him.
Run after him and call him!

Mio. I tried to say it
and it strangled in my throat. I might have known
you'd win in the end.

Miriamne. Is it for me?

Mio. For you?
It stuck in my throat, that's all I know.

Miriamne. Oh, Mio,
I never asked for that! I only hoped
Garth could go clear.

Mio. Well, now he will.

Miriamne. But you—
It was your chance!

Mio. I've lost
my taste for revenge if it falls on you. Oh, God,
deliver me from the body of this death
I've dragged behind me all these years! Miriamne!
Miriamne!

Miriamne. Yes!

Mio. Miriamne, if you love me
teach me a treason to what I am, and have been,
till I learn to live like a man! I think I'm waking
from a long trauma of hate and fear and death
that's hemmed me from my birth—and glimpse a life
to be lived in hope—but it's young in me yet, I can't
get free, or forgive! But teach me how to live
and forget to hate!

Miriamne. He would have forgiven.

Mio. He?

Miriamne. Your father.

   [*A pause*]

Mio. Yes.

   [*Another pause*]
   You'll think it strange, but I've never
   remembered that.

Miriamne. How can I help you?

Mio. You have.

Miriamne. If I were a little older—if I knew
   the things to say! I can only put out my hands
   and give you back the faith you bring to me
   by being what you are. Because to me
   you are all hope and beauty and brightness drawn
   across what's black and mean!

Mio. He'd have forgiven—
   Then there's no more to say—I've groped long enough
   through this everglades of old revenges—here
   the road ends.—Miriamne, Miriamne,
   the iron I wore so long—it's eaten through
   and fallen from me. Let me have your arms.
   They'll say we're children—Well—the world's made up
   of children.

Miriamne. Yes.

Mio. But it's too late for me.

Miriamne. No.

   [*She goes into his arms, and they kiss for the first time*]

Then we'll meet again?

Mio. Yes.

Miriamne. Where?

Mio. I'll write—
or send Carr to you.

Miriamne. You won't forget?

Mio. Forget?
Whatever streets I walk, you'll walk them, too,
from now on, and whatever roof or stars
I have to house me, you shall share my roof
and stars and morning. I shall not forget.

Miriamne. God keep you!

Mio. And keep you. And this to remember!
if I should die, Miriamne, this half-hour
is our eternity. I came here seeking
light in darkness, running from the dawn,
and stumbled on a morning.

> [*One of the* YOUNG MEN IN SERGE *strolls in casually from the
> right, looks up and down without expression, then,
> seemingly having forgotten something, retraces his steps
> and goes out.* ESDRAS *comes in slowly from the left.
> He has lost his hat, and his face is bleeding from a
> slight cut on the temple. He stands abjectly near the
> tenement*]

Miriamne. Father—what is it?

> [*She goes towards Esdras*]

Esdras. Let me alone.

> [*He goes nearer to Mio*]

He wouldn't let me pass.
The street's so icy up along the bridge
I had to crawl on my knees—he kicked me back
three times—and then he held me there—I swear
what I could do I did! I swear to you
I'd save you if I could.

Mio. What makes you think
that I need saving?

Esdras. Child, save yourself if you can!
He's waiting for you.

Mio. Well, we knew that before.

Esdras. He won't wait much longer. He'll come here—
he told me so. Those damned six months of his—
he wants them all—and you're to die—you'd spread
his guilt—I had to listen to it—

Mio. Wait—

[*He walks forward and looks casually to the right, then returns*]

There must be some way up through the house and out
across the roof—

Esdras. He's watching that. But come in—
and let me look.—

Mio. I'll stay here, thanks. Once in
and I'm a rat in a deadfall—I'll stay here—
look for me if you don't mind.

Esdras. Then watch for me—
I'll be on the roof—

[*He goes in hurriedly*]

Mio.

[*Looking up*]

Now all you silent powers
that make the sleet and dark, and never yet
have spoken, give us a sign, let the throw be ours
this once, on this longest night, when the winter sets
his foot on the threshold leading up to spring
and enters with remembered cold—let fall
some mercy with the rain. We are two lovers
here in your night, and we wish to live.

Miriamne. Oh, Mio—
if you pray that way, nothing good will come!
You're bitter, Mio.

Mio. How many floors has this building?

Miriamne. Five or six. It's not as high as the bridge.

Mio. No, I thought not. How many pomegranate seeds
did you eat, Persephone?

Miriamne. Oh, darling, darling,
if you die, don't die alone.

Mio. I'm afraid I'm damned
to hell, and you're not damned at all. Good God,
how long he takes to climb!

Miriamne. The stairs are steep.

[*A slight pause*]

Mio. I'll follow him.

Miriamne. He's there—at the window—now.
He waves you to go back, not to go in.

Mio, see, that path between the rocks—
they're not watching that—they're out at the river—
I can see them there—they can't watch both—
it leads to a street above.

Mio. I'll try it, then.
Kiss me. You'll hear. But if you never hear—
then I'm the king of hell, Persephone,
and I'll expect you.

Miriamne. Oh, lover, keep safe.

Mio. Good-bye.

> [*He slips out quickly between the rocks. There is a quick ma-
> chine gun rat-tat. The violin stops.* MIRIAMNE *runs
> toward the path.* MIO *comes back slowly, a hand pressed
> under his heart*]

It seems you were mistaken.

Miriamne. Oh, God, forgive me!

> [*She puts an arm round him. He sinks to his knees*]

Where is it, Mio? Let me help you in! Quick, quick,
let me help you!

Mio. I hadn't thought to choose—this—ground—
but it will do.

> [*He slips down*]

Miriamne. Oh, God, forgive me!

Mio. Yes?
The king of hell was not forgiven then,
Dis is his name, and Hades is his home—
and he goes alone—

Miriamne. Why does he bleed so? Mio, if you go
   I shall go with you.

Mio. It's better to stay alive.
   I wanted to stay alive—because of you—
   I leave you that—and what he said to me dying:
   I love you, and will love you after I die.
   Tomorrow, I shall still love you, as I've loved
   the stars I'll never see, and all the mornings
   that might have been yours and mine. Oh, Miriamne,
   you taught me this.

Miriamne. If only I'd never seen you
   then you could live—

Mio. That's blasphemy—Oh, God,
   there might have been some easier way of it.
   You didn't want me to die, did you, Miriamne—?
   You didn't send me away—?

Miriamne. Oh, never, never—

Mio. Forgive me—kiss me—I've got blood on your lips—
   I'm sorry—it doesn't matter—I'm sorry—

   [ESDRAS *and* GARTH *come out*]

Miriamne. Mio—
   I'd have gone to die myself—you must hear this, Mio,
   I'd have died to help you—you must listen, sweet,
   you must hear it—

   [*She rises*]

   I can die, too, see! You! There!
   You in the shadows!—You killed him to silence him!

   [*She walks toward the path*]

But I'm not silenced! All that he knew I know,
and I'll tell it tonight! Tonight—
tell it and scream it
through all the streets—that Trock's a murderer
and he hired you for this murder!
Your work's not done—
and you won't live long! Do you hear?
You're murderers, and I know who you are!

[*The machine gun speaks again. She sinks to her knees.* GARTH
runs to her]

Garth. You little fool!

[*He tries to lift her*]

Miriamne. Don't touch me!

[*She crawls toward Mio*]

Look, Mio! They killed me, too. Oh, you can believe me
now, Mio. You can believe I wouldn't hurt you,
because I'm dying! Why doesn't he answer me?
Oh, now he'll never know!

[*She sinks down, her hand over her mouth, choking.* GARTH
kneels beside her, then rises, shuddering. The HOBO
comes out. LUCIA *and* PINY *look out*]

Esdras. It lacked only this.

Garth. Yes.

[ESDRAS *bends over Miriamne, then rises slowly*]

Why was the bastard born? Why did he come here?

Esdras. Miriamne—Miriamne—yes, and Mio,
one breath shall call you now—forgive us both—

forgive the ancient evil of the earth
that brought you here—

Garth. Why must she be a fool?

Esdras. Well, they were wiser than you and I. To die
when you are young and untouched, that's beggary
to a miser of years, but the devils locked in synod
shake and are daunted when men set their lives
at hazard for the heart's love, and lose. And these,
who were yet children, will weigh more than all
a city's elders when the experiment
is reckoned up in the end. Oh, Miriamne,
and Mio—Mio, my son—know this where you lie,
this is the glory of earth-born men and women,
not to cringe, never to yield, but standing,
take defeat implacable and defiant,
die unsubmitting. I wish that I'd died so,
long ago; before you're old you'll wish
that you had died as they have. On this star,
in this hard star-adventure, knowing not
what the fires mean to right and left, nor whether
a meaning was intended or presumed,
man can stand up, and look out blind, and say:
in all these turning lights I find no clue,
only a masterless night, and in my blood
no certain answer, yet is my mind my own,
yet is my heart a cry toward something dim
in distance, which is higher than I am
and makes me emperor of the endless dark
even in seeking! What odds and ends of life
men may live otherwise, let them live, and then

go out, as I shall go, and you. Our part
is only to bury them. Come, take her up.
They must not lie here.

[LUCIA *and* PINY *come near to help.* ESDRAS *and* GARTH *stoop
to carry Miriamne*]

CURTAIN

High Tor

CHARACTERS

(In the order of their appearance)

THE INDIAN	A SAILOR
VAN VAN DORN	DEWITT
JUDITH	DOPE
ART. J. BIGGS	ELKUS
JUDGE SKIMMERHORN	BUDDY
LISE	PATSY
CAPTAIN ASHER	A. B. SKIMMERHORN
PIETER	BUDGE

DUTCH CREW OF THE *Onrust*

ACT ONE

SCENE I

SCENE: *A section of the broad flat trap-rock summit of High Tor, from which one looks out into sky and from which one might look down a sheer quarter mile to the Tappan Zee below. A cluster of hexagonal pillared rocks masks the view to the left and a wind-tortured small hemlock wedges into the rock floor at the right. Light from the setting sun pours in from the left, and an ancient* INDIAN, *wearing an old greatcoat thrown round him like a blanket, stands in the rays from a cleft, making his prayer to the sunset.*

The Indian. I make my prayer to you, the falling fire,
   bearing in mind the whisper in my ears
   from the great spirit, talking on the wind,
   whispering that a young race, in its morning,
   should pray to the rising sun, but a race that's old
   and dying, should invoke the dying flame
   eaten and gulfed by the shark-toothed mountain-west,
   a god that dies to live. As we have died,
   my race of the red faces and old ways,
   and as we hope to rise. I give you thanks
   for light, for the coming summer that will warm
   my snake's blood, cold and crawling; for the rain
   that fed the ripe May apples in the woods
   in secret for me; for the waterfall
   where the trout climb and pause under my hand,
   taken in silence; for quiet on the hills
   where the loud races dare not walk for fear
   lest they be lost, where their blind hunters pass
   peering with caps and guns, but see no game,
   and curse as they go down, while the raccoon waits,
   the woodchuck stands erect to catch the wind,

3

the partridge steps so lightly over leaves
the listening fox hears nothing, the possum hangs
head down, looking through his hands, and takes no
breath,
the gray squirrel turns to stone against the rock,
watching the owl, the rabbit holds his ears
steady above the trembling of his heart
and the crow mocks down the shellbark. I am fed
and sheltered on this mountain where their hands
are helpless. But I am old as my race is old;
my eyes hunt day and night along the ground
the grave where I shall lie; my ears have heard
dead women calling upward from the earth,
mother and wife and child: "You are welcome here;
you are no longer welcome where you walk,
but here you are most welcome." I shall go,
and lie and sleep, and I shall give you thanks,
O God that dies, that my last night is dark
and long, for I am tired, but yet I ask
one summer more, that I may be warm again,
and watch the nestlings grown upon the crag,
and hear the wild geese honking south by night,
if this may be, but if it may not be
then is my prayer, that when I lie to sleep
I may lie long, sleep soundly, hear no step,
hear only through the earth your step in spring,
O God of the dying fire!

[VAN DORN *and* JUDITH *come in from the right.*]

Van Dorn. Evening, John.

The Indian. Evening.

Van Dorn. Had any luck so **far?**

The Indian. Yes. Plenty of luck.

Van Dorn. Found it?

The Indian. Yes.

Van Dorn. O.K., John, let me know.
Let me know in time.

The Indian. I will. Good night.

Van Dorn. Good night.

[*The* INDIAN *slips away through the rocks to the left.*]

Judith. Who is it, Van?

Van. Just an Indian.

Judith. Are there Indians?
I didn't know there were any Indians left.

Van. Well, there's one. There's not much left of him,
and he's the last around here.

Judith. He's hunting something?
You asked him if he'd found it.

Van. Um—yes, you see,
he's looking for a place to make his grave,
and he's kind of captious about it—folks get that way
along toward the end, wanting their bones done up
in some particular fashion. Maybe because
that's all you've got to leave about that time
and you want it the way you want it.

Judith. Did he tell you this?

Van. We've got an understanding. When he feels it
coming over him he's going to die

he'll let me know, and I'll go dig him in
so the crows and foxes can't get at him. See,
he's all alone in the world. We fixed this up
a couple of years ago.

Judith. But you couldn't Van,
without a permit. A burial permit.

Van. Oh,
I guess you could. This getting old and dying
and crawling into the ground, that was invented
back before medical examiners
and taxes and all that. The old boy's clean.
He'll go right back to dirt.

Judith. But, Van, you can't!
People can't die that way!

Van. I guess they can.
What the hell good's being wrapped in cellophane?
You don't keep anyway.

Judith. You're impossible
to live with! Why do you say such things? If I
should die—you'd get a pine box!—

Van. If you should die
the old boy that drives the sun around up there,
he'd unhitch, and put the cattle out
to grass, and give it up. He'd plumb lose interest
if you should die. Maybe I would myself,
I don't say. Maybe I would.—Fetch out that supper.
We want to see what we eat.

Judith.
    [*Opening a lunch box*]

It's dinner, Van,
not supper.

Van. That's what I said. Fetch out that dinner.
When it gets a little darker what's black's pepper
and what's green's parsley; still you can't be sure.
It might be ants.

Judith. Just the same we'll quarrel.
We'll always quarrel.

Van. Oh, no. We've both got sense.
What's the sense fighting?
   [*He looks at a paper that was round the lunch.*]

Judith. And you shouldn't read at table.

Van. I never do. The Nanuet bank's been robbed.
My God, there's not enough money in Nanuet
to buy their gas for a get-away. One night
pap and me sat in on a poker game
in Nanuet and took twenty-seven dollars
out of town. Next day they couldn't do business.
The place was clean.

Judith. There were troopers at the train
tonight, and sirens going through Haverstraw,
but the robbers got away.

Van. They took twenty-five thousand.
How'd twenty-five thousand get to Nanuet?
It's against nature.

Judith. It didn't stay there long.

Van. No—I understand that.
But just to have it there in passing, just

to look at, just to fool the customers,
how do they do it?

Judith. Maybe it wasn't real.

Van. Federal money, that's it. Some of the stuff
Jim Farley prints in Washington with the stamps
to pay you for voting straight. Only now you see it
and now you don't.

Judith. They say it buys as much
as if you earned it.

Van. Bad for the stomach, though,
to live on humble pie.

Judith. I'd rather work.

Van. Well, as I said, don't work if you don't feel like it.
Any time you want to move up in the hills
and sleep with me, it's a bargain.

Judith. Van!

Van. Why not?
We'll get married if that's what you mean.

Judith. You haven't any job. And you make it sound
like animals.

Van. I'm fond of animals.

Judith. You shoot them all the time.

Van. Well, I get hungry.
Any man's liable to get hungry.

Judith. Van,
I want to talk to you seriously.

Van. Can't be done.
  Listen, things get serious enough
  without setting out to do it.

Judith. Van, this spring
  you had three weeks' work, laying dry wall.
  You could have had more, but you didn't take it.
  You're an expert mason—

Van. I'm good at everything.

Judith. But you work three weeks in the year—

Van. That's all I need—

Judith. And all the rest of the year you hunt or fish
  or sleep, or God knows what—

Van. Ain't it the truth?

Judith. Last fall I came looking for you once, and you
  were gone—gone to Port Jervis hunting—deer,
  you said on the postcard—

Van. Sure, I was hunting deer—
  didn't I bring you half a venison?

Judith. But not a word to me till I got the postcard
  ten days later—

Van. Didn't have a minute—

Judith. Then last winter there's a note nailed to a tree
  and you're in Virginia, down in the Dismal Swamp
  tracking bear. Now, for God's sake, Van,
  it's no way to live.

Van. Jeez, it's a lot of fun.

Judith. Maybe for you.

Van. You want me to take that job.

Judith. Why don't you, Van?

Van. Porter in a hotel, lugging up satchels,
opening windows, maybe you get a dime.
I'd choke to death.

Judith. I'd see you every day.

Van. Yeah, I could see you on the mezzanine,
taking dictation from the drummer boys,
all about how they can't get home. You can stand it,
a woman stands that stuff, but if you're a man
I say it chokes you.

Judith. We can't live in your cabin
and have no money, like the Jackson Whites
over at Suffern.

Van. Hell, you don't need money.
Pap worked that out. All you need's a place to sleep
and something to eat. I've never seen the time
I couldn't find a meal on the mountain here,
rainbow trout, jugged hare, something in season
right around the zodiac.

Judith. You didn't like
the Chevrolet factory, either?

Van.
  [*Walking toward the cliff edge*]

Look at it, Judy.
That's the Chevrolet factory, four miles down,
and straight across, that's Sing Sing. Right from here

you can't tell one from another; get inside,
and what's the difference? You're in there, and you
                                work,
and they've got you. If you're in the factory
you buy a car, and then you put in your time
to pay for the goddam thing. If you get in a hurry
and steal a car, they put you in Sing Sing first,
and then you work out your time. They graduate
from one to the other, back and forth, those guys,
paying for cars both ways. But I was smart.
I parked at a polis station and rung the bell
and took to the woods. Not for your Uncle Dudley.
They plugged the dice.

Judith. But one has to have a car.

Van. Honest to God now, Judy, what's the hurry?
Where in hell are we going?

Judith. If a man works hard,
and has ability, as you have, Van,
he takes a place among them, saves his money,
works right out of the ruck and gets above
where he's safe and secure.

Van. I wouldn't bet on it much.

Judith. But it's true.

Van. All right, suppose it's true. Suppose
a man saves money all his life, and works
like hell about forty years, till he can say:
good-bye, I'm going, I'm on easy street
from now on. What's he do?

Judith. Takes a vacation.

Van. Goes fishing, maybe? I'm on vacation now.
Why should I work forty years to earn
time off when I've got it?

Judith. It's not always easy,
you know it's not. There was that time last winter
when I helped you out.

Van. Why, sure, you helped me out.
Why wouldn't you? But if you didn't help me
I'd get along.

Judith. Yes, you would. I know you would.
But you don't even seem to want money. You won't
                    take it
when they bring it to you.

Van. When did they bring me any?

Judith. And what if there was a child?

Van. Why he'd be fine—
the less they have the better they like it.—Oh,
you mean the trap-rock company, wanting to buy
High Tor? They offered seven hundred dollars—
and they offered pap ten thousand before he died,
and he wouldn't sell.

Judith. He wouldn't?

Van. They want to chew
the back right off this mountain, the way they did
across the clove there. Leave the old palisades
sticking up here like billboards, nothing left
but a false front facing the river. Not for pap,
and not for me. I like this place.

Judith. But, Van Van Dorn!
  Ten thousand dollars!

Van. Well, it's Federal money.
  Damn stuff evaporates. Put it in a sock
  along with moth balls, and come back next year,
  and there's nothing left but the smell. Look, Judy, it's
  a quarter mile straight down to the Tappan Zee
  from here.—You can see fifteen miles of river
  north and south. I grew up looking at it.
  Hudson came up that river just about
  three hundred years ago, and lost a ship
  here in the Zee. They say the crew climbed up
  this Tor to keep a lookout for the fleet
  that never came. Maybe the Indians got them.
  Anyway on dark nights before a storm,
  they say you sometimes see them.

Judith. Have you seen them?

Van. The Dutchmen? Maybe I have. You can't be sure.
  It's pretty wild around here when it storms.
  That's when I like it best. But look at it now.
  There was a Jaeger here from Switzerland
  last year. He took one squint at this and said
  they could keep their Alps, for all him. Look at the
                              willows
  along the far breakwater.

Judith. It's beautiful.

Van. Every night I come back here like the Indian
  to get a fill of it. Seven hundred dollars
  and tear it down? Hell, no.
    [BIGGS *and* SKIMMERHORN *come in from the right, a bit be-*

draggled, and wiping their brows. SKIMMERHORN *carries a brief-case. It is growing darker.*]

Biggs. Hey listen, Mac, any houses round here?

Van. Guess you're off the beat, buddy; never heard of any houses on the mountain.

Skimmerhorn. Come on, Art; we're doing well if we're down at the road before dark.

Biggs. Look, Mac, maybe you can help us out. You familiar with this region, at all?

Van. I've been around here some.

Biggs. Well, we're all afternoon hunting a cabin that's somewhere along the ridge. Ever hear of it?

Van. Anybody live in it?

Biggs. Fellow named Van Dorn.

Van. Oh, yes, sure.

Biggs. You know where it is?

Van. Sure. You climb down the face of the cliff here and keep left along the ledge about a hundred yards, then you turn sharp left through a cleft up the ridge. Follow the trail about half a mile and there you are.

Skimmerhorn. Down the face of the cliff?

Van. Down through the rocks there, then turn left—

Skimmerhorn. A monkey couldn't go down there, hanging on with four hands and a tail!

Van. Well, you can always walk along back toward Little Tor, and cut down from there through the gulch.

There's a slough at the bottom of the ravine, but if you get through that you can see the cabin up on the side-hill. About four miles that way.

Skimmerhorn. Yeah, we'll set right out. I always did want to get lost up here and spend a night in the hills.

Van. Oh, you'll get lost, all right.

Biggs. Any snakes?

Van. No, you might see a copperhead, or a timber rattler.

Skimmerhorn. Coming back down?

Biggs. Yeah, we'd better go down. Thanks.

Van. Don't mention it.

[BIGGS *and* SKIMMERHORN *go out to the right.*]

Judith. But they were looking for you?

Van. Yeah.

Judith. Why didn't you tell them?

Van. What?

Judith. Who you were!

Van. They didn't ask about that.

Judith. But out of common courtesy!

Van. Well, you see, I know who they are.

Judith. Who are they?

Van. Art J. Biggs, Junior, and Skimmerhorn, Judge Skimmerhorn.

Judith. But why not talk to them?

Van. Oh, we communicate by mail. I've got
a dozen letters stacked up from the firm:
Skimmerhorn, Skimmerhorn, Biggs and Skimmerhorn,
and maybe two or three Skimmerhorns I left out
printed across the top. They're realtors,
whatever that is, and they own the trap-rock company,
and one of the Skimmerhorns, he's probate judge,
and goes around condemning property
when they want to make a rake-off. Take a letter:
Dear Skimmerhorn—

Judith. But they're the trap-rock men!

Van. That's what I said.

Judith. I'll call them!

Van. Oh, no; oh, no!
I've got nothing to say to those two buzzards
except I hope they break their fat-back necks
on their own trap-rock.

Judith. You take a lot for granted.

Van. Do I?

Judith. You think, because I said I loved you once,
that's the end; I'm finished.

Van. Oh, far from it.

Judith. Oh, yes—you think because a girl's been kissed
she stays kissed, and after that the man
does her thinking for her.

Van. Hell, it's all I can do
to handle my own thinking.

Judith. If we're married
   I'll have to live the way you want to live.
   You prefer being a pauper!

Van. Get it straight!
   I don't take money nor orders, and I live
   as I damn well please.

Judith. But we'd live like paupers!
   And you could have a fortune!

Van. Seven hundred dollars?

Judith. You could get more!

Van. I don't mean to sell at all.

Judith. You see; it's your place, and your thinking! You
                decide,
   but I'd have to stand it with you!

Van. What do you want?

Judith. Something to start on; and now, you see, we could
                have it,
   only you won't!

Van. I can't, Judy, that's the truth.
   I just can't.

Judith. They'll get it anyway.
   They've worked right up to where your land begins,
   and they won't stop for you. They'll just condemn it
   and take it.

Van. They'll be in trouble.

Judith. You can't make trouble
   for companies. They have a dozen lawyers

and ride right over you. I've worked for them.
It's never any use.

Van. Well, I won't sell.

Judith. We'll call it off then.

Van. What?

Judith. Between you and me.

Van. Only you don't mean it.

Judith. I know I do, though.
You haven't thought about it, and so you think
I couldn't do it. But it's better now
than later.

Van. You don't know what it means to me
if you can say it.

Judith. It means as much to me,
but I look ahead a little.

Van. What do you see?

Judith. Two people growing old
and having children, running wild in the woods
with nothing.

Van. There's no better place to run.
But I've been counting on you. More than you know.
More than—Judy, this is the kind of night
we've been in love most.

Judith. Yes, we could be in love,
but that's not everything.

Van. Well, just about.
What else do we get?

Judith. I think I'd better go.
It's getting dark.

Van. You could find your way by the beacon.

Judith. I'd better go.
[BIGGS *and* SKIMMERHORN *come back from the right.*]

Biggs. Listen, Mac, would you do something for us?

Van. I don't know.

Biggs. Could you take a paper round to Van Dorn and leave it with him?

Van. A summons?

Biggs. A sort of notice.

Van. Yeah, a notice to appear. No, I couldn't.

Biggs. It's worth a dollar to me.

Van. I'd be cheating you.

Skimmerhorn. Make it two dollars.

Van. You'd be throwing away money.

Skimmerhorn. Never mind that part of it. Will you do it?

Van. You'll take a running jump over the edge of the cliff and think things over on the way down before I serve any papers for you.

Biggs. What's the matter with us?

Van. Might be hoof and mouth disease, for all I know. You certainly brought an awful stench up here with you.

Skimmerhorn. Not much on manners, these natives.

Van. My rule in life is keep away from skunks.

Biggs. You'll get the tar kicked out of you one of these days.

Van. Make it today.

Judith. If you gentlemen care to know, this is Mr. Van Dorn.

Biggs. Say, are you Van Dorn?

Van. Sure I am.

Biggs.
   [*Extending a hand*]

   Oh, in that case, forget it—you're the fellow we want to see!—Boy, we apologize—
   [*He uncovers*]

   and to the lady, too! Listen, I don't know what to say but you've got us all wrong. We want to buy this place!

Van. You like the view, I suppose?

Biggs. Certainly is a view.

Van. You wouldn't spoil it, of course? You wouldn't move in with a million dollars worth of machinery and cut the guts out of the mountain, would you?

Skimmerhorn. We always leave the front—the part you see from the river.

Van. But you take down all the law allows.

Skimmerhorn. Well, we're in business.

Van. Not with me.

Judith. Do you mind if I ask how much you're offering?

Biggs. We said seven hundred. but I'll make it a thousand right here and now.

Skimmerhorn. As a matter of fact, we'll make it two thousand.

Biggs. Yeah, all right. Two thousand for the hundred and seven acres.

Judith. But you offered Mr. Van Dorn's father ten thou. sand before he died.

Skimmerhorn. His father had a clear title, right down from the original Dutch patroon to the original Van Dorn. But unfortunately the present Mr. Van Dorn has a somewhat clouded claim to the acreage.

Van. My father's title was clear, and he left it to me.

Skimmerhorn. The truth is he should have employed a lawyer when he drew his will, because the instrument, as recorded, is faulty in many respects. It was brought before me in my capacity as probate judge at Leden-town.

Van. And in your capacity as second vice-president of the trap-rock company you shot it full of holes.

Skimmerhorn. Sir, I keep my duties entirely separate.

Van. Sure, but when your left hand takes money your right hand finds out about it. And when there's too much to carry away in both hands you use a basket. You're also vice-president of the power company, and you stole right-of-ways clear across the county north and south—

Skimmerhorn. We paid for every foot of land—

Van. Yes, at your own price.

Biggs. Let's not get in an argument, Mr. Van Dorn, because the fact that your father's will was improperly drawn means he died intestate and the land goes to his heirs. Now we've found twenty-seven Van Dorns living at Blauvelt, all claiming relationship and all willing to sign away their rights for a consideration.

Van. The best you can do you'll need my name in your little paper, and you won't have it.

Skimmerhorn. To put it straight, you'll take three thousand dollars, and I'll hold the will valid.

Van. Oh, it's three thousand, now?

Biggs. You'll say that's crooked, but it's not. It's perfectly legal—and it's what you get.

Van. I'm still waiting to hear what you do about my signature.

Skimmerhorn. It's quite possible you'll be held incompetent by the court and a guardian appointed.

Van. Me, incompetent.

Skimmerhorn. But I've got the validation in my pocket, naming you executor, if you'll sell.

Biggs. And by God, anybody that won't take money when it's offered to him is incompetent! And you'll take it

now or not at all! I don't go mountain-climbing every
day with a blank check in my pocket!

[*A pause*]

Come on: It's bad enough sliding down that trail by
daylight.

Van. Well, I wouldn't want to make you nervous,
a couple of eminent respectables
like you two—but a dog won't bite a Dutchman—
maybe you've heard that—and the reason is
a Dutchman's poison when he don't like you. Now,
I'm Dutch and I don't like you.

Skimmerhorn. That's a threat?

Van. Not at all. Only don't try to eat me
or you'll curl up. I'm poison to a hound-dog,
and you're both sons-of-bitches.

Biggs. Come on.

[*The daylight is now gone. The airplane beacon lights the scene
from the right.*]

Van. What's more
there's something funny about this mountain-top.
It draws fire. Every storm on the Tappan Zee
climbs up here and wraps itself around
High Tor, and blazes away at what you've got,
airplane beacon, steam-shovels, anything
newfangled. It smashed the beacon twice. It blew
the fuses on your shovel and killed a man
only last week. I've got a premonition
something might happen to you.

Biggs. God, he's crazy.

Skimmerhorn. Yeah, let him talk.
   [*There is a sudden rumbling roar of falling rock.*]

Biggs. What's that?

Van. That's nothing much.
   That's just a section of the cliff come down
   across the trail. I've been expecting it
   this last two years. You'd better go down this way.

Biggs. This way?

Van. Yeah.

Biggs. No, thanks.

Van. Just as you say.
   But there's something definitely hostile here
   toward you two pirates. Don't try that trail in the dark.
   Not if you want to be buried in your vaults
   in Mount Repose. Your grieving families
   might have to move two thousand tons of rock
   to locate your remains. You think High Tor's
   just so much raw material, but you're wrong.
   A lot of stubborn men have died up here
   and some of them don't sleep well. They come back
   and push things round, these dark nights. Don't blame
                              me
   if anything falls on you.

Skimmerhorn. Oh, what the hell!
   Let's get out of here.
   [*Another long rumble of falling rock*]

Van. Another rock-fall.
   Once they start there's likely to be more.
   Something hanging round in the dark up here

doesn't like you boys. Not only me.
Better go down this way.

Biggs. Thanks.

> [BIGGS *and* SKIMMERHORN *go out to the right.*]

Judith. What do you mean?

Van. I don't know.

Judith. They'll say you threatened them.
Good-bye, Van.

Van. You'll be up tomorrow?

Judith. No.

> [*She steps down into a cleft.*]

Van. You'd better let me see you down.

Judith. Oh, no.
I can climb. Stay here and guard your rock—
you think so much of it.

Van. When will I see you?

Judith. Never.
We'll forget about it. You had a choice
and you chose High Tor. You're in love with your
mountain.
Well, keep your mountain.

Van. All right.

Judith. Good night.

Van. Good night.

> [*She disappears down the rocks.* VAN *sits in the shadow, look-
ing into darkness. After a moment a barely perceptible*
FIGURE *enters from the gloom at the right and crosses the*

*stage toward the rocks at the left. At the foot of the climb
he pauses and his face is caught in the light of the beacon.
He is seen to be young or middle-aged, bearded, and
wearing the costume of a Dutch sailor of the sixteen
hundreds. He climbs the rocks, and* ANOTHER SAILOR, *a
small cask strapped to his shoulders, follows.* THREE MORE
cross the stage similarly, then the CAPTAIN *and* HIS WIFE
pause, like the others, in the light of the beacon. The
CAPTAIN *is like his men, only younger perhaps;* HIS WIFE
*is a tiny figure, with a delicate girlish face looking out
from under the Dutch bonnet. They too pass up the
rocks, and are followed by a rolling* SILENUS *in the same
garments. As they vanish* VAN *rises, looking after them.*]

Uh—huh—going to rain.

CURTAIN

ACT ONE

Scene II

SCENE: *The curtain goes up on complete darkness enfolding the summit of the Tor. There is a long cumbrous rolling, as of a ball going down a bowling alley, a flash of white light, a crackling as of falling pins and a mutter dying into echo along the hills. The flash reveals the outline of the Tor, black against the sky, and on it the figures of the DUTCH CREW. Again the roll, the flash, the break and the dying away. The beam of the airplane beacon steals into the scene sufficiently to suggest the bowlers, some of them standing, some sitting about the keg, the CAPTAIN's WIFE a little apart from the rest. Beyond the peak is a moving floor, the upper side of blown cloud.*

The Captain's Wife. I'm weary of it, Martin! When you drink
there should be one on guard to watch the river
lest the ship come, and pass, and we must haunt
the dark another year!

The Captain. To humor her,
Pieter, old son, climb down and post the Zee,
and mind you keep good lookout.

Pieter. Ships, aye, ships—
when the ball's rolling and there's gin in hand
I go to post. My luck!

The Captain. When you shipped with me
you signed the voyage.

Pieter. Is this sea or land?
I'm no foot soldier!

The Captain. March!

27

Pieter. Aye, aye. I'm going.

    [PIETER *detaches himself from the group and goes down the
    rocks.*]

The Captain. Are you content?

The Captain's Wife. When the *Half Moon* returns
and we have boarded her, and the wind scuds fair
into the east—yes, when we see the wharves
of Texel town across the Zuyder Zee,
with faces waiting for us, hands and cries
to welcome our returning, then perhaps
I shall be content.

A Sailor. Now God, for Texel town.

Another Soldier.

    [*Rising*]

I'll drink no more.

DeWitt.

    [*The Silenus*]

Drink up, lads, and forget.
It's a long way to the Texel. Drink your drink
and play your play.

The Captain. Drink up and play it out.

The Captain's Wife. Have you forgotten how the cobbled
                            street
comes down by cranks and turns upon the quay,
where the *Onrust* set sail? The traders' doors
under the blowing signs, bright colors hung
to catch unwary eyes? The bakers' ovens
and the long, hot brown loaves? The red-coal fires
and silver under candles? There your wives

wait for you, their sharp roofs in Amsterdam
cut on a rainy sky.

The Captain. Be quiet, Lise.
You were so much in love you must come with me;
you were so young that I was patient with you,
but now day long, night long you carp and quarrel,
a carping wife.

Lise. We stay so long—so long;
Asher, at first the days were years, but now
the years are days; the ship that set us down
to watch this river palisade becomes
alike with supper-stories round a hearth
when we were children. Was there this ship at all,
was there a sailor-city, Amsterdam,
where the salt water washed the shallow piers
and the wind went out to sea? Will the ship return,
and shall I then see the Netherlands once more,
with sabots clattering homeward from the school
on winter evenings?

Asher. Aye, there was a ship,
and we wait here for her, but she's long away,
somewhere up-river.

Lise. And now you drink and drink,
distill your liquor on the mountain-top
and bowl against the light. But when you break it
these new strange men come build it up again;
and giant shovels spade the mountain down,
and when you break them still the new strange men
rig them afresh and turn them on the rock,
eating the pillared stone. We must go back.
There's no safety here.

A Sailor. We must go back.

Asher. These muttering fools!

Lise. Oh, Asher, I'm afraid!
For one thing I have known, and never told
lest it be true, lest you be frightened, too,
lest we be woven of shadow! As the years
have gone, each year a century, they seem
less real, and all the boundaries of time,
our days and nights and hours, merge and are one,
escaping me. Then sometimes in a morning
when all the crew come down the rocks together,
holding my breath, I see you in the light,
and back of you the gray rock bright and hard,
seen through figures of air! And you, and you,
and you were but cloud-drift walking, pierced by the
                                    light,
translucent in the sun.

DeWitt. Now damn the woman!

Lise. Love, love, before our blood
be shadow only, in a dark fairyland
so far from home, we must go back, go back
where earth is earth, and we may live again
and one day be one day!

Asher. Why, then, I knew it,
and I have known it, now that you know it, too.
But the old Amsterdam of our farewells
lies in another world. The land and sea
about us on this dark side of the earth
is thick with demons, heavy with enchantment,
cutting us off from home.

Lise. Is it enchantment?
  Yes, it may be. At home there were tulips growing
along my bordered path, but here the flowers
are strange to me, not one I knew, no trace
of any flower I knew; no, seedlings set
upon a darkened, alien outer rim
of sea, blown here as we were blown, enchanted,
drunken and blind with sorcery.

Asher. And yet
  what we're to have we shall have here. Years past
the demons of this air palsied our hands,
fixed us upon one pinnacle of time,
and on this pinnacle of stone, and all
the world we knew slid backward to the gulf,
stranding us here like seaweed on the shingle,
remembering the sea. In Texel town
new houses have gone up, after new fashions;
the children of the children of our days,
lying awake to think of what has been,
reach doubtfully beyond the clouds of years
back to our sailing out of Texel. Men
are like the gods, work miracles, have power
to pierce the walls with music. Their beacon light
destroys us. You have seen us in the sun,
wraithlike, half-effaced, the print we make
upon the air thin tracery, permeable,
a web of wind. They have changed us. We may take
the fire-balls of the lightning in our hands
and bowl them down the level floor of cloud
to wreck the beacon, yet there was a time
when these were death to touch. The life we keep
is motionless as the center of a storm,

yet while we can we keep it; while we can
snuff out to darkness their bright sweeping light,
melt down the harness of the slow machines
that hew the mountain from us. When it goes
we shall go too. They leave us this place, High Tor,
and we shall have no other. You learn it last.
A long while now we've known.

A Sailor. Aye, aye, a long while.

Asher. Come, we'll go down.

> [*The* CAPTAIN *and his* MEN *go out, leaving only* DEWITT *with*
> LISE.]

Lise. That's why they drink.

DeWitt. It's enough to drive a sailor-man to drink, by the
great jib boom, marooned somewhere on the hinder
parts of the earth and degenerating hourly to the status
of a flying Dutchman, half-spook and half God-knows-
what. Maps and charts we have, compass and sextant,
but the ships these days are bewitched like ourselves,
spanking up and down the Mauritius with sails struck,
against wind and tide, and on fire from below. Drink?
Why wouldn't we drink? A pewter flagon of Hollands
gin puts manhood into the remnants and gives a sailor
courage to look out on these fanciful new devils that
ride sea, land and air on a puff of blue smoke. They're
all witches and mermaids, these new-world devils, dancing around on bubbles, speaking a language God never
heard, and nothing human about them except when
they fall they break like the rest of us.

Lise. If I had known. It's not too late. The sun
still rises in the east and lays a course

toward the old streets and days. These are my hands
as when I was a child. Some great magician,
binding a half-world in his wiles, has laid
a spell here. We must break it and go home.
I see this clearly.

DeWitt. Lise, little heart, the devils are too much for us.
God knows it's a hard thing to say, and I'd help you
if I could help myself, but all hell wouldn't know
where we are nor where we ought to go. The very
points of the compass grow doubtful these latter years,
partly because I'm none too sober and partly because
the great master devil sits on top of the world stirring
up north and south with a long spoon to confuse poor
mariners. I've seen him at it, a horned bull three times
the size of Dundenberg and with more cloven feet than
the nine beasts in Revelations. Very clearly I saw him,
too, as clear as you see the east and a path across the
waters.

Lise. Are we to wait till all the color steals
from flower and cloud, before our eyes; till a wind
out of the morning from the Tappan Zee
lifts us, we are so light, for all our crying,
and takes us down the valleys toward the west,
and all we are becomes a voiceless cry
heard on the wind?

DeWitt. We'll see the time, if they continue to work on
us, when we'll be apparent in a strong light only by
the gin contained in our interior piping. The odor itself, along with that of church-warden tobacco, should
be sufficient to convince a magistrate of our existence.—
You tremble, little Lise, and you weep, but look now,

there's a remedy I've had in mind. Fall in love with one of them. Fall in love with one of these same strange new-world magicians. I shall choose me out one of their female mermaid witches, and set my heart on her, and become a man again. And for God's sake let her love me strongly and hold on, lest I go down the brook like a spring freshet in the next pounding rain.

Lise. I gave my love long ago, and it's no help.
I love enough.

DeWitt. Aye, but he's in a worse case than you are, the Captain. Saving his captaincy, there's not enough belief in him to produce half a tear in a passion of sobbing. You'll make me weep, little one, and what tears I have I shall need, lest my protestation turns out to be a dry rain.

Lise. Aye, we were warned before we came away
against the cabalistic words and signs
of those who dwell along these unknown waters;
never to watch them dance nor hear them sing
nor draw their imprecations—lest their powers
weave a weird medicine throughout the air,
chilling the blood, transfixing body and mind
and we be chained invisibly, our eyes darkened,
our wrists and breasts pulseless, anchored in time,
like birds blown back in a wind. But we have listened,
and we are stricken through with light and sound,
empty as autumn leaves, empty as prayers
that drift in a godless heaven. Meaningless,
picked clean of meaning, stripped of bone and will,
the chrysalids of locusts staring here
at one another.

DeWitt. If it's true it's enough to make a man weep for himself, Lise, and for all lost mariners, wherever they are, and for us more than any, here on these spellbound rocks, drawing up water from time past—the well growing deeper, and the water lower, till there be none.

[*He turns away to go down the path.*]

CURTAIN

ACT ONE

Scene III

Scene: *Another section of the Tor, in darkness save for the airplane beacon. A large steam shovel reaches in from an adjacent excavation and hangs over the rock, the control cables dangling. Van is alone on the stage looking at the machinery. He reaches up, catches a cable, and swings the shovel a little. Biggs and Skimmerhorn enter from the right.*

Biggs. Hey, what are you doing with that shovel?

Van. Did you know you're trespassing? Also when a man owns land he owns the air above it and the rock below. That means this damn shovel of yours is also trespassing.

Biggs. Oh, it's Van Dorn. We'll have that moved tomorrow, Mr. Van Dorn. Somebody's made a miscue and left it hanging over the line.

Skimmerhorn. By the way, that trail's gone out completely, Mr. Van Dorn; there's a fifty foot sheer drop there now, where it was. Now we've got to get off, if you can think of any way to manage it.

Van. I'm not worrying about it. Spend the night. No charge.

Skimmerhorn. The truth is I have to be in court early tomorrow, and a man needs his sleep.

Van. Afraid you'd doze off on the bench and somebody else might take a trick? Oh, you'd wake up before they got far with anything. The Skimmerhorns are automatic that way.

36

Biggs. You don't know any other trail down?

Van. I showed you the one I knew, and you both turned green looking at it. What am I supposed to do now? Pin wings on you?

[*He goes out to the right.*]

Skimmerhorn. I think I'll swear out a warrant for that squirt. He's too independent by half.

Biggs. On what ground?

Skimmerhorn. He threatened us, didn't he?

Biggs. And where'll that get us?

Skimmerhorn. He might be easier to talk to in jail.

Biggs. That's true.

Skimmerhorn.

[*Sitting on a rock*]

This is a hell of a mess.

Biggs. You're explaining to me?

Skimmerhorn. What did we ever come up here for?

Biggs. Twenty-two thousand dollars.

Skimmerhorn. Will we get it?

Biggs. It'll look all right on the books.

Skimmerhorn. It's not good enough, though.

Biggs. What are you grousing about?

Skimmerhorn. Because I want my dinner, damn it! And because I'm tired of taking forty per cent and giving you sixty on all the side bets! I want half!

Biggs. You're a damn sight more likely to get your dinner. You're overpaid already.

Skimmerhorn. The will's perfectly good. I could find holes in it, but I've probated plenty much the same.

Biggs. What of it?

Skimmerhorn. A judge has some conscience, you know. When he sets a precedent he likes to stick to it.

Biggs. I never knew your conscience to operate except on a cash basis. You want half.

Skimmerhorn. Yes, I want half.

Biggs. Well, you don't get it. Any other judge I put in there'd work for nothing but the salary and glad of the job. You take a forty per cent cut and howl for more. The woods are full of shyster lawyers looking for probate judgeships and I'll slip one in at Ledentown next election.

Skimmerhorn. Oh, no, you won't, Art; oh, no, you won't. You wouldn't do that to an old friend like me; because if you did, think what I'd do to an old friend like you.

Biggs. Well, maybe I wouldn't. Not if you're reasonable. Look, what's the difference between forty per cent and fifty per cent? Practically nothing!

Skimmerhorn. Then why don't you give it to me?

Biggs. Because, try and get it!—

Skimmerhorn. Damn it, I'm hungry.—I ought to telephone my wife, too.

Biggs. Why don't you?

Skimmerhorn. Maybe it's fun for you—nothing to eat, no place to sleep, cold as hell, black as Tophet and a storm coming up! Only I'm not used to it!

Biggs. You're pulling down forty per cent of twenty-two thousand dollars for the night's work. I say it's worth it.

Skimmerhorn. Think we could slide down one of those cables?

Biggs. Maybe you could, Humpty-Dumpty, but not me.

Skimmerhorn. I'm going to look at it.

> [*He goes out left,* Biggs *following. After a moment* Three Men *climb in through the rocks at the right, one of them carrying a small zipper satchel. They throw themselves down wearily on the rock. They are, in brief, the Nanuet bank robbers,* Elkus, Dope *and* Buddy.]

Dope. God, I got no wind.

> [*A siren is heard faintly, far down on the road.*]

Elkus. Sons a' bitches a' troopers.

Dope. What'd you want to wreck the car for?

Elkus. Want to get caught with the stuff on you?

Buddy. We'll get four hundred years for this.

Elkus. Shut up!

Dope. You didn't need to wreck the car, though.

Elkus. Didn't you hear the trooper slam on the brakes when he went by? You'd be wearing bracelets right now if I hadn't dumped the old crate over the embankment! The way it is he thinks he's following us, and he'll blow that fire alarm all the way to Bear Mountain

Bridge. Only hope he meets something solid head-on at ninety miles an hour.

Dope. What I want to know is where we go from here.

Elkus. Down the other side and pick up a car.
[*The siren is heard receding.*]

Buddy. We'll get four hundred years for this.

Elkus. What do you think you are, a chorus? Go on back to St. Thomas's and sing it to the priest. You're about as much help as a flat tire.

Buddy. I never wanted to be in it. I was only lookout— you're both witness to that.

Elkus. What good do you think that does you, you poor fish? Brace up and take it like a man. There's twenty-five thousand in that bag and some of it's yours.

Dope. How do you know it's twenty-five thousand?

Elkus. It's the Orangeburg pay roll.
[Buddy *looks off left.*]

Buddy. Before God, it's Judge Skimmerhorn!

Elkus. What? Where?

Buddy. There. Coming round the rocks. Judge Skimmerhorn of Ledentown.

Elkus. Does he know you?

Buddy. Sure, he knows me.

Elkus. We're out climbing, see? Hikers, see? On a picnic.
[*They stand.* Elkus *holds the satchel behind him casually.* Biggs *and* Skimmerhorn *come in.*]

Biggs. Hello.

Elkus. How are you?

Biggs. Out walking?

Elkus. That's right. Climbed up on a bet.

Skimmerhorn. Isn't that Buddy?

Buddy. Yes, sir. Evening, Judge.

Skimmerhorn. You're a long way from home.

Buddy. Yes, sir.

Biggs. Think you could show us a way down? We're stuck up here.

Buddy. There's a path down the cliff. Yes, sir.

Skimmerhorn. No, thanks. I saw that one. Going to camp here?

Elkus. Might as well. Sure.

Skimmerhorn. Bring anything to eat?

Elkus. Matter of fact, we didn't.
   [*He sets the satchel down behind the rock, unobtrusively.*]

Skimmerhorn. Not a thing?

Elkus. Not a thing.

Skimmerhorn. That's funny. Camping with nothing to eat.

Elkus. Yeah, it is kinda funny.

Dope. We ate before we started.
   [*He smiles cunningly.*]

Elkus. That's right. The Dope's right for once. We ate before we started.

Skimmerhorn. Wish I had.

Buddy. You—you staying up here tonight, sir?

Skimmerhorn. Seems that way. We came up looking for somebody.

Elkus. Looking for somebody?

Skimmerhorn. That's what I said.

Elkus. Who was it?

Biggs. That's our business.

Elkus. I see.

Skimmerhorn.
[*Coming near the three*]

Listen, Buddy, you're young and ambitious. Would you do something for me if you got well paid?

Buddy. I guess so, Judge.

Skimmerhorn.
[*Sitting on the rock and incidentally over the satchel*]
We're done in, traipsing around the rocks. Would you climb down the Tor and get to Haverstraw and telephone my wife I can't come home?

Buddy. I guess so, wouldn't I, Elkus?

Elkus. Up to you.

Skimmerhorn. And while you're there will you buy **a** dozen sandwiches and some beer?

Buddy. Yes, sir.

Skimmerhorn. There's another thing you could do. Call up the state troopers for me, and tell them I'm here and I want them to come up and make an arrest.

Buddy. You—want to arrest somebody?

Skimmerhorn. You get it. What do you say?

Buddy. I—I guess so. Is it all right, Elkus?

Dope. Oh—no. Oh—no.

Elkus. Sure it's O.K. Why not?

Buddy. It'd take about five hours—to get down and back.

Skimmerhorn. Damn it—I'll starve to death.

Dope. What do you want to make an arrest for?

Biggs. That's our business.

Buddy. All right. I'll go.

Skimmerhorn. Here's five dollars for you. And another when you get back. And make it fast, will you?

Buddy. Yes, sir.
   [*He starts out right.*]

Elkus. Just a minute, Bud.
   [ELKUS *and* DOPE *follow* BUDDY *out to converse with him.*]

Biggs. You might have made it two dozen sandwiches.

Skimmerhorn. I guess I will.
   [*He starts to rise, places his hand on the satchel, and jumps.*]
Christ, what's that?
   [*He kicks the satchel, then flips it up into the rocks.*]

Biggs. Yeah?

Skimmerhorn. I thought it was a snake. Somebody's mouldy luggage. People are always throwing truck around.

[*He calls.*]

Say, for God's sake, get started, will you?

Buddy.

[*Outside*]

Yes, sir. Right away.

[ELKUS *and* DOPE *return.*]

Elkus. I guess we'll all go.

[*He looks nonchalantly where the satchel was.*]

Skimmerhorn. Fine. Will you make it two dozen sandwiches?

Elkus. What the hell's going on here?

Skimmerhorn. We're hungry, that's all.

Elkus. Are you two finnegling with us? Because if you are—!

Biggs. What are you looking for?

Elkus. Nothing. Who said I was looking for anything?

Dope. Hey, Elkus! They got the troopers up here!

[DEWITT's *broad Dutch hat appears above the rocks in the rear, looking, for the moment, remarkably like that of a state trooper.* ELKUS *and* DOPE *freeze, looking at it.*]

Elkus.

[*Drawing a gun*]

Why, you fat pimps!
[DEWITT *disappears.*]

Dope. Beat it, you fool!
[ELKUS *and* DOPE *scatter out to the right.*]

Biggs.
[*Looking at the rocks*]

What was all that about?

Skimmerhorn. I hope they bring those sandwiches.
[*He also stares toward the rear.*]

Biggs. Sandwiches? They're not bringing sandwiches for anybody, those two.
[*He calls.*]

Hey! Hey, you! Anybody there?—What did he mean by troopers?

Skimmerhorn. Want to take a look?

Biggs. I'm plenty unhappy, right where I am.
[SKIMMERHORN *climbs up on the rocks.*]

Skimmerhorn. Wish to God I did see a trooper.

Biggs. Nobody there?

Skimmerhorn. Not a thing. Hey! Hey, you!
[*A silence.*]

Nope. Nobody.

Biggs. Looks to me as if we just missed being stuck up by a couple of lunatics.

Skimmerhorn. If I can't eat I'm going to sleep.

Biggs. Maybe you've never tried adjusting yourself to igneous limestone.

Skimmerhorn. I'm about to try it now.

Biggs. You have my sympathy.

.   [SKIMMERHORN *stretches out on the rock, takes off his coat for
        a pillow and lies down.*]

Skimmerhorn. Thanks.

Biggs. Beautiful shape you have. A lot of slop tied up
with a piece of string.

Skimmerhorn.

   [*Sitting up*]

   God it's cold. Listen, we could use one coat for a pillow
and put the other one over us.

Biggs. What other one?

Skimmerhorn. Yours.

Biggs. A proposition, huh?

Skimmerhorn. You going to sit up all night?

Biggs. In some ways it might be preferable.

Skimmerhorn. You can't prop yourself on end forever,
like a duck on a rock.

Biggs. Pull yourself together, then. You stick out behind
like a bump on a duck. All right. Move over.

Skimmerhorn. Your coat's bigger than mine.

   [*They pull* BIGGS' *coat around them and lie down.*]

Biggs. Just a couple of perfect forty-nines. Where the hell am I supposed to put my hip bone?

Skimmerhorn. You juggle your own hip bones.
[DEWITT *appears on the rocks at the rear, looking down.*]

Biggs. If you snore, you probate judge, I'll have you disbarred.

Skimmerhorn. Go to sleep.

Biggs. Wish I thought I could. On bed rock. Wake me early, mother dear.

Skimmerhorn. Shut up.
[DEWITT *meanwhile has opened the satchel and now brings it down into the light to examine the contents. He sits down, takes out five packets of bills, shakes the satchel, then begins to go through the inner pockets. He finds a roll of pennies, which he breaks open into his hands.*]

DeWitt. Copper pieces, by the great jib boom, enough to purchase a new wig, if a man ever got back to a place where money was useful to him. A counting-house full of them wouldn't buy a ship from one of these semi-demi-demi-semi-devils, so that's no good.
[*Two snores rise in concert from* BIGGS *and* SKIMMERHORN. DE-WITT *goes over to them, dropping the money.*]

What kind of demi-semi-devil do you think you are, with four legs and two faces, both looking the same direction? Jesu Maria, it's a kind of centaur, as big one way as another, no arms, and feet the size of dishpans.

Biggs. What's that?

DeWitt.

    [*Backing away*]

It's the rear end that talks, evidently, the front being fast asleep in the manner of a figure-head.

Biggs. Who's there? Did somebody speak?

DeWitt. None too clear in the back thinker, I should say, which would be a natural result of lugging two sets of brains, fore and aft. I'd incline to communicate with the front end, but if necessary I'll converse with the posterior.

Biggs.

    [*Sitting up, looking at* DEWITT]

Skimmerhorn!

Skimmerhorn. What's the matter?

Biggs. I'm damned if I know.

Skimmerhorn. Go to sleep, then.

Biggs. Do you believe in apparitions?

Skimmerhorn. No.

Biggs. Well, there's a figure of fun sitting talking to me, right out of a masquerade ball.

Skimmerhorn. You been drinking?

Biggs. What would I find to drink?

DeWitt. If the forecastle wakes now I shall play both ends against the middle, like a marine auctioneer. I want to buy a boat.

Biggs. You've come to the wrong shop, sailor. I'm in the real-estate business, and it's a long mile down to sea level.

[SKIMMERHORN *sits up suddenly.*]

DeWitt. You have no boats?

Biggs. No boats.

Skimmerhorn. What in the hell?—

Biggs. I told you I'm damned if I know.

DeWitt. And the front end has no boats?

Biggs. You're the front end, see. He wants to know if you've got boats.

Skimmerhorn. No, stranger, no boats.

DeWitt. Ah.

[*He shakes his head mournfully, turns him about and goes to the right, still muttering.*]

The great plague on them, the lying, two-headed fairies out of a witch's placket. What chance has an honest man against a two-faced double-tongued beast, telling the same tale—

[*He disappears through the rocks.*]

Biggs. Did you see what I saw?

Skimmerhorn. Not if you saw what I saw. What I saw wasn't possible.—Did you fake that thing?

Biggs. Fake it? I saw it.

Skimmerhorn. Oh, no—! Nobody saw that—what I saw. I didn't either. I've got a family to support. They aren't going to put me away anywhere.

Biggs. Whatever it was, it left a calling card. Looks as if he ate his lunch here, supposing a thing like that eats lunch. Maybe he left some for us.

Skimmerhorn. I don't want any of that.

Biggs.
> [*Rising and turning the packages over with his foot*]

There's something in it.

Skimmerhorn. Help yourself.

Biggs.
> [*Opening a package, tossing the cover away*]

You know what this is?

Skimmerhorn. Probably a sheaf of contracts with the devil, all ready to sign.

Biggs. No, it's money.

Skimmerhorn. Money!
> [*He leaps to his feet.*]

Biggs. Fives and tens.
> [*He opens another package.* SKIMMERHORN *does the same.*]

Skimmerhorn. Well, bless the poor little Dutchman's heart—after all we said about him, too!

Biggs. Think he left it?

Skimmerhorn. It wasn't there before.

Biggs. No.

Skimmerhorn. Were you born with a caul, or anything?

Biggs. Always before I had to work for it, or steal it. Never till tonight have I been waked up by a little man in a big hat, fetching it to me in packages.

Skimmerhorn. Are you asleep?

Biggs. I probably am, asleep and dreaming.

Skimmerhorn. If you're dreaming, you're dreaming that I found money.

Biggs. Oh, you found it now?

Skimmerhorn. Fifty-fifty.

Biggs. Wait a minute. You know what money this is?

Skimmerhorn. No.

[BIGGS *picks up a discarded envelope.*]

Biggs. It came out of the Nanuet bank.

[SKIMMERHORN *takes the envelope from him.*]

Skimmerhorn. If that little guy's a bank robber he's certainly careless with the proceeds.

Biggs. That's where it came from.

Skimmerhorn. In that case we ought to give it back. For the reward.

Biggs. No reward offered yet.

Skimmerhorn. Maybe we ought to give it back anyway.

Biggs. Think so?

Skimmerhorn. Might be marked bills.

Biggs. No, it's not. I was talking with the president of the bank on the 'phone. Made up for a pay roll. No marks on any of it.

Skimmerhorn. It ought to be returned, though.

Biggs. Sure, it should. Question is, will it be?

Skimmerhorn. I think so, don't you?

Biggs. I'm inclined to think so. Bank robbing's away out of my line.

Skimmerhorn. Mine, too, as a matter of fact. The president of the bank's a friend of yours?

Biggs. Yes, he is, in a way. Oh, he's gypped me a couple of times, same as you would.

Skimmerhorn. He wouldn't lose anything.

Biggs. Oh, no, he's insured.

Skimmerhorn. Has it occurred to you the little Dutchman that was here might not mean any good to us?

Biggs. Did you see a little Dutchman?

Skimmerhorn. I thought I did, there for a minute.

Biggs. I don't believe that any more.

Skimmerhorn. Certainly doesn't sound very likely.

Biggs. We'd better count it. Man never ought to carry money around without knowing how much it is.

Skimmerhorn. Yeah, let's count it. It said twenty-five thousand in the paper.

Biggs. You know, nobody in the world would ever know who had it?

Skimmerhorn. No, they wouldn't.

Biggs. What do you say?

Skimmerhorn. I say fifty-fifty.

Biggs. Damn you, Skimmerhorn, if I hadn't been in business with you for twenty years I'd say you were a crook!

Skimmerhorn. If I wasn't a crook after twenty years with you I'd be slow in the head and hard of hearing!

Biggs. What's fifty per cent of twenty-five thousand? Twelve thousand five hundred? And what's forty per cent? Ten thousand! Are you going to hold up the deal for two thousand five hundred?

Skimmerhorn. I certainly am.

Biggs. All right, take it. Fifty-fifty on this one deal.

Skimmerhorn. And on the Van Dorn deal, too.

Biggs. Why, you fat louse—
   [Van Dorn *comes in from the right out of the shadows.*]

Van. Sorry to bother you gentlemen, but—

Biggs.
   [*As they stuff the bills into their pockets*]
   Where the hell did you come from?

Van. Why, you're not friends of mine, but there's a storm blowing in and it occurred to me I might show you where you could keep dry under a ledge.

Biggs. Thanks. Much obliged.

Van. Want me to go with you?

Biggs. No, thanks—Let's get a little nearer the **light**.

Skimmerhorn. Good idea.

> [BIGGS *and* SKIMMERHORN *go out right.* VAN *looks after them, then picks up one of the discarded envelopes and studies it. He sits.* LISE *comes up the rocks in the rear and stands looking out to the river, shading her eyes from the beacon.*]

Lise. You who have watched this river in the past
till your hope turned bitterness, pity me now,
my hope gone, but no power to keep my eyes
from the mocking water. The hills come down like
sand,
and the long barges bear them off to town,
to what strange market in what stranger town,
devouring mountains? but never, in all days,
never, though I should watch here without rest,
will any ship come downward with the tide
flying the flag we knew.

> [VAN *rises.* LISE *draws back an instant, then comes down a step toward him.*]

Do you hear my voice?

Van. Yes, lady.

Lise. Do you see me in the light,
as I see you?

Van. Yes.

Lise. You are one of those
the earth bears now, the quick, fierce wizard men
who plow the mountains down with steel, and set
new mountains in their sky. You've come to drive
machines through the white rock's heart.

Van. Not I. I haven't.
I hate them all like poison.

Lise. You're against them—
   the great machines?

Van. I'd like to smash the lot,
   and the men that own them.

Lise. Oh, if there were a friend
   among so many enemies! I wish
   I knew how to make you friend. But now my voice
   shrinks back in me, reluctant, a cold thing,
   fearing the void between us.—I have seen you.
   I know you. You are kind.

Van. How do you know?

Lise. When I have been most lonely in the spring,
   the spring rain beating with my heart, I made
   a wild flower garden; none of these I knew,
   for none I knew are here, flowers of the woods,
   little and lovely, nameless. One there was
   like a pink moccasin, another low
   with blotted leaves, wolf-toothed, and many more
   rooted among the fern. I saw you then
   come on this garden, secret as the tears
   wept for lost days, and drew my breath in dread
   that you should laugh and trample it. You smiled
   and then went on. But when I came again
   there was a new flower growing with the rest,
   one I'd not seen. You brought and placed it there
   only for love of gardens, ignorant whose
   the garden you enriched. What was this flower?

Van. Wild orchid. It was your garden?

Lise. Yes. You know
   the names of all the flowers?

Van. Yes.

Lise. But then
  you'd teach them to me?

Van. Yes.

Lise. Teach me the names.
  What is the tall three-petaled one that's black
  almost, the red's so dark?

Van. That's trillium.
  Speaking of flowers, tell me your name.

Lise. It's Lise,
  or used to be.

Van. Not now?

Lise. I'm weary of it,
  and all things that I've been. You have a lover?
  She'll be angry?

Van. She's angry now. She's off
  and gone. She won't come back.

Lise. Love me a little,
  enough to save me from the dark. But if
  you cannot give me love, find me a way!
  The seas lie black between your harbor town
  and mine, but your ships are quick. If I might see
  the corner where the three streets come to an end
  on sundial windows, there, a child by a fire—
  no, but it's gone!

Van. I've seen you on the hills
  moving with shadows. But you're not shadow.

Lise. No.
Could one live and be shadow?

Van. Take my hand.

Lise. I dare not.

Van. Come, let me see your garden.

Lise. No.
I dare not. It is your race that thins our blood
and gathers round, besieging us with charms
to stay the feet of years. But I know you kind.—
Love me a little. Never put out your hand
to touch me, lest some magic in your blood
reach me, and I be nothing. What I am
I know not, under these spells, if I be cloud
or dust. Nor whether you dream of me, or I
make you of light and sound. Between this stone
and the near constellations of the stars
I go and come, doubting now whence I come
or when I go. Cling to me. Keep me still.
Be gentle. You were gentle with the orchid—
Take my hand now.

Van. You're cold.

Lise. Yes.

Van. Here on the Tor
the sun beats down like murder all day long
and the wind comes up like murder in the night.
I'm cold myself.

Lise. How have I slipped so far
from the things you have? I'm puzzled here and lost.
Is it so different for you? Keep my hand

and tell me. In these new times are all men shadow?
All men lost?

Van. Sometimes I stand here at night
and look out over the river when a fog
covers the lights. Then if it's dark enough
and I can't see my hands or where the rock
leaves off against the cloud, and I'm alone,
then, well I'm damned if I know who I am,
staring out into that black. Maybe I'm cloud
and maybe I'm dust. I might be old as time.
I'd like to think I knew. A man gets that way
standing staring at darkness.

Lise. Then—you do know.
It's better now.—Somewhere along a verge
where your life dips in dusk and my gray days
lift to the light a moment, we walk there
and our eyes meet.—Look, when the wizards come
to tear the mountain down, I'll have no place.
I'll be gone then.

Van. Child, they won't get our mountain!
Not if I have to shoot them as they come
they won't get our mountain! The mountain's mine,
and you're to make your garden where you like;
their feet won't step across it! All their world's
made up of fat men doing tricks with laws
to manage tides and root up hills. The hills
can afford to laugh at them! A race of grubs
bred down from men!

Lise. Is it the light I feel
come flooding back in me? Light or their charms
broken here, seeing your face?

Van. Your hands are warm.

Lise. I'm not cold now; for an instant I'm not cold,
seeing your face. This is your wizardry.
Let me stand here and see you.

Elkus.

[*Outside*]

Somewhere around here it was. Over toward the crane.

Dope.

[*Outside*]

What'd you go and put down the satchel for?

Elkus.

[*Outside*]

How did I know he'd sit on top of it?

[VAN *and* LISE *slip out through the rocks at the rear.* ELKUS *and*
DOPE *come in furtively from the right.*]

Dope. That's where. Under that rock.

Elkus. Keep your eye peeled. They're probably beating
the woods for us.

Dope. What's that?

[*He picks up an envelope.*]

Elkus. They got it.

Dope. God damn the rotten business! Now we will get
four hundred years.

Elkus. Now you're saying it—

Dope. What are we going to do?

Elkus. I'm going to send Buddy back with sandwiches to
see if the Judge got the money. If he did we'll stick
him up.

Dope. Hey, how about the troopers?

Elkus. If that was troopers I'm Admiral Dewey. Troopers would a' used the artillery. Come on.

Dope. O.K. Some pennies here.

Elkus. To hell with 'em.

[DOPE *flings the pennies to the left along the ledge.*]

Dope. Get going.

[ELKUS *and* DOPE *go out right.* BIGGS *and* SKIMMERHORN *come in along the ledge.*]

Biggs. Now it's raining money. I got the price of a morning paper square in the eye.

Skimmerhorn. I've got two thousand five hundred in a breast pocket, five thousand in a side pocket, and five thousand in the billfold.

[*He slaps his rear.*]

How do I look?

Biggs. No different. Just a lot of slop tied up with string. I've got five thousand in each side pocket and two thousand five hundred in the back. How do I look?

Skimmerhorn. You? All you need now's a pair of wings.

Biggs. Wish I could find the little guy with the big heart that gave us the money. Maybe he'd help us down off this devil's belfry.

Skimmerhorn. How about that shovel? Any possibility of making it pick us up and set us down below there?

Biggs. Well—if anybody was running it, sure. If it swung us over on that dump we could slide the rest of the way. You might wear out that last five thousand of yours, the five thousand that's bringing up the rear there.

Skimmerhorn. When do they come to work in the morning?

Biggs. They won't come to work tomorrow. They can't do any more till we buy this land.

Skimmerhorn. That's fine. That's just dandy.

Biggs. Nice idea though. Somebody might come along that could run the engine.

Skimmerhorn. You don't think that boy's coming back with the sandwiches?

Biggs. No, I don't.

Skimmerhorn. The way I feel inside I may never live to spend the money.

Biggs. Who you going to leave it to?

Skimmerhorn. Yeah?

Biggs. Oh, all right. Nothing personal.

> [*They sit facing the audience. The* CAPTAIN *and* HIS CREW, *including* DEWITT, *seep in through the rocks about them and stand quietly looking on.*]

There was something in that—what you said about needing a pair of wings.

Skimmerhorn. I should say that wings was the last thing likely to grow on you. You might grow horns, or a cloven hoof, or a tail, but wings, no. Not unless somebody slipped up behind you and bashed you over the head.

Biggs. You know, you'd murder me for what I've got in my pockets?

Skimmerhorn. You thought of it first. Who am I going to leave it to, you said.

Biggs. Just the same I wouldn't feel right if you were standing behind me with a rock in your hand.
   [*The* Crew *move in a little.*]

Skimmerhorn. You wouldn't?

Biggs. No. At the moment I wouldn't like to think anybody was creeping up behind me.
   [*He stiffens.*]

And by God there is somebody behind me.

Skimmerhorn.
   [*Without turning*]

What makes you think so?

Biggs.
   [*Running a hand over his hair*]

I just feel it. Turn around, will you? Take a look.

Skimmerhorn.
   [*Shivering*]

I will not.—Now you've got me worried.—Or else I'm getting light-headed for lack of food.
   [Biggs *ducks suddenly, as if from an imaginary blow.* Skimmer-
   horn *dodges in sympathy, and with their heads drawn in
   like turtles they creep forward on hands and knees.*]

Biggs. See anything?

Skimmerhorn. There's nothing there, you ass! What are you dodging? Want to scare me to death? Go on, turn around and face it like a man!

Biggs. Now!

Skimmerhorn. Now!
[*They whirl in concert, on their knees, facing the* CREW. *They look at each other.*]

Biggs. You're crazy!

Skimmerhorn. I certainly am. And so are you.

Biggs. That isn't there at all. There's nothing there.

Skimmerhorn. All right, you go up and hit it. I'll stay right here, and you go punch it in the nose.
[BIGGS *stands up.*]

Biggs. Uh—how do you do?—Maybe you—wanted to give us something, huh?
[*To* DEWITT.]

Uh—I see you brought your friends with you.—If you want the money back you can have it, you know. We don't want the money.
[*He sticks a hand in his pocket.*]

How much was it now?
[*The* CREW *look at each other gravely, tapping their foreheads.* SKIMMERHORN *rises.*]

Anything we could do, you know, we'd be glad to do. We're just trying to get down off here.

Skimmerhorn. You know what it is, Art; it's a moving picture company. And have they got the laugh on us?

Thinking they're real. It's all right, boys, we're onto you.

Biggs. Is that so? Say, I guess that's so. Was that moving picture money, you gave us, you fellows? We thought that was real. Ha ha! That's a good one. I guess you must have thought we were pretty funny, backing up that way and jumping around. You had us scared stiff!

[*The* CREW *shake their heads at each other.*]

Skimmerhorn. Come on, now, you aren't bluffing us at all. We've seen the pictures work over at Suffern. We were right out on location there with actors and producers and everything. Some of those girls didn't care whether they wore clothes or not. You're probably used to that where you come from, but I certainly got a kick out of pictures. Fifty chorus girls changing clothes in the bushes over there.

A silence. DEWITT *goes over to the* CAPTAIN *and whispers in his ear.*]

Asher. Lay a hand to it.

[DEWITT *catches hold of the dangling cable.*]

DeWitt. Lay a hand to it, lads. Heave.

[*The* CREW *catch the rope and haul on it, sailor-fashion. The shovel begins to descend.*]

The Crew.

[*Pulling down*]

> Heave! Heave! Heave! Heave!
> Coming a blow, coming a blow;
> Sea runs black; glass runs low;
> Heave! Heave!

Yardarm dips; foam's like snow!
Heave!

[*The shovel touches ground.*]

Biggs. Say, that's an act if I ever saw one. What kind of picture you putting on?

[*The* CAPTAIN *points to the interior of the shovel, looking at* BIGGS *and* SKIMMERHORN.]

What's up, anyway? Want us to go aboard? You know, we were just saying if somebody could run that thing we might get across to the dump and slide down out of here. Think you could swing it across there?

[*The* SAILORS *maneuver behind the two, edging them into the machine.*]

You might haul us up there and not be able to get us down, you know. It's mighty friendly of you to try it, but you'll have your work cut out. Sure, I'll get in. I'll try anything once.

[*He steps in,* SKIMMERHORN *follows reluctantly. The* CAPTAIN *and* DEWITT *guard their retreat. The* SAILORS *catch hold of the cable.*]

Take it easy, now.

The Crew.
Hoist! Hoist! Hoist! Hoist!
Tar on a rope's end, man on a yard.
Wind through an eye-bolt, points on a card;
Hoist! Hoist!
Weevil in the biscuit, rats in the lard,
Hoist!

[*They haul the two up as far as seems necessary, and swing the crane out over the abyss. Then they stop to contemplate their handiwork.*]

Biggs. I'll tell you what—if you catch that line over there some of you can hold back while the rest pull and that'll swing it around.—If that don't work you'd better pull it down again and we'll just wait till morning.

[*The* CREW *continue to stare silently.*]

Skimmerhorn. I'm getting sick at my stomach, boys; you better make it snappy. It gives me the megrims to look down this way.

[*He draws his feet up suddenly.*]

Biggs. Hey, don't rock the boat, you fool! It's a thousand miles straight down!

Skimmerhorn. I'm going to be sick.

Biggs. You better take us down, fellows. It's no good. You can't make it.

DeWitt. How about a game of bowls?

[*The* CAPTAIN *nods.*]

Pieter. Aye, a game of bowls.

[*Led by the* CAPTAIN, *the* CREW *begin to file out.*]

Biggs. Hey, you wouldn't leave us up here, would you? Hey, listen! You! You can have that money back, you know! We don't want the money! What in the name of time?—Listen, what did we ever do to you?—A joke's a joke, after all, but this thing might let go any minute! What's more you're responsible if anything happens to us! There's such a thing as laws in this country!

[*But they have all gone.*]

Skimmerhorn. I'm sick.

Biggs. You'll be sicker before you're out of this mess.— What do you think they meant by that?

Skimmerhorn. I don't know.—Quit kicking me, will you? I'm sick.

Biggs. Well, keep it to yourself.

Skimmerhorn. I wish I thought I could.

Biggs. Help, somebody! Help! We're stuck up here!

Skimmerhorn. What good's that going to do?

Biggs. You don't think they'll leave us here, do you?

Skimmerhorn. I don't know. I don't care. I wish I was dead!—Say, keep away from me, will you? What are you trying to do, pick my pocket?

Biggs. Pick your pocket, you fish? All I ask is keep your feet out of my face.

Skimmerhorn. Well, where in hell's my bill-fold?

Biggs. How do I know? Do you think I took it?

Skimmerhorn. Come on, now. Where is it?
   [*He searches his clothes frantically.*]

Biggs. You're probably sitting on it.—You are sitting on it. There it is.

Skimmerhorn.
   [*Finding it.*]
Jeez, I might have lost it.

Biggs. Now you'd better count it. Just to make sure it's good.

Skimmerhorn. I think I will.
   [*He begins to count the bills.*]

It's good money, Art. Look at it.

Biggs. Not a bad idea, either.

> [*He takes out money and counts it. There is a flash, a long roll and a crash of thunder. Then another and another.*]

Isn't that coming pretty close?

Skimmerhorn. What?

Biggs. The lightning, you fool! Put your money away before you get it wet. You know what I think?

Skimmerhorn. No.

Biggs. There's something up there taking pot shots at us.

Skimmerhorn. There's one thing about money you find. You don't have to pay income tax on it.

Biggs. That's true.

> [*There is a terrific flash, a crash, and the stage is in darkness.*]

That one got the beacon!

> [*Another flash runs right down the crane.*]

Good God, will you quit that? That's close enough!—Say, do you know any prayers?

Skimmerhorn. I know one.

Biggs. Say it, will you?

Skimmerhorn. Matthew, Mark, Luke and John,
Bless the bed that I lie on.

Biggs. That's not much good, that one.

Skimmerhorn. It's the only one I know.—Hey, catch it—hey!

Biggs. What?

> [*The lightning is now an almost perpetual illumination, the thunder a constant roll.*]

Skimmerhorn. I dropped fourteen ten dollar bills!

Biggs. Do you know we're going to die here?

Skimmerhorn. We're going to what?

Biggs. Will you quit counting money? We're going to be killed! We're going to die right here in our own steam shovel!

Skimmerhorn. Oh, no. I can't die now. I'm not ready to die!

Biggs. I wish you'd put up your money, then, and pray!

Skimmerhorn. I don't know how to pray.

> [*A crash*]

Biggs.

> [*On his knees*]

Oh, God, I never did this before, and I don't know how, but keep me safe here and I'll be a better man! I'll put candles on the altar, yes, I'll get that Spring Valley church fixed up, the one that's falling down! I can do a lot for you if you'll let me live! Oh, God—

> [*A crash*]

Skimmerhorn.

> [*On his knees, his hands full of money*]

Oh, God, you wouldn't do a thing like that, hang us up in our own steam shovel, wet through, and then strike us with lightning! Oh, God, you've been kind to us to-

night, and given us things we never expected to get so
easy; don't spoil it now!—God damn it, there goes another batch of bills!

[*He snatches at the falling money, and is hauled back by* BIGGS.]

I don't know how to pray! What makes you think
there's anybody up there, anyway?

[*Another crash*]

Biggs. Say the one you know then, for God's sake—say it!

Skimmerhorn. Matthew, Mark, Luke and John,
Bless the bed that I lie on!

Biggs. Matthew, Mark, Luke and John,
Bless the bed—Oh, God, I've got an old mother de-
pendent on me; please let me live! Why don't you tell
him you'll give the money back?

Skimmerhorn. Because I won't! And you won't, either!

[*A crash*]

Biggs. Now you've done it! Can't you keep anything to
yourself? There's such a thing as being politic, even
when you're talking to God Almighty!

[*Thunder again*]

CURTAIN

HIGH TOR
ACT TWO

ACT TWO

Scene I

SCENE: *The Tor and the steam shovel as before, only five or six hours later. It's still pitch dark, and* BIGGS *and* SKIMMERHORN *are still in the shovel. They are, however, fast asleep in much the same postures they took formerly on the ground. Under the shovel sits* DEWITT, *picking up and smoothing on his knee a few bills which he has found blowing loose on the rock. The beacon light flashes into the scene.*

DeWitt. There comes on the light again, too, the sweeping light that withers a body's entrails. No sooner out than lit again.—

[*Two snores rise from the sleeping pair.*]

Aye, take your ease and rest, you detachable Doppelgangers, swollen with lies, protected by the fiends, impervious to lightning, shedding rain like ducks—and why wouldn't you shed rain? your complexions being pure grease and your insides blubber? You can sleep, you can rest. You of the two-bottoms. You make nothing of the lightning playing up and down your backbones, or turning in on cold iron, but a poor sailor out of Holland, what rest has he?—

[*He smooths a bill.*]

These will be tokens and signs, these will, useful in magic, potent to ward off evil or put a curse on your enemies. Devil's work or not, I shall carry them on me, and make myself a match for these fulminating latterday spirits.

[*He pouches the bills.*]

I'm hanged if it's not noticeable at once, a sort of Dutch courage infused into the joints and tissues from the mere pocketing up of their infernal numbered papers.

[*He takes out a bill and looks at it.*]

That's sorcery, that's witchcraft, that's black art for you—that's a trick after the old one's heart; why, this stuff would make a man out of a cocked hat and a pair of crutches!

[*He slaps his chest.*]

Now I shall face destiny and take it like a pinch of snuff! Which reminds me I could use a pinch of snuff.

[*He takes out his snuffbox.*]

Snuff? When have I reached for snuff? It would seem to me I haven't gone after snuff in something like two hundred years!

[*He ladles into both nostrils and sneezes violently.*]

Aha, DeWitt! You're a man, DeWitt! A man and a devil! And what shall we wish for now that we have wishing papers in the pockets of our pantaloons? What but a woman, one of these new female furies of theirs, wearing pants like a man, and with nothing to indicate her sex but the general conformation!

[*He draws out bills.*]

Let my woman appear, god of the numbered papers, and let her wear what she likes, so long as a man can make out how she's made. Let her appear within this next three minutes, for God knows how long this mood will last in an old man!

[*He takes another pinch of snuff.*]

Aha! Destiny, present occasions!

[BUDDY *enters carrying beer and sandwiches.*]

Buddy. Hello.

DeWitt. What answer would a man make to that now? That's a strange greeting.

Buddy. Seen a couple of old fat men around anywhere?

DeWitt. Boy, I have seen nothing else all night.

Buddy. Where are they?

DeWitt. You wish to find a couple of old fat men?

Buddy. That's right.

DeWitt. I begin to doubt the supernal powers of these new angel-demons. Here he stands in their presence and asks very foolishly if old DeWitt has seen them.

Buddy. What's foolish about that?

DeWitt. A very cheap, witless little cabin boy unless all signs fail. One who carries packages and lives very badly by the day on half a skilling. A cabin boy.

Buddy. What's the matter with you?

DeWitt. What do you carry in the bag?

Buddy. That's my business.

DeWitt. He has a business then. He is not perhaps so witless as he appears.

Buddy. Are you going to tell me where those two are or do you want me to blow your brains out?

DeWitt. Is my carcass so thin you think to puff my brains out with a breath? Look, 'prentice devil, I am one of

you. I bear your signs and symbols. Here you see your
own countersign, a cabalistic device of extreme rarity
and force. What have you in the bag?

Buddy. Nothing but sandwiches. What do you mean,
you're one of us?

DeWitt.

[*Waving a sheaf of bills*]

You should recognize the insignium.

Buddy. Where'd you get it?

DeWitt. It blew away from these same two fat men,
'prentice devil, but now I have it, and it's mine and I
obtain power over you. Let me see these sandwiches.

Buddy. It blew away from the fat men, huh? All right,
that's what I want to know. It's mine, see? Hand it over.

DeWitt. You reveal yourself a very young and tender
'prentice.

Buddy. Hand it over or I'll fill you full of holes.

[*He sets down his packages and draws a gun, but* DeWitt *is
beforehand with two flintlock pistols.*]

DeWitt. You will drop your child's armory on the ground,
cabin boy, or I shall pull both triggers at once and
blast you halfway to the water.

[BUDDY *drops the gun.*]

I tell you I am now a great devil and violent. When I
wish merely I have my way.

[BUDDY *suddenly takes to his heels.* DeWitt *pulls the triggers
one after another; the hammers click but there is no ex-
plosion.*]

Why, this new world is not so bad. I am left in possession of the field.

[*He picks up the automatic and the bag and retreats to his
rock.*]

They fight with the weapons of children. Why, this
new world begins to be mine, to do as I please with.
Whatever kind of witch a sandwich may be come out
and let me interrogate you.

[*He takes out sandwiches.*]

If it be the food eaten by witches and wizards so much
the better, for I am now a wizard myself, and by the
great jib boom I haven't tasted food in God knows
when.

[*He eats.*]

A sweet and excellent morsel, very strong with garli*
and salami, medicinal for the veins and bladder.

[*He looks at his pistols.*]

A little glazed powder in the priming now, and these
two will speak with more authority if it becomes neces·
sary to defend my position.

[*He opens his powder horn and renews the priming.*]

We have seen the time, these blunderbusses and mysel*,
when we could defend a crow's nest against a whol*
crew in mutiny.

[*He pushes away the beer bottles with his foot.*]

I will eat your rations, cabin boy out of the new age,
and I will master you all, men and maids, now that my
strength comes back, but I will not drink your drink.
As Pastor Van Dorf observed very wisely before we
sailed; you may eat the food of the salvages, said he,
when you have voyaged to the new lands overseas; you

may share their rations, you may even make up to their
females after the fashion of sailors when the flesh is
weak, but drink none of their drink, said he, lest it
prove to be Circe's liquor and turn you all to hogs.

[*He eats.*]

Now I have small inclination to be a hog, but a man
I will be, and a very good man, too, of the fieriest
model.

[*He hears* Judith's *step.*]

Take care now, take care! I'm an armed man and a
man of blood!

[Judith *enters.*]

Judith.

[*At some distance*]

I beg your pardon, sir—

DeWitt. A woman, by the great tropical cross, a salvage
woman, come in answer to my unspoken desires.

[*He rises.*]

Your humblest servant, lady salvage; don't run away,
please. I'm a poor lost little man, wouldn't hurt a fly.

Judith. Who are you?

DeWitt. I'm a poor bosun, ma'am, but grown, God knows
how, to something of a person this last quarter hour.

Judith. Are you lost?

DeWitt. Completely adrift, ma'am, on my own mountain.

Judith. I don't think I've seen you before.

DeWitt. That may be, though I'm by way of being one

of the earliest inhabitants, not counting Indians and Patagonians.

Judith. You live on the mountain?

DeWitt. I maintain a residence here, though the situation eludes me at the moment.

Judith. Then you are acquainted with Van—Van Dorn?

DeWitt. I have seen him about.

Judith. Have you seen him tonight? I want to find him.

DeWitt. A mere blind, I should say, a maidenly defense, not to be too forthright; but sent by the talisman she is.

Judith. You have seen him?

DeWitt. God help him, I have, and in none too sanctified an attitude, saving your ladyship, for the lad was obviously a bit taken with the captain's wife, and she a married woman of some years' standing, young though she appear.

Judith. Where was he?

   [*She takes a step nearer to him.*]

DeWitt. I was never one to break in on a budding romance, sweetheart, and out of sheer delicacy I looked the other way.

Judith. No, but where was he, please? I can show you the path.

DeWitt. If you hunt out a very pretty little mistress in a bonnet somewhat behind the fashion, and look under the bonnet, you may chance to find him there.

Judith. Who are you?

DeWitt. Alpheus DeWitt, your most humble, bosun in the King's navy.

Judith. Forgive me—I shall look elsewhere—

DeWitt. Oh, but I assure you the lad's head over ears, ma'am, and loathe you'd be to interrupt him. Now a pretty lass like yourself should have no trouble replacing one sailor man with another in these stirring times. They come and go like a run of salmon.

Judith. Thank you.

DeWitt. I am myself a notionable lad. Salt tears have been wept for me by one and another.

Judith. No doubt.

DeWitt. I'm a blunt man, but constant and of considerable substance on my own wharf. Could you find it in your heart to love me?

Judith. I'm sorry, no.

DeWitt. To save a sad and desperate man from such a death as the lines of frost on a window? This is a kindly face, this of mine, and a kindly heart under a worn jerkin. These are real tears on my cheeks, too, and I weep them for you, lady.

Judith. I've never seen you till this moment.

DeWitt. Yet you could save me from their sorcery, with' one touch of your hand. I waited here for you, and you came.

Judith. You're horrible. Your face is horrible!

DeWitt. Is it, truly?

Judith. Ancient and terrible and horrible!—Tell me, where he is. I must know.

DeWitt. I don't know where he is.—You will think better of it. You need only pity me a little at first, or even laugh at me—so you do it kindly—

Judith. I'm in no mood for laughing, though you're ridiculous enough in that get-up.

DeWitt. It's not the latest, I know. And I'm a sad and broken man, lady, lost here among the lesser known peaks on the west side of the world, and looking only for a hand to help me.

Judith. I don't think you're lost at all.

DeWitt. Yes, lady, quite lost.—Nevertheless they run from me! You should have seen the lad run when I snapped my pistols at him.

Judith.

[*Stepping back*]

I should think he would.—Isn't there someone coming there now?

[*She points to the right.* DEWITT *faces about, reaching for his pistols.* JUDITH *slips away left.*]

DeWitt. If there be, watch what soldierly stand old De-Witt makes in defense of a lady! Come out, children of the new Satan, show yourselves in the light!

[ELKUS *and* DOPE *appear at right.*]

Elkus. Stick 'em up, bo!

[*They train automatics on him.*]

DeWitt. More toys! Stand back, you cheap new devils!

Elkus. Keep your hands down or I'll let you have it!

DeWitt. Watch now how a man holds off the fiends.
[*He lifts his pistols.*]

Elkus. Give it to him!
[*They fire a fusillade at* DEWITT, *who stands unmoved.*]

DeWitt. Firecrackers! You think me a devil like your-selves, to be exorcised with firecrackers?

Elkus. Give it to him again!
[*They fire once more.*]

DeWitt. Look, you puny devils, I'm a patient man, but in one moment I shall blow you both into the Tappan Zee!

Elkus.
[*Stepping up and pouring bullets into him*]

Too bad about you!
[*To* DOPE]

Take the money off him.

Dope. There's something funny about this guy! I can see right through him!

Elkus. No wonder. He's full of holes as a tennis racket.

Dope. No, by God, I can see through him! Look!
[*They step back together.*]

Elkus. What kind of a thing are you?

DeWitt. I'm not a man to be daunted by loud noises and firecrackers, Beelzebub! Go seek your place with the new father of hell before I send you there! Wizards!

Elkus. Where's the money?

DeWitt. I have a talisman and I ate a sandwich, devils!

Dope. Look, he's a moving picture! He's a regular church window! Look!

DeWitt. Disperse or I fire!

Elkus. Keep out of the way of that sawed-off shotgun!
   [DOPE *suddenly runs in and shoots* DEWITT *through the head, then retreats.*]

DeWitt. I warn you I begin to be annoyed!

Dope. It's no use, chief. I blew his brains out, and he's standing right there!

Biggs.
   [*Looking over the side of the shovel*]

   It's a war.

Elkus. Who said that?

Dope. Damned if I know.

Elkus. Beat it.

Dope. Yeah, beat it. Let the money hang. I'm for Canada.

Elkus You said it.
   [*They turn tail. As they are going* DEWITT *fires his pistols in the air.*]

DeWitt. Now am I master of the world of things,
   a buccaneer, a devil and a rake!
   Women love mastery, and they ran from me;
   they ran, these minor devils, ran from DeWitt!
   Look where they go there, sweetheart!
   [*He turns.*]

God, she's gone!
Lady! New-world lady! Are you lost?
[*He follows her.*]

Look now, I've dispersed them, brats and wizards,
spawn out of hell, they ran! I'm master here,
I'm master of the world! Look, lady!
[*He goes out left.*]

Skimmerhorn. Are you awake?

Biggs. I hope not. I hope this is a nightmare and I wake
up at home in bed.

Skimmerhorn. How did we get here?

Biggs. It must have been something we ate.

Skimmerhorn. I didn't eat anything.

Biggs. There's a bag of sandwiches down there on the
ground.

Skimmerhorn. That's a pleasant thought.

Biggs. Look for yourself.

Skimmerhorn. You're right. It's a bag of sandwiches.

Biggs. Didn't we send somebody for sandwiches and beer,
away back there before all this started?

Skimmerhorn. I don't know. I'm all wet, and I'm stuck
to the shovel.

Biggs. You do seem to be kind of going to pieces. What's
the matter with your toupee?

Skimmerhorn. The glue must have melted.
[*He takes off his wig.*]

Now I'll catch cold.

Biggs. If any of your constituency sees you in that condition you're out of office for good.

Skimmerhorn. I don't even care if I fall out. I feel terrible.

Biggs. Might be more comfortable for me if you did fall out.
[*He shifts his weight.*]

Skimmerhorn. Sit down! Quit rocking the boat!

Biggs. I've got a cramp. O ıch!

Skimmerhorn. Don't shove me!
[*He pushes* BIGGS.]

Biggs.
[*Pushing back*]

You want to pitch me overboard?

Skimmerhorn. Hey! You know I might have gone out?

Biggs. What do you care?

Skimmerhorn. I'll show you what I care!
[*They lock in a deadly struggle on the verge.*]

Biggs. Wait, Skimmer, look now! If one of us goes down the other goes too. Look at the drop. You don't want to splash on those rocks and I don't either.

Skimmerhorn. Let go then.

Biggs. I'll let go when you do. I'll count three **and we'll** both let go.

Skimmerhorn. All right.

Biggs. One—two—three.
  [*They let go and catch the ropes over the swinging basket.*]

That's better. Now take it easy, buddy. You woke up feeling like poison this morning. After this you count ten when you get an impulse to push anybody.

Skimmerhorn. Same to you.

Biggs. Fine.
  [*They sit down cautiously.*]

Skimmerhorn. How in hell did those sandwiches get there?

Biggs. How in hell did we get here?

Skimmerhorn. You haven't got a fishing hook on you, have you?

Biggs. No, I haven't.
  [*They sit gloomily looking at the sandwiches.* LISE *and* VAN *come in from the left.*]

Van. Nothing in all the woods
is silent as the owl; you see his shadow
but never hear his wings. The partridge now,
every time he takes off he creaks and cranks
like an old Ford. You never heard such a fuss;
but he's quiet on the ground.

Lise. And is there a squirrel
that flies, bird-fashion?

Van. Well, there's a flying squirrel,
but he's more the glider type. No engine, see,

but he'll do thirty yards. He's on the way
to be a bat if he's not careful.

Lise. How?

Van. He'll leave off tail and put on wing until
he's mostly wing. No doubt the bat was once
some kind of flying mouse.

Lise. Some men have wings.
I've seen them overhead.

Van. That's all put on.
They've no more wings than a goat. When they come
down.

Lise. I've hoped that it was true that men had wings.

Van. Why?

Lise. Oh, they've lived so long, and tried so hard,
and it all comes to nothing.

Van. Having wings,
would that be something?

Lise. Yes, it seems so. And yet
a bird has wings.

Van. And he gets nowhere.

Lise. Yes.
Nothing but just to be a bird, and fly,
and then come down. Always the thing itself
is less than when the seed of it in thought
came to a flower within, but such a flower
as never grows in gardens.

Biggs. Eh—Van Dorn!

Van.

   [*Looking up*]

   What are you doing on the roost, you birds?
   Building a nest?

Biggs. We can't get down.

Van. I'd say
   it ought to be just as easy to get down
   as it was to get up there.

Skimmerhorn. Will you help us out?

Van. You look all right to me. What happened to you?

Biggs. Everything.

Van. How did you get there?

Biggs. God,
   it's a long story.

Van. You've been there all night?

Biggs. Yes, all night.

Van. I wouldn't want to spoil it.
   It's too good to be true. You see those two,
   Lise, there in the scoop?

Lise. They're pitiful.
   Shouldn't you help them?

Van. No. Since time began
   there haven't been two fat-guts that deserved
   a hoisting like those two. In their own machine—
   that makes it perfect.

Lise. What have they done?

Van. They've been
  themselves, that's all. Two thieves, a probate judge
  and a manipulator, hand and glove
  to thieve what they can get. They've got High Tor
  among other things, and mean to carve it down,
  at three cents a square yard.

Lise. These poor old men?

Van. Yes, these poor old men.

Lise. Let them hang there then!

Van. They'll hang there for all me.
  [LISE *and* VAN *turn to go.*]

Skimmerhorn. I'll tell you what,
  Van Dorn, I'll let you have that validation
  if you'll help me down.

Van. That means I'd own the land?

Skimmerhorn. Yes, you'd own it.

Van. Only you'd cancel it,
  once you got down.

Skimmerhorn. To tell the truth I couldn't,
  not if you had the paper.

Van. Toss it over;
  I'd like to see it.
  [SKIMMERHORN *gets out an envelope and throws it to* VAN.]

Biggs. You're a simple judge!
  Now the land's his.

Van. There's a bond goes with this,
  a bond signed by the court. Oh, I looked it up.
  I've read that much law.

Skimmerhorn. Yes, I'll keep the bond
  till we're on your level.

Van. Then I'd advise you both
  to make yourself a nest with two-three sticks,
  like a couple of crows, and settle down to see
  what you can hatch—or maybe lay an egg—
  you'll have plenty of time.

Biggs. Come now, Van Dorn,
  we're in a bad way. It drops off straight down
  a thousand feet here, and Judge Skimmerhorn
  has vertigo. Why, just to save a life,
  out of common humanity, lean on that cable
  and pull us in.

Van. This one?
    [*He pulls. The shovel dips.*]

Biggs. Oh, no, no! God,
  do you want to dump us out!

Van. You said to pull it.

Biggs. Not that one! This! Pull up on that again!
  We're sliding!

Van. Sure.
    [*He rights the shovel.*]

  Now you know how it feels
  when you kick out the props from under men
  and slide 'em on the relief rolls. Ever think
  how that might feel?

Biggs. You don't know what we've both
  been through, Van Dorn. Rained on and struck by
                lightning,

no dinner; we're half-crazy; we've had nightmares,
funny people in hats; that's how we got here,
one of those nightmares!

Van. You sound disconnected.
Maybe you've lost your minds; still I'm not melting
down in my shoes with compunction. The fact is
he's clinging to the bond, Judge Skimmerhorn;
he's not too sunk for that. Now here's my bargain:
You're hanging onto life by one steel cable,
but that's much safer than the spider web
most men have to trust to. Toss me the bond,
Judge Skimmerhorn, or I'll give this line a yank
and you won't even hang.

Skimmerhorn. You wouldn't do it.

Van. Oh, wouldn't I? For a two-cent lollipop
I'd pull the chain right now!

Skimmerhorn. You wouldn't do it!

Van. Hang on, then! Just for a taste, how's the incline
now?
A little steep?
 [*He pulls the line. The shovel tips as before.*]

Biggs. Pull it up! Take the God damn bond!—
throw it to him!

Skimmerhorn. I will not!

Van. Try this then.
 [*He tips the shovel further.*]

Biggs. Give him his bond! I'm slipping!

Skimmerhorn. I will not!

Biggs. I say you will! What good's the money to you
   if you're bologny?

Skimmerhorn. What money?

Biggs. You know what money!

Skimmerhorn. Straighten it up.

Van. Do I get the bond?

Skimmerhorn. Hell, yes!
   [VAN *restores their equilibrium.*]

You get the bond if you agree to accept
five thousand for your claim.
   [*He brings out a paper.*]

Van. Don't stall with me!
   I'll never have a chance like this again,
   and it's hard to resist!

Skimmerhorn. I'm offering you five thousand!
   Five thousand! Cash!

Van.
   [*Leaping to the rope.*]
   Keep it!

Biggs. Give him his bond!
   [*He wrenches the paper from* SKIMMERHORN *and sails it to* VAN.]

And now you've got it how's five thousand sound?
You settle for it?

Van. Bid against them, Lise. It's a game.
   What would you say, Lise?
   They offer me five thousand.

Lise. Pieces of silver?

Van. Pieces of silver.

Lise.

[*Smiling*]

But I'll give you more!
Only five thousand for this crag at dawn
shedding its husk of cloud to face a sunrise
over the silver bay? For silver haze
wrapping the crag at noon, before a storm
cascading silver levin? For winter rains
that run in silver down the black rock's face
under a gray-sedge sky? For loneliness
here on this crag? I offer you nine thousand!
To be paid in silver!

Van. You hear? I've got nine thousand;
what am I offered?

Biggs. Make it ten thousand—
and let us down in the bargain!

Van. Yes? Ten thousand?
A mountain for ten thousand? Hear them, Lise,
In their despair they lift it by a grand!
Should it go for ten?

Skimmerhorn. We'll never get it back—
but that's all right.

Van. Yes, Lise?

Lise. Will they pay
no more then for the piling of this stone,
set in its tall hexagonals by fire
before men were? Searching a hundred kingdoms

men will not find a site for lodge or tower
more kingly! A hundred thousand, sir, in silver,
this is my offer!

Van. Come now, meet it boys—
I have a hundred thousand!

Biggs. She's a fraud!
She's no dealer; she's a ringer, primed
to put the price up! What do you mean by silver?
She won't pay silver!

Van. Coinage of the moon,
but it's current here!

Skimmerhorn. Ten thousand, cash, and that's
the last. Five thousand out of my pocket, see,
and five from Biggs!
    [*He pulls out a bundle of bills.* BIGGS *does the same.*]

Take a good look at cash,
see how that operates!
    [*He tosses down the roll.* BIGGS *follows suit.*]

Van. You go well-heeled
when you go mountain-climbing. Is it real?

Skimmerhorn. Well, look it over. Count it.
    [VAN *takes up one packet, then another.*]

Van. Where did this come from?

Skimmerhorn. Where would you think?

Van. I'll say I got a shock.
    [*He studies the bills again.*]

I don't want your money.

Biggs. What's wrong with it?

Van. Didn't I tell you I had a hundred thousand?
Take the stuff back. We reckon in moonlight here!
Put up your mitts!
[*He tosses the bundles back.*]

Biggs. It's yours if you want it.

Van. No,
oh, no, I thank you. It's no sale. What's more
I never meant to sell. The auctioneer's
about to take a walk.

Biggs. Well, look, we're sitting
right where we were.

Van. You sit there for your health,
and think it over.

Skimmerhorn. You won't do that, Van Dorn,
just leave us here.

Van. Watch me, if you don't think so.
[*He gives an arm to* LISE.]
Let me tell you about those babes in the wood,
did I say they were thieves?
[*They start out.*]

Biggs. Make it fifteen!

Van. Go to sleep.

Skimmerhorn. Well, twenty! and let us down!

Van. Sweet dreams.

Skimmerhorn. We'll run you out of the state, Van Dorn!

Van. You'll have to get down first!

Skimmerhorn. Is he going away
and leave us sitting?

Biggs. Looks like it.
  [VAN *and* LISE *move off.*]

Skimmerhorn. Say, Van Dorn,
will you pitch us up a sandwich?

Van. Sure; they're soggy,
lying out in the rain.
  [*He returns and tosses sandwiches to them.*]

Biggs. Thanks.

Van. Don't mention it.
  [*He goes out right with* LISE. BIGGS *and* SKIMMERHORN *unwrap
  sandwiches.*]

Skimmerhorn. He got away with that bond.

Biggs. Yeah.

Skimmerhorn. Looks as if we wouldn't make anything on
Van Dorn.

Biggs. That's what it looks like.

Skimmerhorn. Christ.

Biggs. Well, we've still got the windfall.

Skimmerhorn. Yeah, we've got that.

Biggs. And here he comes again.

Skimmerhorn. Who?

Biggs. Our mascot, little rabbit's foot, little good-luck
token, little knee-high with the big heart.

[DeWitt *comes in from the left, looks at the place where the
sandwiches were and then at the two in the shovel. He
mutters.*]

DeWitt. Magic again! More devil's work! And the woman
gone, slipped round a turn, and the scent was cold
for an old dog like me. By the mizzen yards,
it's wearing to the temper of a man
even if he's not choleric!—And those two,
those buzzards of evil omen, brooding there
on how they'll cut the mountain like a pie
and sell it off in slices!

[*He looks at his pistols.*]

One apiece.
It should be just enough, and it's a wonder
I never thought of it.

[*He lifts his pistols, the two drop their sandwiches into the
void, and cower down; he clicks the hammers.*]

Damp again! Well, boys,
we'll fix that.

[*He sits down to freshen the priming.*]

They'll brood over us no more,
those two sea-lions. Damn the rain and mist;
it penetrates the priming! Damn the flint,
and damn the spring! A brace of fine horse-pistols,
that's what the Jew said back in Amsterdam;
it takes a horse to cock 'em. Now then, damn you,
blow 'em off their perch!

[*As he rises his eye catches something out on the Zee. He stands
transfixed for a moment, watching.*]

It can't be there!
    It's there! It's gone! I saw it! Captain Asher!
    Captain! Captain! Captain! Captain Asher!

     [BIGGS *and* SKIMMERHORN *have ducked down again* DEWITT
         rushes out to the right, firing his pistols in the air in his
         excitement. BIGGS *sits up, then* SKIMMERHORN.]

Skimmerhorn. Am I hurt? Do you see blood anywhere?

Biggs. It seems there was nothing there.

     [*They contemplate the place where* DEWITT *stood.*]

                 CURTAIN

ACT TWO

Scene II

SCENE: *Another part of the Tor.* LISE *is sitting high up on a ledge, looking out over the Zee.* VAN *stands near her, looking at her as she speaks. She has his old felt hat in her lap and has woven a wreath of dandelions around the brim. The beacon light strikes athwart her face.*

Lise. But nobody likes this flower?

Van. I like it now.
I used to think it was a weed, but now,
well, it's a flower now.

Lise. The dandelion.
Where will you find another prodigal
so merry or so golden or so wasteful,
pouring out treasure down the sides of hills
and cupping it in valleys?

Van. Buttercups
and touch-me-nots. The touch-me-not's a shoe,
a tiny golden shoe, with a hair-spring latchet
for bees to loosen.

Lise. When did you part from Judith?

Van. Judith?

Lise. When did she go away?

Van. Last evening.
But it seems longer.

Lise. Why?

99

Van. Why, a lot's happened.—
    It's almost morning.

Lise. How do you know?
    [*He steps up to the ledge.*]

Van. See that star,
    that heavy red star back in the west? When that
    goes down, then look for the morning star across
    Long Island Sound, and after that the lights
    dim down in the gray.

Lise. You loved her, very much?

Van. Yes.

Lise. I loved someone too. I love him still.

Van. No, you're mine now.
    [*He sits beside her.*]

Lise. See the great gulf that lies
    between the heavy red star down the west
    and the star that comes with morning? It's a long way.
    There's that much lies between us.

Van. Not for me.

Lise. Even for you.—You're weary?

Van. Well, the truth is
    I sometimes sleep at night.

Lise. Put your head down.
    I'll hold you.
    [*He lays his head on her knees and stretches out.*]
Now I'll wish that I could sing
    and make you sleep. Somehow they're all forgotten,

the old songs. Over and over when the birds
begin at morning I try hard to catch
one tune of theirs. There's one that seems to say:

> Merrily, merrily, chirr, chirr,
> Lueté, lueté, stee—
> Merrily, merrily, chirr, lueté,
> Chirr, lueté, stee.

That's only what it says; for what it sings
you'll have to ask the bird.

Van. I know it, though.
That's the song sparrow.

Lise. Have I come so near?

Van. Say it again.

Lise. I can't. May I ask you something?

Van. Yes.

Lise. There's so much that's changed now men can fly
and hear each other across seas, must men
still die—do they die still?

Van. Oh, yes, they die.
Why do you ask?

Lise. Because I'm still so young,
and yet I can't remember all the years
there must have been.—In a long night sometimes
I try to count them, but they blow in clouds
across the sky, the dancing firefly years,
incredible numbers.—Tell me how old you are
before you go to sleep.

Van. Lying here now
there's not much logic in arithmetic.

Five, or six, maybe. Five or six thousand, maybe.
But when I'm awake I'm twenty-three.

Lise. No more?

Van. No more.

Lise. Tell me why it is I am as I am
and not like you?

Van. I don't know, Lise.

Lise. But tell me.
Have I been enchanted here? I've seen
the trap-rock men, there in the shovel, seeming
so stupid and so pitiful. Could these
use charms and rites to hold wrecked mariners
forever in a deep cataleptic spell
high on a mountain-fringe?

Van. The trap-rock men?
They're no more wizards than I am. They buy
and sell, and when they've had their fill of dust
they die like the rest of us.

Lise. But they laid spells
about us?

Van. There are no wizards and no spells.
Just men and women and money and the earth
the way it always was. The trap-rock men
don't know you're here.

Lise. It's not sorcery then. If I had died
and left my bones here on the mountain-top
but had no memory of it, and lived on
in dreams, it might be as it is. As children

sure we were told of living after death,
but there were angels there, and onyx stone
paving an angel city, and they sang
eternally, no darkness and no sun,
nothing of earth. Now can it be men die
and carry thence no memory of death,
only this curious lightness of the hands,
only this curious darkness of the mind,
only to be still changeless with the winters
passing; not gray, not lined, not stricken down,
but stamped forever on the moving air,
an echo and an image? Restless still
with the old hungers, drifting among men,
till one by one forgotten, fading out
like an old writing, undecipherable,
we lose our hold and go? Could it be true?
Could this be how men die?

Van.

   [Half asleep]

It may be, Lise.
I love you when you speak.

Lise. And I love you.
But I am dead, and all the crew is dead;
all of the *Onrust* crew—and we have clung
beyond our place and time, on into a world
unreal as sleep, unreal as this your sleep
that comes upon you now. Oh, you were cruel
to love me and to tell me I am dead
and lie here warm and living! When you wake
we shall be parted—you will have a world
but I'll have none! There's a chill falls on me,
the night-dew gathering, or my mind's death chill—

knowing at last I know.—You haven't heard.
You told me this in a half-dream. You've been kind.
You never thought to hurt me. Are you asleep?

Van. I think I was.

Lise. Sleep, sleep. There was once a song,
if only I could call back air and words,
about a king who watched a goblet rising
and falling in the sea. It came to land
and on the rim the king's name was inscribed
with a date many years before. Oh, many years,
a hundred or three hundred. Then he knew
that all his life was lived in an old time,
swept out, given to the waters. What remained
was but this goblet swimming in the sea,
touching his dust by chance.—But he's asleep.
And very well he might be with dull stories
out of old songs.—Sleep, sweet; let me have
your head here on my knees, only this night,
and your brown hair round my finger.

[*A girl's shadowy figure comes in from the right, walking lightly, pauses, as if at seeing them, and turns to go, the face still unrevealed.*]

Are you Judith?

Judith. Yes.

Lise. The lad's asleep, but when he wakes
you'll have him back.

Judith. Do you dispose of him
just as you please?

Lise. No. It's not what I please.
It's what will happen.

Judith. I don't know who you are.

Lise. I'm but a friend of his. You left him bitter
  going away so lightly. I was bitter—
  and so we tried to play at being lovers,
  but it won't do. He'll wake, and he'll be yours,
  all as it was. Only if I may hold him
  while he lies here asleep, it helps a little
  and I'll be happier.

Judith. You'll keep him then
  after he wakes.

Lise. No.

Judith. Then why are you crying?

Lise. Am I crying?
  Well, they're not for him, nor you, these tears;
  something so far away, so long ago,
  so hopeless, so fallen, so lost, so deep in dust
  the names wash from the urns, summons my tears,
  not love or longing. Only when you have him,
  love him a little better for your sake,
  for your sake only, knowing how bitterly
  I cried, for times past and things done.

Judith. You're strange—
  the dress you wear's strange, too.—Who are you then?
  I'm—afraid of you!

Lise. Afraid of tears
  and a voice out of long ago? It's all I have.

Judith. No—no—I'm not afraid. Only for him.
  I've done my crying, too.—Shall I come back?

Lise. Don't wake him now. Come back at dawn. You'll find him
here alone.

[Two *or* THREE SAILORS *appear on the rocks at the rear, looking out over the Zee.*]

Pieter. Look for yourself.

A Sailor. Aye.

Pieter. Do you make her out?

The Sailor. She's the square top-yards.

Another Sailor. Now, God, if it were she!

Pieter. It's the brigantine! The *Onrust* from up-river
tacking this way!

Asher.
    [*Outside*]
Lise! Lise! Lise!
    [*The* CAPTAIN *comes in at the rear with* DEWITT.]

Lise, the ship's on the river! Quick, there's haste!
She must catch the tide down-stream!

Lise. Hush! Hush! You'll wake him!

Asher. But look across the Zee! The *Onrust's* in
and waiting for us!

Lise. But you say it, Asher,
    only to comfort me. There is no ship,
    nor are we caught in spells here, or enchanted,
    but spectres of an old time. The life we live
    is but a lingering, a clinging on,

our dust remembering. There is no ship,
only a phantom haunting down the Zee
as we still haunt the heights.

Asher. Look! The *Onrust!*
Look, Lise!

Lise. Yes, I see it.

Asher. Will you come?

Lise. Why would I stay? Why would I go? For go
or stay we're phantoms still.

Asher. But will you come?
Who is this lad?

Lise. Her lad. But he was hurt
and fell asleep.
  [VAN *wakes and lifts his head.*]

Asher. Come quickly!

Lise. Yes, for his sake
it's better I should go.

Van. Where must you go?
  [*She rises.*]

Lise. The *Onrust's* on the river
and we must catch the tide.

Van. Would you leave me now?

Lise. Yes, I must leave you.

Van. You'll go back with him?

Lise. Yes.

Van. And was nothing meant of all we said?

Lise. What could we mean, we two? Your hurt's quite
cured
and mine's past curing.

Van. Let me go with you then.

Lise. I should have told you if I'd only known
how we stood at the tangent of two worlds
that touched an instant like two wings of storm
drawn out of night; touched and flew off, and, falling,
fall now asunder through a wide abyss,
not to touch again.
> [*She steps back among the rocks.*]

Van. Let them go if they like!
What do I care about worlds? Any world you have
I'll make it mine!

Lise. You told me in your sleep.
There is no witchcraft. Men are as they were;
we're parted now.

Van. Give me your hand again!
They dare not take you from me, dare not touch **you**
no matter who they are, or where they come from—
they have no hold on us!

Lise. If I could stay!
If I could stay with you. And tend my garden
only a little longer!

Van. Put out your hand!

Lise. There were too many, many, many years.

Van. I'll be alone here—

Lise. No, not alone. When you must walk the air,
    as all must walk it sometime, with a tread
    that stirs no leaf, and breathe here with a breath
    that blows impalpable through smoke or cloud,
    when you are as I am, a bending wind
    along the grain, think of me sometimes then
    and how I clung to earth. The earth you have
    seems now so hard and firm, with all its colors
    sharp for the eye, as a taste's sharp to the tongue,
    you'll hardly credit how its outlines blur
    and wear out as you wear. Play now with fire
    while fire will burn, bend down the bough and eat
    before the fruit falls. For there comes a time
    when the great sun-lit pattern of the earth
    shakes like an image under water, darkens,
    dims, and the clearest voices that we knew
    are sunken bells, dead sullen under sea,
    receding. Look in her eyes.

> [VAN *looks at* JUDITH.]

Asher. Come!

Lise. See, the dawn
    points with one purple finger at a star
    to put it out. When it has quite gone out
    then we'll be gone.

> [VAN *looks at the dawn, then turns back toward* LISE.]

Van. Lise! Lise!

> [*But even as he speaks* LISE *and the* CREW *have disappeared.*]

Lise.

> [*Unseen*]

This is your age, your dawn, your life to live.
The morning light strikes through us, and the wind

that follows after rain tugs at our sails—
and so we go.

DeWitt.

    [Still half-seen]

And welcome you are to the age, too, an age of witches
and sandwiches, an age of paper, an age of paper money
and paper men, so that a poor Dutch wraith's more
                         man
than the thickest of you!

    [He steps back and vanishes. It is now dawn.]

Van. She never said good-bye.

Judith. There is a ship.

Van. Yes?

Judith. Tiny, with black, square sails;
low and small.

Van.

    [Still looking after Lise]

She'll be a phantom too
like all the rest. The canvas casts no shadow;
the light sifts through the spars. A moonlight rig
no doubt they call it.

Judith. I think I hear their voices
as they go down the crag.

Van. But you won't see them.
No matter what you hear.

The Sailors.

    [A wisp of chantey in the distance]

    Coming a blow, coming a blow,
    sea runs black, glass runs low.

Van. Just voices down the wind.
    Why, then they were all mist, a fog that hangs
    along the crevices of hills, a kind
    of memory of things you read in books,
    things you thought you'd forgotten. She was here,
    and she was real, but she was cloud, and gone,
    and the hill's barren of her.

Judith. There are no ghosts.

Van. I know—but these were ghosts or I'm a ghost,
    and all of us. God knows where we leave off
    and ghosts begin. God knows where ghosts leave off
    and we begin.

Judith. You were in love with her.

Van. She leaves the mountain barren now she's gone.
    And she was beautiful.

Judith. I came to tell you
    that I was wrong—I mean about the land—
    what you have here is better than one buys
    down in the towns. But since I come too late
    I'll say it and then go.—Your way was best.
    I think it always would be.—So, good night, Van—
    or, rather, it's good morning.

Van. Yes, it's morning.—
    Is it too late?

Judith. Oh, Van, I think it is.
    It was for Lise you were calling, not
    for Judith. I can't say I blame you much,

because she is more beautiful. And yet
you love her, and not me. You'll say they're ghosts
and won't come back. Perhaps. I'm not so certain
about the way of ghosts. She may come back.
And you still love her.

Van. There's no ship at all.
It faded in the dawn. And all the mists
that hung about the Tor, look how they lift,
pouring downstream with the wind. Whatever it was,
was said, or came between us, it's all gone
now it's daylight again.

Judith. I came to say
if only I could keep you, you should keep
the Tor, or what you wished. I'm sorry I went.
I'm sorry this has happened. But it has.
And so—

Van. Should I keep the Tor?

Judith. Yes, if you like.

Van. God knows they haven't left me much of it.
Look, where the new road winds along the ledge.
Look at the jagged cut the quarries make
down to the south, and there's a boy scout trail
running along the ridge Mount Ivy way,
where they try out their hatchets. There's the light,
and steps cut into stone the linesmen blew
for better climbing. The crusher underneath
dumps road rock into barges all day long
and sometimes half the night. The West Shore tunnel
belches its trains above the dead lagoons
that line the brickyards. Their damned shovel hangs

across my line, ready to gouge the peak
we're standing on. Maybe I'm ghost myself
trying to hold an age back with my hands;
maybe we're all the same, these ghosts of Dutchmen
and one poor superannuated Indian
and one last hunter, clinging to his land
because he's always had it. Like a wasp
that tries to build a nest above your door—
and when you brush it down he builds again,
then when you brush it down he builds again—
but after a while you get him.

Judith. Then you'll sell?

Van. I guess if you were with me then we'd sell
for what we could, and move out farther west
where a man's land's his own. But if I'm here
alone, I'll play the solitary wasp
and sting them till they get me.

Judith. If it's your way
then it's your way.

Van. I'll sell it if you'll stay.
Won't you stay with me, Judith?

Judith. I think I'd always hear you calling Lise
while I was standing by. I took a wrong turning
once, when I left you and went down the hill,
and now it may not ever be the same.
   [*She turns.*]

CURTAIN

HIGH TOR

ACT THREE

ACT THREE

SCENE: *The shovel still hangs over the verge, and* BIGGS *and* SKIM-MERHORN *still occupy it. The rising sun sends level rays across the rock, lighting their intent faces as they stare downward.* BIGGS *has torn a handkerchief into strips and tied them together into a string. He appears to be fishing for something which lies below the ledge, out of view of the audience. Over and over he tries his cast.*

Skimmerhorn. Little to the left.

Biggs. You don't say?

Skimmerhorn. Little to the right.

Biggs. Put it to a tune and sing it, why don't you?

Skimmerhorn. There! Almost!

Biggs. I don't need any umpire.

Skimmerhorn. Let me try it.

Biggs. Oh, no. You always were a butter-fingers.
   [*The string tightens.*]
   By Golly!

Skimmerhorn. It's on!

Biggs. You're explaining to me?
   [*He pulls up. A bottle of beer emerges from below.*]

Skimmerhorn. Fifty per cent!

Biggs. What?
   [*He pauses, the bottle in air.*]

117

Skimmerhorn. You tore up my handkerchief! Fifty per cent. That's the natural division between capital and labor.

Biggs. Oh, now I'm labor and you're capital.
> [*He pulls up carefully.*]

Skimmerhorn. Fifty per cent!

Biggs. I get the first pull at it. That's all I ask.
> [*The string parts, and the bottle descends silently into the void.*]

That's that.

Skimmerhorn. You should 'a let me handle it.

Biggs. Yeah. No doubt.

Skimmerhorn. Am I thirsty?

Biggs. Wait till the sun gets up a little. We'll be pan-fried in this thing.

Skimmerhorn. Look!
> [*He points down the rocks.*]

Biggs. If it's more of those little people I give up.

Skimmerhorn. It's a trooper.

Biggs. What do you know? Up early for a trooper, too. Listen, about that stuff in our pockets?

Skimmerhorn. Yeah?

Biggs. Do we say anything about it?

Skimmerhorn. Do you?

Biggs. Do you?

Skimmerhorn. No.

Biggs. Neither do I, then.

Skimmerhorn. Beautiful morning.

Biggs. I always say it's worth while being up early just to catch the sunrise.

[*A* TROOPER *climbs in followed by* SKIMMERHORN SENIOR.)

The Trooper. Hello!

Biggs. Hello, Patsy.

Patsy. Say, you boys had the wives worried down in Leden-town. Been looking for you all night. There they are, Mr. Skimmerhorn.

Skimmerhorn, Sr.
[*Winded*]

Good God!
[*He sits, a hand to his heart.*]

And I climbed up here. We thought you were under that rock slide.

Skimmerhorn. I guess you're disappointed.

Senior. The next time you two go on a bat and spend a night up a tree you can stay there and sober up.

Skimmerhorn. We haven't been drinking.

Senior.
[*Pointing to a bottle*]

What's that?

Skimmerhorn. Beer. But we didn't have a drop to drink. I'd certainly appreciate a swallow of that now.

Patsy.

[*Tossing up bottle*]

Here you are. Hair of the dog that bit you.

Biggs. We're not drunk. We're dry. We didn't have a drop to drink nor a bite to eat.

Patsy. All right. All right. Only the ground's covered with beer and sandwiches.

Biggs. You tell 'em how it was, Skimmer.

Skimmerhorn. You tell 'em.

Biggs. Well, you see, the whole thing's pretty complicated.

Patsy. I know. I've been through it. You wake up in the morning and you can't believe it yourself.

Biggs. I don't mean that. I'm sober as a judge.

Patsy. Yeah, what judge?

[*He hauls at a cable.*]

Can you lend me a hand with this, A.B.?

Senior. Give me a minute.

[*The shovel tips.*]

Biggs. Hey, not that one! The other one!

Patsy. Sorry. Not much of a mechanic.

Biggs. Straighten it up again.

[*Patsy does so.*]

Skimmerhorn. Are we never getting off this? My legs are paralyzed sitting here.

Biggs. So are mine.

Patsy.

[*Hauling down*]

It's too much for me alone.

Skimmerhorn. Got your wind yet, A.B.?

Senior. I don't know whether I want you down yet. You had your good time, now you can put in a few minutes paying for it.

Skimmerhorn. Oh, we had a good time, did we?

Senior. What were you doing? You came up here to buy Van Dorn's property; you're gone all night, and the whole damn town's up all night hunting for you! And we find you up in a steam shovel enjoying a hang-over!

Patsy. And now I know what a hang-over looks like.

Biggs. I tell you we didn't even have a drink of water!

Senior. I believe that!

Biggs. And we're thirsty! Have you got an opener?

Patsy. No, I haven't.

Senior. Before you open anything tell me what you were doing last night. Did you see Van Dorn?

Skimmerhorn. Sure we saw him.

Senior. Well, what did he say?

Skimmerhorn. He said no.

Senior. And I suppose that took all night?

Skimmerhorn. We had an argument.

Senior. And then he chased you up the crane, I suppose?

Skimmerhorn. No.

Senior. Well, how did you get up there?

Skimmerhorn. We were hauled up.

Senior. All right. Who hauled you up?

Skimmerhorn. You tell him, Art.

Biggs. Oh, no. You tell him.

Skimmerhorn. As a matter of fact, I don't think it happened.

Senior. You're there, aren't you?

Skimmerhorn. Yes, we're here.

Senior. Well, if you weren't drunk how did you get there?

Skimmerhorn. Well, you see, first we tried to negotiate
with Van Dorn.

Senior. And he wouldn't take the money?

Skimmerhorn. That's right.

Senior. Did you tell him he didn't really own the land?
Till the will was validated?

Skimmerhorn. Yes, we told him that.

Senior. And he still wouldn't talk business?

Skimmerhorn. He's stubborn. Stubborn as a mule.

Senior. Did you tell him you could take the land away
from him?

Skimmerhorn. Oh, yes.

Senior. And you offered him the twenty-five thousand?

Biggs. We offered him a fair price.

Senior. You were authorized to say twenty-five thousand.

Biggs. We didn't quite get to that. We offered ten.

Skimmerhorn. You see, we thought we'd save the company some money.

Senior. I'll bet you did. You thought you'd make a little on the side, and I'd never know.

Skimmerhorn. Oh, no.

Biggs. Oh, no.

Senior. All right, you offered ten and he wouldn't take it. Then what happened?

Skimmerhorn. Well, we couldn't get down because of the slide, so some sailors offered to let us down in this thing.

Senior. Sailors—up here?

Skimmerhorn. Little men, in big hats.

Biggs. Might have been a moving picture company.

Senior. Yeah? Any elephants? Or snakes?

Skimmerhorn. We're trying to tell you the truth!

Patsy. Certainly sounds like delirium tremens, boys.

Senior. Never mind, you were hauled up by pink ele phants, and then what?

Skimmerhorn. Van Dorn came along and started to dump us down the cliff.

Senior. What's Van Dorn look like? Kind of an octopus, with long feelers?

Skimmerhorn. Are you going to let us down out of this basket?

Senior. No. Not till you come across with what's been going on.

Skimmerhorn. All right. I'll talk when I'm down.

Senior. Can a grown man get pie-eyed on beer?

Patsy. Must have been something stronger.
    [VAN DORN *comes in from the right.*]

Senior. Who are you?

Van. Oh, I'm nobody. I just own the property.

Senior. What property?

Van. This.

Senior. Are you Van Dorn?

Van. I am.

Senior. I'm A. B. Skimmerhorn, Mr. Van Dorn, president of Igneous Trap-rock, and I'm glad to meet you.
    [*He puts out a hand.*]

Van.
    [*Ignoring the hand*]
    Are these friends of yours?

Senior. One's a nephew and one's a partner. Why?

Van. Because any friend of theirs is no friend of mine.

[JUDITH *and* THE INDIAN *enter at the rear. She is leading him.*]

Patsy. Who do you think you're talking to?

Van. A. B. Skimmerhorn, of Skimmerhorn, Skimmerhorn, Biggs and Skimmerhorn, small-time crooks and petty thieving done. Cheap.

Senior. Now, to be frank, there may have been some misunderstanding, Mr. Van Dorn. Those two were hardly in condition to negotiate. But I can offer you a fair price for your land, and if you don't take it we may have to push you a little, because we want this acreage and we intend to have it.

Skimmerhorn. He's got the validation papers.

Senior. You gave him the validation papers?

Biggs. We had to. He started to trip the machine.

Senior. That puts us in a sweet mess, that does. Will you take twenty-five thousand?

Van. No.

Senior. Will you take fifty thousand?

Van. No.

Senior. Then we go home, and the machinery can rust here. That's the best I can do.

Van. Fine. Let it rust.

Judith. Van?

Van. Yes, Judith.

Judith. There's someone here to see you.

Van. You want to see me, John?

The Indian. But I can wait. I have time enough.

Van. I'll be right with you.

Judith. I had to bring him, Van, because he said
his eyes were bad. He couldn't see the way.

Van. Thanks, Judith.

Senior. Look, Van Dorn, you know the saying,
every man has his price. I've heard it said
God has his price, if you'll go high enough.
Set a figure.

Van. I'm not thinking of prices.
I don't want to sell. Hell, fifty thousand's
too much money for me.

Senior. We'll give you less.

Van. I don't want less or more. It's not a matter
of money.

Senior. Will you take a partnership
in the company?

Van. No.

Senior. Good God, what do you want?

Van. I want to have it back the way it was
before you came here. And I won't get that. I know
what kind of fool I look to all of you,
all but old John there. But I'll be a fool
along with John, and keep my own, before

Van. I let you have an inch. John, fifty thousand
or this old hill-top. Is it worth keeping?

The Indian. No.

Van. No?

The Indian. It's gone already. Not worth keeping.

Van. I thought you'd say it was. I counted on you
to be my friend in that.

The Indian. It's an old question,
one I heard often talked of round the fire
when the hills and I were younger. Then as now
the young braves were for keeping what was ours
whatever it cost in blood. And they did try,
but when they'd paid their blood, and still must sell,
the price was always less than what it was
before their blood was paid.

Van. Well, that may be.

The Indian. I wish now I had listened when they spoke
their prophecies, the sachems of the tents;
they were wiser than I knew. Wisest of all,
Iachim, had his camp here on this Tor
before the railroad came. I saw him stand
and look out toward the west, toward the sun dying,
and say, "Our god is now the setting sun,
and we must follow it. For other races,
out of the east, will live here in their time,
one following another. Each will build
its cities, and its monuments to gods
we dare not worship. Some will come with ships,
and some with wings, and each will desecrate

the altars of the people overthrown,
but none will live forever. Each will live
its little time, and fly before the feet
of those who follow after." Let them come in
despoiling, for a time is but a time
and these will not endure. This little hill,
let them have the little hill, and find your peace
beyond, for there's no hill worth a man's peace
while he may live and find it. But they fought it out
and died, and sleep here.

Senior. Why, this is a wise Indian.
A little pessimistic about the aims
of civilization, but wise anyway.
What do you say, Van Dorn?

The Indian. You too will go
like gnats on the wind. An evening and a day,
but still you have your day. Build monuments
and worship at your temples. But you too
will go.

Senior. You're on my side, so I don't mind,
but you have a damned uncomfortable way
of speaking. I'm a Republican myself,
but I don't go that far! What do you say, Van Dorn?
Can we do business?

Van. Judith?

Judith. I'm out of it.
It's your decision. I'd say keep it though
if you want to keep it.

Van. I'll sell it. Fifty thousand.
On one condition. There's a burying ground
I want to keep.

Senior. Sure. That can be arranged.
It's settled, then. Come down to Ledentown
tomorrow and get your money.

Van. Yes, I'll come.

Senior. Why three cheers, boys. We're out of the woods.
Take hold,
Van Dorn, and swing these topers off the limb.
Then they can sign the pledge.

[*A* TROOPER *appears with* ELKUS *and* DOPE.]

Budge (The Trooper). Help me keep an eye on these
two, will you, Patsy? I've got a confession out of them
on the Nanuet bank robbery, and they say the money's
up here.

Patsy. Up here? Whereabouts?

Budge. They left it in a satchel.

Patsy. There's the satchel, all right.

[*He examines it.*]

Empty.

Budge. Looks like a stall, you guys. You buried it.

Elkus. Didn't keep a cent, officer. Somebody up here got it.

Budge. Well, who?

Elkus. Last time I saw it one of those birds sat down on it.

[*He points to* BIGGS *and* SKIMMERHORN.]

Patsy. You know who they are? That's Judge Skimmerhorn of the Probate Court, and Arthur Biggs of the
Trap-rock Company.

Elkus. Well, one of them sat down on it.

Budge. Why didn't he pick it up?

Elkus. I don't know whether he saw it.

Dope. And then there was a little guy in a big hat that had some of it.

Patsy. Yeah? Who?

Budge. That's right. Buddy said something about a little guy in a big hat.

Patsy. You think he got away with it?

Elkus. He had some of it, and we haven't got a cent.

Budge. So now we have to look for a little guy in a big hat. Any other description?

Elkus. Short and fat, had two sawed-off shotguns, and wore knee-pants.

Dope. And you could see right through him.

> [BUDGE *is writing in a notebook.*]

Patsy. What?

Dope. You could see right through him.

Budge. I'm beginning to think I can see right through you.

Patsy. Check on that. Elkus, you saw him. Could you see through him?

Elkus. Certainly was a funny-looking guy. Looked as if you could see right through him.

Budge. You expect me to send that out over the country: "Look for a short, fat man with a big hat and two sawed-off shotguns. Dangerous. You can see right through him."?

Patsy. They buried the money, Budge. Or else they're screwy.

Elkus. I thought I was screwy. You couldn't hurt him with a gun.

Budge. What do you mean?

Dope. We bored him full of holes and he wouldn't even sit down.

Budge. You mean he kept on running?

Dope. Running? He just stood there and let us shoot him.

Like shooting through a window.

Budge. Must have been wearing a vest.

Dope. I shot him through the head! Two feet away! And it just made him mad!

Patsy. Take 'em away, Budge. They're nuts.

Elkus. But he had the money! Buddy saw him with the money!

Patsy. They're all three nuts.

Budge. I never heard a line like that before.

Patsy. Who lives around here?

Van. I guess I'm the only one that lives near-by.

Patsy. Did you hear any shooting last night?

Van. Plenty of it.

Patsy. Did you take a look round?

Van. Yes, I did.

Patsy. Did you see a little guy in a big hat?

Van. Six or seven of them.

Budge. What!

Van. Six or seven of them.

Budge. I suppose you could see right through them?

Van. Once in a while.

Budge. I'm going to quit writing this down. There's enough here to get me fired already.

Patsy. If you saw six or seven where did they go?

Van. Down the river.

Patsy. In a car?

Van. In a ship.

Patsy. Sounds like a motor-boat gang. Well, that's something. They went down the river.

Van. But I can tell you where there's thirty dollars of the money.

Budge. Where?

Van. On the ledge there below the shovel.
    [BUDGE *and* PATSY *step over to look.*]

Budge. There it is. Three ten dollar bills. How did it get there?

Van. I don't know. I just happened to see it.

Budge. Did you try to get it?

Van. No. I thought it probably belonged to the gentle-men up there in the scoop.

Patsy. Did one of you drop some money, Judge?

Skimmerhorn. I don't think so. Not me.

Biggs. Not me.

Patsy. Did either of you see a little man in a big hat?
[*The two look at each other.*]

Skimmerhorn. Why, yes, we did.
[PATSY *and* BUDGE *look at each other.*]

Budge. Well, if they say so he must have been here.

Patsy. What was he doing?

Skimmerhorn. He was fighting with those two.
[*He points to* ELKUS *and* DOPE.]

Biggs. A regular war.

Patsy. Say, listen to that.

Budge. Do you know if he took anything out of the satchel?

Skimmerhorn. Yes, I think he did. He had the satchel.

Budge. Now we're getting somewhere.

Patsy. You don't know where he went?

Skimmerhorn. No.

Patsy. If you saw anything else that might give us a clue—?

Skimmerhorn. No, not a thing.

Patsy. It beats me.

Van. Want me to suggest a question?

Patsy. What?

Van. Ask the Judge if he gained any weight during the night.

Patsy. What's the matter with you?

Van. Looks to me like he picked up a good deal.

Patsy. I'll think up my own questions, thanks. Might as well trundle the yeggs back to jail, Budge. Whoever got the stuff it's gone.

Budge. That's what it looks like.

Van. Aren't you going to help the Judge down before you go?

Biggs. Oh, don't bother. We'll get down.

Skimmerhorn. No hurry. We're all right. You take care of your prisoners.

Patsy. Might as well lend a hand while we're here.

Biggs. Run along, boys. We're all right. Don't worry about us.

Patsy.

[*To* BUDGE]

Want to wait a minute?

Budge. Well, I'm due back, if they can make it themselves.

Biggs. Sure.

Van. Oh, don't leave those poor fellows up on that crane!
They've been there all night!

Skimmerhorn. We're fine. You run along.

Budge. Well, take a drag on the rope, Patsy. I'll wait.
   [PATSY *and* VAN *haul the shovel down.*]

Skimmerhorn. No need to go to all this trouble.

Patsy. No trouble at all.

Van. A pleasure. Why you were asking me all night to
get you out of this.
   [*The shovel touches ground. The two sit still.*]

Patsy. What's the matter?

Skimmerhorn. Guess my legs are asleep.

Biggs. Mine too.

Patsy. I'll help you up.
   [*They are pulled to their feet, staggering. Their pockets are very
   obvious.*]

Budge. How about it? O.K.?

Patsy. All set. Say, you are loaded down. Carried plenty
of lunch, I guess?

Biggs. Oh, we brought plenty.

Van.
   [*Tapping* BIGGS' *pocket*]

I told you they gained weight. Something in the air
up here.

Elkus. Couldn't be money, could it?

Biggs. As a matter of fact, some of it is. We were carrying cash to pay Van Dorn for his farm.

Patsy. Cash?

Biggs. Yeah, cash.

Patsy. How much?

Biggs. Just what we were authorized to pay. Twenty-five thousand.

Van. Funny thing, too. It's got the Orangeburg pay roll stamp on it.

Biggs. Well, hardly.

Patsy. What makes you think so?

Van. I saw it. They offered me ten thousand.

Patsy. Just for the record, I'd better look at it, Judge.

Skimmerhorn. I wouldn't if I were you. I'm hardly under suspicion of bank robbery.

Patsy. I'll take a look at it.

> [*He holds out a hand.* BIGGS *passes him a package.*]

Senior. I don't get this at all.

Patsy. It's got the Orangeburg stamp on it, all right.

Skimmerhorn. Must be some mistake. They must have got the money mixed at the bank.

Patsy. Sure. Well, if that's all we can easy check on that.

Van. Sure. You'd better check on it.

Skimmerhorn. Are you under the impression that we robbed the bank?

Van. You explain it. I can't.

Senior. You say you drew the money to pay Van Dorn?

Skimmerhorn. That's right, A.B.

Senior. And it's got the Orangeburg label on it?

Skimmerhorn. That's what they say.

Senior. I'll have something to say to the bank about that.

Skimmerhorn. Oh, I'll take care of it. Just a clerical error.

Patsy. I'm afraid I'll have to take the money, though. Oh, you'll get your own money back, but if this is the Orangeburg money—

Biggs. Sure, take it.
   [*They unload.*]

Patsy. And I guess I really ought to put you both under arrest.

Biggs. What? Under arrest?

Patsy. Wouldn't you say so, Budge?

Budge. Don't see any way out of it. Doesn't mean anything. Just an examination.

Skimmerhorn. I'd like to keep it out of the papers, if possible, of course. An examination might be very embarrassing—you see, I have political enemies.

Biggs. Always ready to think the worst of a man, and print it, too.

Patsy. Still, I guess we'll have to have an examination. Just for the record.

Skimmerhorn. You know who we are, of course?

Patsy. Yes, sir.

Skimmerhorn. I won't submit to an examination! It's preposterous!

Patsy. I don't see how we can get out of it, though. Because we had a robbery, and here's the money, and we've got to explain it somehow.

Skimmerhorn. I won't submit to it!

Patsy. You got an extra pair of handcuffs there, Budge?

Budge. Yeah.

Skimmerhorn. All right. I'll go.

Biggs. Sure. We'll go. And we'll make a lot of people sorry!

Patsy. Go on ahead, Budge.
    [BUDGE *starts out with his prisoners.*]

Dope. But how about the little guy with the big hat? How about him?

Budge. I'll tell you about him. It's entirely possible there wasn't any little guy in a big hat.

Dope. But we all saw him!

Budge. Oh, no, you didn't see him. You saw right through him. And the reason was he wasn't there.
    [BUDGE, ELKUS *and* DOPE *go out.*]

Biggs. You don't think we made that up, about the man in the big hat?

Patsy. Well, you have to admit it doesn't sound exactly plausible.

[PATSY, BIGGS *and* SKIMMERHORN *go out.*]

Senior.

[*As he goes*]

It shakes a man's faith in evidence.

[*To* VAN]

See you tomorrow.

Van. I'll be there.

[SKIMMERHORN SENIOR *goes out.*]

So now—I've sold the Tor.

The Indian. Yes, but it's better.

Van. Better than living on a grudge, I guess.
It might come down to that.

The Indian. There's wilder land,
and there are higher mountains, in the west.

Van. Out Port Jervis way.

The Indian. Perhaps. You'll find them.

Judith. He came to tell you, Van—this is his death-day.
I'll go now.

Van. All right, John.

The Indian. Could I keep it?
The hand I held? It's a new thing, being blind,
when you've had an Indian's eyes.

[JUDITH *returns and gives him her hand again.*]

Judith. I'll stay a while.

The Indian. When I had lost the path
  halfway along the ridge, there at my feet
  I heard a woman crying. We came on
  together, for she led me. There'll be time
  for crying later. Take her west with you.
  She'll forget the mountain.

Van. Will you come?

Judith. I'd remember Lise!

Van. Was there a Lise?
  I think she was my dream of you and me
  and how you left the mountain barren once
  when you were gone. She was my dream of you
  and how you left the Tor. Say you'll come with me.

Judith. Yes.

The Indian. It's a long day's work to dig a grave
  in stony ground. But you're young and have good
                    shoulders.
  It should be done tonight.

Van. I'll have it done
  even if you don't need it. Tell me the place.

The Indian. There's still an Indian burying ground that
                    lies
  behind the northern slope. Beneath it runs
  a line of square brown stones the white men used
  to mark their dead. Below still, in a ring,
  are seven graves, a woman and six men,
  the Indians killed and laid there. In the freshet,
  after the rain last night, the leaf-mould washed,
  and the seven looked uncovered at the sky,

white skeletons with flintlocks by their sides,
and on the woman's hand a heavy ring
made out of gold. I laid them in again.

Van. Seven graves—a woman and six men—
Maybe they'll rest now.

The Indian. Dig them in deeper, then.
They're covered only lightly.

Van. I'll dig them deeper.

The Indian. But you must make my grave with my own
people,
higher, beneath the ledge, and dig it straight,
and narrow. And you must place me in the fashion
used by the Indians, sitting at a game,
not fallen, not asleep. And set beside me
water and food. If this is strange to you,
think only I'm an Indian with strange ways,
but I shall need them.

Van. Don't worry. You shall have it
just the way you want it.

The Indian. Shall we go?

Van. One last look at the rock. It's not too late
to hold out on the bargain. Think of the gouge
they'll make across these hills.

Judith. If it's for me
you sell, we'll have enough without it, Van.
We'll have each other.

Van. Oh, but you were right.
When they wash over you, you either swim
or drown. We won't be here.

The Indian. And there's one comfort.
    I heard the wise Iachim, looking down
    when the railroad cut was fresh, and the bleeding earth
    offended us. There is nothing made, he said,
    and will be nothing made by these new men,
    high tower, or cut, or buildings by a lake
    that will not make good ruins.

Judith. Ruins? This?

The Indian. Why, when the race is gone, or looks aside
    only a little while, the white stone darkens,
    the wounds close, and the roofs fall, and the walls
    give way to rains. Nothing is made by men
    but makes, in the end, good ruins.

Van. Well, that's something.
    But I can hardly wait.

CURTAIN